To [illegible]

Pirke Avot

With Best Wishes

William Berk...

PIRKE AVOT
TIMELESS WISDOM FOR MODERN LIFE

WILLIAM BERKSON
TRANSLATION WITH
MENACHEM FISCH

THE JEWISH PUBLICATION SOCIETY
PHILADELPHIA
2010 · 5771

Jewish Publication Society is a nonprofit educational association and the oldest and foremost publisher of Judaica in English in North America. The mission of JPS is to enhance Jewish culture by promoting the dissemination of religious and secular works, in the United States and abroad, to all individuals and institutions interested in past and contemporary Jewish life.

The Jewish Publication Society, 2100 Arch Street, 2nd floor, Philadelphia, PA 19103
www.jewishpub.org

Design and Composition by William Berkson
Set in Williams Caslon and Hadasa MFO
Cover design by Claudia Cappelli
Manufactured in the United States of America

11 12   10 9 8 7 6 5 4 3 2

ISBN:978-0-8276-0917-4
Library of Congress Cataloging-in-Publication Data

Berkson, William.
  Pirke Avot: timeless wisdom for modern life / William Berkson; translation with
  Menachem Fisch.
    p. cm.
  Includes the text of Pirke Avot in Hebrew and English translation.
  ISBN 978-0-8276-0917-4 (alk. paper)
  1. Mishnah. Avot--Commentaries. I. Fisch, Menachem. II. Mishnah. Avot. English. III.
Mishnah.
  Avot. IV. Title.
  BM506.A23B346 2010
  296.1'234707--dc22
                        2010024632

JPS books are available at discounts for bulk purchases for reading groups, special sales, and fundraising purchases. Custom editions, including personalized covers, can be created in larger quantities for special needs. For more information, please contact us at marketing@jewishpub.org or at this address: 2100 Arch Street, Philadelphia, PA 19103.

Contents

Acknowledgments

I AM grateful to Dr. Menachem Fisch for a delightful collaboration on the translation, and for his critique, support and encouragement. I am also grateful to Ellen Frankel, former editor-in-chief of The Jewish Publication Society and to the editorial committee for believing in the project, and for excellent suggestions for strengthening the book. My thanks for conscientious and able editing of the text by Julia Oestreich, and to Robin Norman for her understanding in managing production with an author who is also a designer.

Finally, my deep gratitude goes to my wife Isabelle for her support throughout the years that I have been blessed to work on the commentary for this great and sacred text.

Note on the Text

THE VERSION of the sayings of *Pirke Avot* printed in the siddur, the traditional Jewish prayer book, and the version printed with the Mishnah are numbered differently and the texts are slightly different in a few places. Here, the numbering and text follow the siddur version. For ease of discussion, this guide groups together some of these *mishnayot* with the same theme and divides those that contain several different themes. Subdivisions are indicated with A, B, C (for example, 2:6A, 2:6B).

For the sake of concision, neither the introductory comments, such as "Rabbi X used to say," nor the prooftexts from the TANAKH, are included in the large English quotations at the tops of the pages. The complete text of *Pirke Avot* in both Hebrew and English, including the supplementary sixth chapter in the siddur, follows the text of the commentary.

Here "Sages" with a capital "S" refers to authors of the Talmud, including *Pirke Avot*, who are traditionally referred to as "our Sages of blessed memory," or by the Hebrew acronym *Ḥazal*. The Sages' names are transliterated following their pronunciation in Modern Hebrew, except for those with Greek names. The "ḥ" transliterates ח and is pronounced as the "ch" in "J. S. Bach." The "kh" transliterates כ and is pronounced the same way as the "ḥ" is. The "a" is pronounced as it is in "father," the "u" as "oo" in "too," and the "i" as "ee" in "see."

All Hebrew words are grammatically either masculine or feminine. The translations here are generally gender-neutral where the Hebrew uses the masculine gender. However, the translations sometimes follow the original gendered Hebrew for the sake of authenticity or for a more graceful rendering of the text.

The Sages often cite "prooftexts" from the TANAKH, and give them an unconventional reading to support their point. TANAKH translations that to illustrate a point do not precisely follow the standard JPS translation have their citations italicized. These incorporate phrases from the *Jerusalem Bible* (Koren), trans. Harold Fisch, or *The Five Books of Moses* (Schocken), trans. Everett Fox. Talmudic quotations are based on the *Soncino Talmud*. Quotations from Maimonides' commentary on *Avot* and from his *Mishneh Torah* are from the Moznaim editions, trans. Rabbi Eliyahu Touger. Quotations from other medieval commentators are based on Judah Goldin's *The Living Talmud* (Yale), and those from *Avot de-Rabbi Natan* are from Judah Goldin's *The Fathers According to Rabbi Nathan* (Yale).

Abbreviations

Citations of Talmudic tractates are as a rule from the Babylonian Talmud. A 'P' added before the abbreviations of Talmudic tractates listed below indicates that the reference is instead to the Palestinian Talmud.

I KINGS *First Kings*, Bible
I SAM *First Samuel*, Bible
II SAM *Second Samuel*, Bible
ARN *Avot de-Rabbi Natan*,
      Talmud [minor tractate]
AR *Arakhin*, Talmud
AZ *Avodah Zarah*, Talmud
BB *Bava Batra*, Talmud
BER *Berachot*, Talmud
BM *Bava Metzi'a*, Talmud
DEUT *Deuteronomy*, Bible
ECCL *Ecclesiastes*, Bible
EJ *Encyclopedia Judaica* (1972)
ER *Eruvin*, Talmud
ES *Esther*, Bible
EZEK *Ezekiel*, Bible
EX *Exodus*, Bible
GEN *Genesis*, Bible
GEN RAB *Genesis Rabbah*, Midrash
GIT *Gittin*, Talmud
HAG *Hagigah*, Talmud
IS *Isaiah*, Bible

JER *Jeremiah*, Bible
JOEL *Joel*, Bible
KID *Kiddushin*, Talmud
LEV *Leviticus*, Bible
LEV RAB *Leviticus Rabbah*,
      Midrash
MAK *Makkot*, Talmud
MT *Mishneh Torah*,
      Maimonides
NUM *Numbers*, Bible
PEAH *Pe'ah*, Mishnah
PROV *Proverbs*, Bible
PS *Psalms*, Bible
RH *Rosh Hashanah*, Talmud
SAN *Sanhedrin*, Talmud
SHAB *Shabbat*, Talmud
SOT *Sotah*, Talmud
SUK *Sukkah*, Talmud
TA'AN *Ta'anit*, Talmud
YEV *Yevamot*, Talmud
YOM *Yoma*, Talmud
ZECH *Zechariah*, Bible

Introduction

PIRKE AVOT (peer-KAY ah-VOHT) is an anthology of the sayings of the greatest post-biblical Jewish Sages. It is one of the great wisdom books of world literature, with its only peers being such classics as the *Analects* of Confucius, from ancient China, the *Enchiridion* of Epictetus, from ancient Greece, and the *Dhammapada* of Buddha, from ancient India. Like those other works, in some respects it shows its ancient origins. Yet, like these, it also speaks straight to the heart with a timeless immediacy and power. It speaks to each one of us, in each stage of life, with a direct applicability to the important decisions we face.

Avot (the original, brief title) is, in contrast to the wisdom books of Confucius and Epictetus, a deeply religious book. It tightly weaves together the three strands of spirituality, right conduct, and learning, forming a seamless fabric, a pattern for life. The Sages whose sayings are collected in it were not trying simply to give good advice in pithy phrases, but were trying to etch the outlines of a divine plan for humanity, a "*torah*." They tried to identify principles that would not only improve people's quality of life, but also would imbue lives and relationships with a sense of the sacred, with holiness.

The purpose of this guide to *Avot* is to make the book accessible to today's readers, and enable them to apply its wisdom in making their own life decisions. Each saying—printed in large script—is followed by a guide. The first part of the guide focuses on the original meaning of the saying, or *mishnah*, as intended by the author in his day. The second part, entitled "Modern Life" explores questions such as: What should this saying mean to us today? Can we accept it or not? How does it hold up to competing views? Does it need to be modified or extended? And if we accept it in some form, what difference will it make in the way we look at life, and in our actions in love, work, family, and community?

To help readers explore Jewish wisdom, this guide looks at the sayings in *Avot* from three different perspectives. The first perspective is that of the "insider": how traditional Jewish commentators, such as Maimonides, have interpreted the sayings.

The second perspective is historical. From the conquest of Judea by Alexander the Great in 332 BCE through the historical period in which the Sages of *Avot* lived (200 BCE to 200 CE), the evolution of Judaism is a story of interaction with ancient Greek culture—both reaction against it, and adoption and transformation of some of its features.

The third perspective is contemporary and comparative. The main sources that people in the West turn to today in seeking wisdom, and that we will compare to the Sages' ideas, are: modern psychology, Positivism (which treats science as a substitute for religion), Christianity, and Buddhism.

The most famous comparative book in Jewish history is Maimonides' *Guide for the Perplexed* (12th century). It took a broad cultural perspective, comparing the views of the Jewish Sages with those of the ancient Greeks and the Islamic sages. Our time, like that of Maimonides—and like that of the Sages of *Avot*—is a time of cultures meeting and clashing. Young Israeli soldiers, upon completing their army service, go off to South Asia seeking Eastern wisdom. American Jews seeking guidance on relationships do not think of the Jewish Sages, but rather avidly read modern psychology. And in the United States there is a vigorous "Jewbu" movement, combining Judaism and Buddhism. While culture clash can be stressful, it has also been one of the great wellsprings of creative thinking and human advancement. It was a key factor not only in the brilliantly fertile periods of the Athens of Socrates and Plato, and of the European Renaissance of da Vinci and Copernicus, but also of the Judea of Hillel and Akiva.

So the time is ripe for a new comparison between Jewish thought and competing philosophies. This comparative guide identifies and explores controversial issues, but unlike Maimonides' great work does not attempt to give definitive answers. This approach also has the advantage of directly addressing the questions of Jewish seekers, while making *Avot*, a great classic of world literature, accessible to non-Jews.

Title. Avot literally means "fathers," and may here have a dual meaning. It no doubt refers to the men who are quoted in the tractate—the teachers and judges who are traditionally and aptly referred to as *hakhamim* or "Sages." The title may also refer to the sayings themselves. *Avot* can also mean "a set of basic concepts" used to guide us in making decisions. So *"avot"* here may also refer to the basic ethical concepts of the Sages that give us guidance in a myriad of life situations.

The traditional Jewish prayer book, the siddur, added a sixth chapter, not in the Mishnah, in order to have a chapter to recite on all six of the Sabbaths between Passover and Shavuot. (See the Appendices here for this sixth chapter.) The prayer book refers to all six chapters as

Pirke Avot, literally "Chapters of Fathers." This phrase has been variously interpreted as "Ethics of the Fathers," "Wisdom of the Talmud," "Sayings of the Fathers," and so on. The correct title of the tractate in the Mishnah, to which this book is a guide, is simply *Avot*.

Place in Jewish Literature. Avot was put in nearly final form around 200 CE by one of the last and greatest Sages in the book, Yehudah haNasi. The Sages anthologized here were scholars and teachers of Jewish law and religion, and they also served as judges. During the 1st century, they began to be addressed with the title "Rabbi." *Avot* is part of Yehudah haNasi's definitive compendium of post-biblical legal rulings known as the Mishnah, meaning "recitation" or "repetition." The Talmud, meaning "study," is a collection of extensive commentaries on the Mishnah, known as Gemara, "completion," together with those portions of the Mishnah that have been commented upon. Each saying in *Avot* is also referred to as a "mishnah," with a small "m."

Avot and the Bible. The Sages' outlook was firmly rooted in the Torah, the Five Books of Moses. The Sages' world, however, was very different from that of Moses, and in response to their world, the Sages reconstructed the religion and ethics of the Torah for their era, greatly expanding and sometimes fundamentally changing its ideas.

Avot builds on the Torah's passionate concern with establishing justice, but introduces three key changes: a greater emphasis on love and peace, a devotion to book-centered learning and rational discussion, and a belief in reward and punishment of individuals in "the world to come," as well as in this world. These views fit together to form a unified philosophy. Ethical education based on Torah helps to produce people who are just and kind. Society can thus rely more on education, and less on the punishments laid down in the Torah. God's providence—personal concern for each individual—and rewards and punishments in this life and the next also act as powerful motivations for right conduct. Thus, the different facets of Rabbinic thinking reinforce one another.

The Sages' world was in many ways close to our own. It was already a sophisticated urban world of commerce and international trade, widespread education (including higher education), and contact with many cultures. In particular, Judea was part of the Hellenistic world for hundreds of years, and ancient Greek culture had a decisive influence on it, an influence that is still strong in the Judaism of our own time.

The world of the Sages and our world are, of course, also different. The differences are due to the impact of three new features of modern life: science, representative democracy, and women's equality. The commentary in this book is intended to help the reader explore the implications of these new features of modern life for the wisdom of the Sages.

Avot and Later Judaism. The Judaism of the Mishnah and Talmud was so changed from the religion of the Torah that scholars distinguish between the "ancient Israelite religion" of the Hebrew Bible, on one hand, and the "Classical Judaism" of the Talmud, on the other. While subsequent changes were not quite as radical, the Judaism that developed in the Middle Ages was also profoundly different from the Judaism of the Talmud in a number of ways. In exile, Judaism retreated into a defensive posture, and the dynamism and creativity of the mishnaic period decreased. The approach to Jewish law became increasingly rigid and pedantic.

The blossoming of Jewish mysticism in the Middle Ages was partly a reaction against that rigidity, and an effort to bring back a vibrant experience of holiness. However, these changes were also a reaction to desperate times, and they had an escapist element that is foreign to the Sages' Classical Judaism. For both the mystics of the Kabbalah and the rationalist Maimonides, the highest goal was no longer a life of love and work lived ethically and imbued with holiness. The primary goal was now a direct experience of God. The turn away from daily life, from love, work, and the pursuit of justice, was, in my view, a decay of Judaism resulting from exile and hard times.

Now that Jews' political rights have been restored—the result of a process of emancipation beginning around 1800—and the Jewish state has been restored, I think that the Judaism of the Sages represents a healthier and more dynamic model for Jews to look to for the future.

Ethics and Psychology. The Sages viewed ethics as being central to good human relationships. Two people who are ethical will be able to cooperate effectively for their mutual benefit, and two unethical people will fall into discord and strife. Though many ancient religions and philosophies have shared this view of the centrality of ethics in human relations, in the 20th century, scientific psychology systematically avoided studying the role of ethics in relationships. This avoidance probably resulted from a misguided idea that the impact of ethical conduct on relationships could not be studied scientifically. Whatever the reason for this shift in focus, it had two important results. First, scientific psychology made important advances in understanding many aspects of human emotions and relationships. Second, ethics, a central force in human relationships, was passed over, and progress in understanding this key aspect stagnated.

In this guide to *Avot*, we will put the principles of the Sages and modern psychology side by side, and ask: when taken together, what can they tell us about the challenges of modern life? In considering the ideas of the Sages and of modern psychology side by side, many of those ideas jump out as complementary, whereas others appear to conflict. Psychologist's ideas on skills for problem-solving discussion and communication are particularly complementary to the ideas of the Sages, as these skills promote the Sages' values of compassion and peace.

The Sages' views, however, often conflict with conventional wisdom in popular psychology. Psychologists have generally avoided openly discussing philosophy, but have in fact often fallen into viewing human nature as very depraved, as did Freud, or as naturally good and only corruptible by bad upbringing or trauma, as did Carl Rogers. The Sages, by contrast, had a more balanced view, seeing human nature as having both good and bad tendencies.

Modern psychology, influenced by these unexamined philosophies, and by a reaction against religious views, has tended to be very positive about the expression of all emotions toward others, including anger and desire. However, psychologists have wanted to suppress or eliminate negative emotions toward the self, such as guilt and shame. The Sages, by contrast, saw anger as an extremely dangerous emotion, which usually needed to be curbed, and sexual desire as an emotion to be channeled into the marriage relationship. And they saw guilt as an appropriate emotional reaction to one's own wrongdoing, to be overcome through repentance.

My own view is that all emotions can be appropriate at some times and harmful at others, but need to be managed to be ethical and beneficial to our welfare. One day, scientific research on the role of ethics in relationships may resolve the conflicts between traditional and currently popular views. In the meantime, this guide is designed to help readers sort out these matters for themselves, in their own lives. The Sages' guidelines for living in fact stand up extremely well in our own time.

Reward and Punishment. While the ethics of the Sages have held up remarkably well against competing modern ideas in psychology, the doctrine of reward and punishment is the feature of the Sages' world view that has been most troubling to moderns.

The founding vision of Abraham is of one just God who judges all on earth fairly. In the Torah, God's rewards and punishments are carried out while we are living. During the period of the Maccabean revolt, in which many good and faithful Jews were martyred, the belief in reward and punishment in an afterlife instead of this life became widespread, and this belief was incorporated into the Sages' Classical Judaism. This "old-time religion," which first united the ideas of one God of justice, judgment in an afterlife, and an ethic of love and kindness, became the basis not only for later Judaism, but also for Christianity and Islam. Any challenge to the Sages' views on reward and punishment is thus also a challenge to all the Abrahamic religions.

As we shall see, the Sages are divided on whether there can be any human understanding of why the righteous sometimes suffer and the wicked sometimes prosper. This bafflement has endured to our day, and to this has been added, in the post-Darwin period, skepticism about whether God intervenes to reward and punish as portrayed in the Bible or by the Sages.

Interestingly, this modern skepticism about reward and punishment has not extended to a rejection of belief in God. The inability of science to penetrate the mysteries of human purpose and meaning has led many people to have some degree of religious feeling, to sense and experience holiness behind the mysteries. A diluted form of this religious feeling is "New Age" spirituality, which demands nothing of the individual, because it views religion as a comfort only—not as a commandment to ethical action. This version of "spirituality" is fundamentally at odds with Judaism, which at its core weds ethics and spirituality.

Moderns who reject reward and punishment, but still look to religion for ethical guidance face this challenge: to offer a credible theology that both accepts modern science and supports faith in a God who wants humans to act ethically. Most non-Orthodox Jewish theologians in the 20th century in fact rejected the notion of a God who rewards and punishes individuals, but generally avoided discussing this radical departure from Classical Judaism. This reluctance to discuss such a fundamental change was not good, because "the seal of the Holy One, blessed be He, is truth" (SHAB 55a). By traditional Jewish standards, what is religiously supported should be true, and not just a meaningful myth. Thus, for a vital modern Judaism, the question of God's presence and influence, even if we don't accept divine reward and punishment, has become central.

In writing this book, I long felt reluctant to discuss a religiosity which does not have reward and punishment at its center. Such a religious outlook seemed pale and weak to me in comparison with the inspiring, all-encompassing religion of the Jewish Sages. After all, one could argue that a person can have faith in morality with or without a sense of the transcendent—so what's the difference? Is there any difference between the agnostic who is committed to an ethical life, and one who believes in a God who doesn't reward and punish, but calls upon us to be ethical?

Over the years I've worked on this book, though, the piety of the Sages moved me, and reflecting on it changed my outlook. For even when we don't believe in reward and punishment, the sense of God's Presence (*Shekhinah*) in our lives can make a crucial difference in our *motivations*, in ethics, and in many other areas of our lives.

When we look to do what is right, when it is difficult, do we feel supported by the strong sense that we are part of something greater than ourselves? That feeling is, I believe, divine inspiration to be ethical. When we experience the beauty of nature, do we feel awe and wonder at the mystery of what is behind creation? Do we feel that in the love between husband and wife, parent and child, friend and friend, there is something sacred, of which we are partaking? And do we feel an "attitude of gratitude" for the wonder of life every day? The sense of the sacred both motivates and rewards us. It is a vital spark without which our lives are colder and darker.

In fact, in *Avot*, the Sages actually laid the foundation for a piety without reward and punishment. As we shall see, even while some Sages emphatically affirmed divine reward and punishment (2:1b, 4:29), others put forward the idea that to serve out of love is better than to serve because of thoughts of reward and punishment (1:3). This means that even in view of some of the Sages, a lack of belief in reward and punishment should not change our piety or our devotion to the good.

Each reader will of course draw his or her own conclusions about these theological issues, after studying the Sages' views. Whatever conclusions you come to, you will find here in *Avot,* as a touchstone for your own meditations, the original synthesis underlying Judaism, Christianity, and Islam: the belief in one God, in an ethic of love and kindness, and in divine reward and punishment in this life and the next.

Avot in World Literature and in Judaism. Because of the enmity that broke out between the followers of Jesus and those who followed Rabbinic tradition, *Avot* did not become part of the canon of great ethical works studied in the Christian Western World. However, as some Christian scholars of the 20th century recognized, the tradition of the Sages in fact was the fertile field in which Christian ethics grew. While there are important points of divergence between traditional Christian and Jewish ethics—and these are noted in the commentaries—there is a much larger common heritage.

Next to the Bible itself, *Avot* has been the most beloved and studied sacred text in Judaism. It is reprinted in the traditional prayer book and in most modern ones, and is traditionally studied on the Sabbath. In the Sephardic tradition, it is studied for six weeks, from Passover until Shavuot, and in the Ashkenazi tradition, it is studied from Passover throughout the summer, until the High Holy Days begin in the fall.

In spite of its traditionally important place in Jewish literature, in the 20th century, *Avot* was relatively neglected within non-Orthodox Jewish education. It has not played an important role in the curriculum for Reform or Conservative Jewish youths in America, and in Israel the focus in secular state schools for Jews has been almost exclusively on the Bible. This neglect has been a tragic mistake, for *Avot* is essential to understanding Judaism. Whoever doesn't know *Avot* doesn't know Judaism. And whoever knows *Avot* knows the heart of Judaism, whether they are Jewish or not.

Chapter One

PREAMBLE:

Moses received Torah from Sinai,
And passed it on to Joshua,
And Joshua to the elders,
And the elders to the prophets,
And the prophets passed it on to men of the Great Assembly. (1:1A)

מֹשֶׁה קִבֵּל תּוֹרָה מִסִּינַי וּמְסָרָהּ לִיהוֹשֻׁעַ, וִיהוֹשֻׁעַ לִזְקֵנִים, וּזְקֵנִים לִנְבִיאִים,
וּנְבִיאִים מְסָרוּהָ לְאַנְשֵׁי כְנֶסֶת הַגְּדוֹלָה.

THIS INTRODUCTORY sentence describes the chain of tradition leading up to the sayings in *Avot*. It has two messages. The first is that tradition is a vitally important source of wisdom. *Avot* itself represents the culmination of 1500 years of continuous reflection on the nature of the good life. Each generation has made decisions about what was worthy to preserve from previous generations.

The second message is a bold claim for the divine authority of the post-biblical "Oral Torah"—the record of the discussions and legal decisions that went beyond the Written Torah, the Five Books of Moses. Acceptance of the religious authority of both the Written and Oral Torah defined the Jewish religion for 1600 years following the compilation of *Avot*, and still defines traditional Judaism today. (Because of its dual meaning, the word *Torah,* which literally means "instruction," is often used to refer to all Jewish sacred texts.)

At the end of the 18th and beginning of the 19th centuries, this traditional acceptance of the Oral Torah was challenged by the European Enlightenment in two ways. First, Jews were no longer treated as members of an alien community governed by its own laws, but were accepted, at least in theory, as full citizens. The result, because of the long-standing principle *dina de-malkhuta dina,* "the law of the land is the law," was that secular law largely replaced talmudic civil and criminal law in the countries where Jews were given citizenship. Jewish law, *halakhah*, as a practical matter thus applied only to ritual matters, such as Sabbath observance and *kashrut*, the ritual fitness of foods. *Halakhah* is also still used in some communities for issues of family law as an alternative to the law of the land, and has official status in Israel.

In a second, even more profound challenge to the primacy of Oral Torah, the Enlightenment offered a new standard by which to judge sacred texts: scientific fact. When Jewish sacred literature was examined from the new scientific point of view as a set of historical documents, it became clear that it was not a seamless, consistent whole, but contained evolving and changing views from different generations.

So at the same time that the new social condition of Jews resulted in narrowing the scope of *halakhah*, the new scientific approach to history challenged the divine authority of both the Oral and Written Torahs. In response to this challenge, some Jews tried to preserve the traditional framework in total, while others sought to radically rethink everything; most, though, took a middle course, keeping some traditions and changing others.

Today's worldwide Jewish community is diverse, from the totally secularized to the ultra-Orthodox. *Avot*, with its emphasis on ethical behavior, is a unifying document that can speak to all Jews, no matter their level of observance. And as a book of ethical principles and guidelines, it continues to be revered by all the denominations of Judaism, no matter their views on the authority of the Oral Torah.

MODERN LIFE

OVER THE past century, tradition has proven itself to be much more important and resilient than radical Enlightenment thinkers believed. Still, religious tradition has not been restored to its former position of unrivaled authority, and is not likely to be. As a result, the question of how to deal with tradition remains a central issue for Judaism.

Since about 1800, there have been three basic approaches in Judaism to dealing with tradition. The first is the traditionalist approach, followed by most Orthodox: the whole of Jewish traditional *halakhah* must be followed. Any modification to meet new conditions must be based on past, internal standards, and past rulings cannot be changed.

A difficulty for traditionalism is that, as scholar Menachem Fisch explains in *Rational Rabbis,* the Talmud itself has non-traditionalist voices. It is willing to use the science of its day in halakhic discussions, and to contradict earlier halakhic authorities. It also leaves itself open to future revisions that might revive and recast rejected minority opinions, which then reverse and replace established majority rulings. Thus, the traditionalism of much current Orthodox Judaism is contrary to the spirit of this dominant talmudic voice.

Arguably, a still more fundamental challenge to Orthodoxy comes from the modern historical view of the sacred texts: if they were written at different times, and contradict one another, then they cannot all be true, and so are fallible. This approach removes the divine authority of the text, and the justification for judging the tradition only from within, rather than looking to modern science, social science, and philosophy for insights.

The approach to tradition that is opposite to Orthodoxy is the radical one of rejecting everything in tradition that doesn't agree with reason—the approach of Radical Reform leaders of the mid-19th century. They rejected many ritual rules, including kashrut, and all nationalistic or particularistic elements, which they regarded as not "in accord with the postulates of reason"(*Pittsburgh Platform*, 1885). They rejected the Oral Torah and regarded *halakhah* as outdated, and unworthy of study.

While the Enlightenment has been of huge benefit to humanity, its more radical rationalists were naïve. As with non-Jewish radicals, the Jewish radicals sometimes mistook ideas fashionable in their generation for eternal verities. Time has shown that some of these ideas, once advocated as obvious truths, are in fact mistaken.

In reality, as philosopher Karl Popper used to say, "If we knew only what Adam knew, we would not be able to get further than Adam did." We are all aware that our society relies on past discoveries in science and technology. But we sometimes take for granted our heritage in other fields, such as the inventions of law, money and banking, and representative democracy. We also regularly, without noticing, rely on a precious legacy of spiritual and ethical insights from past sages and prophets.

The third and most popular approach to tradition is to see it as a guide to life, but also be willing to criticize and change it based on standards new to modern times. This reformist approach includes contemporary Conservative, Reform, and Reconstructionist denominations. While these vary in their views of how closely to adhere to tradition, they hold similar philosophies of how to relate to it.

This book approaches the text of *Avot* following this third, reformist philosophy, as it both reverently and critically explores Jewish tradition. However, it resembles the radicals in being willing to critically assess traditional views using modern, external standards, as well as traditional, internal ones. And like the Orthodox, it takes traditional directives as intended: not as metaphors, but as guides to life.

Be deliberate in judging;
Educate many students;
Make a fence around the Torah. (1:1B)

הֵם אָמְרוּ שְׁלֹשָׁה דְבָרִים: הֱווּ מְתוּנִים בַּדִּין, וְהַעֲמִידוּ תַלְמִידִים הַרְבֵּה,
וַעֲשׂוּ סְיָג לַתּוֹרָה.

THESE THREE sayings are addressed particularly to the activities of the scribes who first developed the Oral Torah. They acted as judges and educators, and interpreted the laws in the Written and Oral Torah.

Be deliberate in judging. Here, the Hebrew *m'tunim*, "deliberate," also means slow and careful. This saying warns against dogmatism—the view that the truth is obvious, and that one can make correct judgments quickly and with certainty, whether in court or in ordinary life.

Yet, the saying equally opposes the moral relativism currently popular in America—the view that we shouldn't make moral judgments at all, and that there is really no way to judge between competing principles. In reality, everybody makes moral judgments in their personal lives. Indeed, it is necessary to make judgments about people's actions in order to carry out the commandments in the Torah to pursue justice and to rebuke wrongdoing. And, therefore, the Sages put forward guidance for making good judgments: before judging someone, be careful to weigh the facts and evidence, to put yourself in his or her place (2:5), and to give him or her the benefit of the doubt (1:6).

Whether or not there is divine authority for ethical principles, as Judaism holds, the fact is that some ethical principles promote social harmony and prosperity. And other values, such as callousness and domination, now celebrated in "gangsta rap" music, lead to strife, violence, and poverty. *Avot* contains the principles that the Sages believed best promote a good life for individuals and a peaceful and just society.

Educate many students. The Sages believed that education is vital to producing moral individuals and a good society. They were the first in history (from the 1st century, see BB 21a) to establish a system of universal education for boys. (Education for girls is a modern advancement.) Education must be widespread to sustain the rule of law in a society, as only the educated can make informed and thoughtful judgments about how to pursue their own interests within the law.

Make a fence around the Torah. The "fence" refers to cautionary rules to protect people from temptations to violate the commandments of the Torah. For example, not only is work forbidden on the Sabbath, but so is the handling of work tools. This characteristic activity of the Sages has been praised as preserving Judaism, and has been criticized for creating excessive burdens.

MODERN LIFE

IN THE United States today, if a person expresses a negative opinion about the values or customs of another group, he or she is likely to get a heated rebuttal: "Every group and every person has the right to their own values and ways, and you are being intolerant to make any judgment about their values and customs." In other words, relativism is viewed as the necessary basis of tolerance and thus of peaceful relations among people and nations.

Tolerance has indeed become ever more important in our world, because we now regularly need to interact with others of widely diverse origins and beliefs. However, relativism is, in reality, a fatally flawed foundation for tolerance. For relativism only sustains the weakest kind of tolerance: neutrality toward those we have no contact with.

Once we need to interact with someone who holds different views, relativism gives us no pathway to resolving differences. While we can sometimes avoid talking about contentious issues, at other times differences can be serious obstacles to peace and effective cooperation. Then, it becomes vital to discuss them, and either resolve them or find a way to live with them. And in such situations, relativism leaves us with only power plays, emotional warfare, and violence as options for dealing with differences.

Sages in fact gave us a much better foundation for tolerance. They adopted the Socratic idea that there are truths to be discovered, but that these are difficult to ascertain. Dialogue and debate are key to finding these truths. Following this idea, when the Talmud records a decision on an issue, it also records minority views. For these minority views may also contain some truth, which may be discovered and used by later generations to improve the community and the world (see *Avot* 5:20). As Dr. Joshua Plaskof points out, this system creates a multi-generational "learning community," which cooperatively and creatively arrives at new solutions through respectful disagreement, debate, and dialogue.

Just as importantly, many discussions in the Talmud only render judgments when practical decisions need to be made in particular cases, and issue no rulings on general issues of ethics and theology. This reluctance to make rulings is based on the very sensible notion that many disagreements do not need to be settled immediately; they can be lived with.

This same tolerance for differences in belief is important in one's personal life. Marriage researcher John Gottman has found that the average good marriage has 10 unresolved serious issues. A significant part of conflict resolution in one's personal life involves not resolving differences of opinion, but rather managing them with focused discussions and compromises on practical issues.

The talmudic approach is based on a belief in the reality of right and wrong, and truth and falsity, joined with a deep humility about how difficult it is to discover what is true and right, even with the guidance of scripture. The combination of this approach with institutions for multigenerational learning is a far more powerful basis for tolerance.

How are we to apply this model outside the circle of those who have reverence for the Jewish sacred texts? The answer lies in a humble universalism. We can start with the premise that there are universal ethical values—something that Maimonides advocated—but also acknowledge that it is not easy to determine what they are in practice. This outlook provides the basis for forming communities to engage in respectful dialogue and practical problem-solving across cultures, while leaving the negotiation of more fundamental differences as a long-term project.

As individuals, we often face a difficult choice. We are often tempted to judge too quickly and negatively—and to declare our judgments when we would be wiser keeping them to ourselves. Yet, in other situations, delaying judgment can be disastrous, for the absence of a positive decision on a plan of action can mean we fail to act against a real threat, or we miss an important opportunity:

&❧ Those who are decisive and compassionate, God helps. (ARN 8)

If we weigh options endlessly, we can get "analysis paralysis" and never decide. When should we withhold or delay judgment—and when should we decide immediately? In important cases, we should step back and ask ourselves: "How much time do I have to make this decision?" (a version of *Avot* 1:14). Doing so reminds us to consult those who can help us, and then helps us in choosing the right time to make the decision.

Upon three things the world stands:
Upon the Torah, upon worship,
And upon acts of kindness. (1:2)

שִׁמְעוֹן הַצַּדִּיק הָיָה מִשְׁיָרֵי כְּנֶסֶת הַגְּדוֹלָה. הוּא הָיָה אוֹמֵר: עַל שְׁלֹשָׁה
דְּבָרִים הָעוֹלָם עוֹמֵד עַל הַתּוֹרָה, וְעַל הָעֲבוֹדָה, וְעַל גְּמִילוּת חֲסָדִים.

THE HEBREW begins: "Shimon the Righteous was one of the last from the Great Assembly." The text thus links the first Sage of *Avot* with the unbroken chain of sacred tradition described in 1:1. Shimon believed that for the sake of these three activities—Torah study, worship, and acts of kindness—God created the world.

Shimon's motto in effect paints a portrait of the ideal person we should strive to become: a person both close to God and a boon to humanity. This ideal pious person should learn Torah, fulfill its commandments in both ritual and ethical conduct, and go beyond the strict obligations of the Torah by regularly performing acts of kindness.

This ideal has its roots in the Bible. The paramount importance placed on study—of both the Bible and the post-biblical Oral Torah—and the emphasis upon acts of kindness are, however, characteristics of Rabbinic or "Classical" Judaism. The wedding of learning, spirituality, and ethics is the hallmark of the Classical Judaism that is portrayed in *Avot*.

Upon worship. The commentary in *Avot de-Rabbi Natan* (ARN) says that "worship"—literally "the service"—here refers to the sacrifices at the ancient Temple, where Shimon was high priest. After the fall of the Temple, the Rabbis viewed prayer as a "service of the heart" (TA'AN 2a), which partly served as a substitute for sacrifices. Also, Rabban Yoḥanan ben Zakkai in *Avot de-Rabbi Natan* says that deeds of loving-kindness are as good a means of atoning for sin as the sacrifices had been.

Acts of kindness. In the Bible, *hesed*, "loving-kindness," (also translated as "mercy" or "charity") is one of the basic attributes of God that humanity is to imitate. The rabbinic phrase *gemilut ḥasadim*, literally "the bestowal of kindnesses," refers to a broader category than *tzedakah*, which is the rabbinic term for "charity" in the sense of giving money or goods to the needy. *Gemilut ḥasadim* includes any helpful action done without expectation of reward or recompense.

Another portrait of the ideal Jew in the Talmud also includes acts of kindness as a key virtue:

🕭 Three signs indicate membership in the Jewish nation: compassion, modesty, and acts of kindness. (YEV 79a)

Here "modesty," *baishan* in Hebrew, is the quality of being sensitive and averse to anything that might be seen as shameful. The prooftext given for the importance of this quality is "that the fear of Him may be ever with you" (EX 20:17). In other words, we should be aware of God's presence, and God's call for ethical action, and judgment.

MODERN LIFE

WHY DID Shimon the Righteous single out acts of *hesed*, loving-kindness? I suspect it is because when suspicious or ungenerous feelings arise, these are the first things to go. Couples in love, fond parents, and doting grandparents all find it a joy to help their loved ones, without any thought of recompense. But in many circumstances, people feel uncomfortable taking the initiative to help, or have no inclination to do so. If we keep in mind this most fragile of good impulses, other good acts may follow.

Just actions are based on generous impulses, but that does not guarantee that they will be either welcome or effective. Somerset Maugham said that "no good deed goes unpunished." The reality is that helping others effectively, and without giving offense, is often as complicated and difficult as competing with them.

The Sages' ideals of compassion, modesty, and generosity are high-minded and inspiring, but there is much in our modern, highly competitive society that militates against them. Our society rewards winners, whether it is with grades in school, with money at work, or with renown. And winning a mate is often influenced by winning competitively in other areas.

Some in our society, noticing that some winners are callous and unscrupulous, reject these high-minded Rabbinic values as useless or harmful. And some have gone even further, arguing that no-holds-barred competitiveness, including callousness and selfishness when they help to win, is good for society—a view directly challenging that of the Sages.

The first one to make the case for unfettered competition was Bernard Mandeville, who argued in his *Fable of the Bees* (1714) that the "private vice" of greed becomes a "public virtue" in the free market, because it leads to productivity and prosperity. A more recent and extreme version of Mandeville's idea can be found in the philosophy of Ayn Rand, as articulated in *The Virtue of Selfishness*, which was further popularized through admirers such as Robert Ringer, author of *Winning through Intimidation*. While Rand's philosophy is not usually taken seriously in the academy, its enduring popularity speaks to its wide appeal.

On issues of basic values suitable for a competitive society, it is the Sages who have a deep understanding, and Rand whose views are shallow and destructive. For Rand, the chief value is being "productive," and relationships are simply trades, like a commercial transaction: I give you something of value and you give me something of value in return. In this view, it is foolish and ultimately destructive to give without receiving, because we will be losers. The implication is that any relationship lacking immediate fair trade should be dissolved.

The folly of this commercial model of relationships is that our society presents us with a mixture of situations that call for cooperation, competition, and conflict. And of these, cooperation, particularly in civil life (in contrast to war), is usually most fundamental. Even in competitive situations, our ability to cooperate with others in school or work is key to producing something that succeeds competitively. In one's personal life, cooperation with loved ones and friends is paramount.

Cooperation requires trust and commitment. This is because enduring cooperative relationships involve risk and uncertainty: we never can be sure whether another person's efforts will complement our own, or even if the relationship with that person will endure. And psychological research has found that nothing is so devastating to cooperation as suspicion and mistrust.

Because trust and commitment are keys to successful relationships, personal qualities such as integrity, compassion, and fairness become paramount in our decisions in forming and sustaining relationships. In fact, the Rabbinic values and guidelines here in *Avot* can be seen as a search for the strongest basis for harmony and cooperation among humanity. And this cooperation is not only a practical matter. Most of us experience the sacred in our connection to other people—in love, family, and friendship, in what Martin Buber called "I-Thou" relationships. Thus, the Sages' values are designed to lift our relationships to the level of the sacred, so that love and work are lived on a higher, more fulfilling level.

Be not as servants who serve the master
on condition of receiving a reward;
Be rather as servants who serve the master
without condition of receiving a reward;
And let the fear of Heaven be upon you. (1:3)

אַנְטִיגְנוֹס אִישׁ סוֹכוֹ קִבֵּל מִשִּׁמְעוֹן הַצַּדִּיק. הוּא הָיָה אוֹמֵר: אַל תִּהְיוּ
כַּעֲבָדִים הַמְשַׁמְּשִׁין אֶת הָרַב עַל מְנָת לְקַבֵּל פְּרָס, אֶלָּא הֱווּ כַּעֲבָדִים,
הַמְשַׁמְּשִׁין אֶת הָרַב שֶׁלֹּא עַל מְנָת לְקַבֵּל פְּרָס, וִיהִי מוֹרָא שָׁמַיִם עֲלֵיכֶם.

THE HEBREW begins: "Antigonos of Sokho received from Shimon the
Righteous." Antigonos probably lived through the beginning of the persecutions by Assyria that led to the successful revolt by the Maccabees
in 164 BCE—events which are now celebrated during the festival of
Ḥanukkah.

This mishnah marks an important turning point in the history of
Jewish belief. In the Torah, God promises material rewards—rain, good
harvests, many children, victory in battle, long life—to the Jewish people if they obey God, and punishments if they do not. This traditional
view was challenged in Antigonos' time in two ways.

The first challenge came from the Stoics, whose philosophy developed in the Hellenistic world not long after Alexander the Great con-
quered Judea, in 332 BCE. By Antigonos' time, Stoicism had become
the dominant philosophy of Hellenistic leaders. And as we can see by
Antigonos' Greek name, the Hellenistic influence in Judea was enor-
mous. Indeed, some priests wanted to abandon Judaism, and they invited
Antiochus' repression of Judaism, resulting in the Maccabean rebellion.

The Stoics believed that the world is a "cosmos," an orderly world
governed by natural laws that determine all events. And they believed
that individual happiness is achieved entirely by acting in accordance
with virtue, which in their view meant acting in accordance with nature
and with the duties that accompany one's station in life. This doctrine
is reflected in the saying, "Virtue is its own reward." These Stoic ideas
placed a wise person above any influence by the prospect of reward or
punishment. Antigonos' statement here may be a response, showing
that Jewish piety can and should be just as high-minded. Instead of
serving to receive a reward, we should serve God out of love.

The second challenge came from the persecutions leading up to and during the Maccabean revolt. Faithful Jews were martyred for their religion for the first time in history. Their suffering and death raised the question in the minds of the Jewish people: what happened to our covenant with God, and with God's promises to protect us so long as we were faithful? At the time of the revolt, concepts of the afterlife were widespread in surrounding cultures: individual judgment and resurrection in Persia, and immortality of the soul in Greece. Probably as a result of these influences, many Jews adopted the view that the righteous would be rewarded only in *olam ha-ba*, "the world to come." Indeed, in the view of historians, the first direct references to the world to come, in Daniel 12:2, were written during this period, and are some of the last texts to be included in the TANAKH.

Not long after the revolt, Jews broke into two parties, the Pharisees and Sadducees. Pharisees supported the authority of the Oral Torah and believed in judgment in an afterlife. Sadducees, associated with the priests and the Temple, opposed both of these concepts. Indeed, *Avot de-Rabbi Natan* reports that the Sadducees came to deny belief in the afterlife after their founder Zadok (a student of Antigonos) misinterpreted this saying as a denial of reward and punishment. However, the Sages, who were heirs of the Pharisees, included this mishnah in *Avot*—not as a denial of reward and punishment, but rather as an assertion that other motivations for ethical conduct are preferable.

Be not as servants. Antigonos has carefully worded his saying to shift away from reliance on the earlier belief in rewards for good behavior, without rejecting it outright. Implicit in this saying is the idea that because we may not get rewards in this life, we may be disappointed and lose faith if we rely on them. The later Rabbinic view says that rewards for righteous deeds come only—with a few important exceptions—in the afterlife (KID 39b). Antigonos, however, doesn't mention rewards in the world to come, but instead reconstructs the foundations of the bridge between ethics and spirituality. The Torah commands both love and awe of God (DEUT 10:12), and Antigonos makes these feelings, rather than any reward or punishment, the fundamental motivation for ethical behavior.

The fear of Heaven. Antigonos takes not only feelings of love—which are naturally generous and unselfish, but also the "fear of Heaven," as fundamental. The Hebrew here, *mora shamayim,* can also be translated as "awe of Heaven," and probably does not refer to fear of retribution in an afterlife, but rather to what we feel looking at the starry night—awed, humbled by our smallness and vulnerability, and by the brevity of life.

Modern Life

IN A modern context, Albert Einstein also described "awe of Heaven":

   The most beautiful experience we can have is the feeling of the mysterious; it is the fundamental emotion that stands at the cradle of all true art and true science. ... It was the experience of mystery—even if mixed with fear—that engendered religion. A knowledge of the existence of something we cannot penetrate, our perceptions of the profoundest reason and most radiant beauty, which only in their most primitive forms are accessible to our minds—it is this knowledge and this emotion that constitute true religiosity. (*Ideas and Opinions*, 11)

Einstein continues, "In this sense, and this sense only I am a deeply religious man." And then, like Antigonos, he immediately discusses reward and punishment by God, and in fact rejects the concept: "I cannot conceive of a God who rewards and punishes his creatures."

Jewish philosopher Martin Buber also did not accept the notion of individual reward and punishment. He found awesome mystery and beauty in human relationships. In open and honest relationships there is, he said, a mysterious creative, transcendent element that at times leads us to experience holiness, a divine presence in our lives—a presence such as that which Einstein felt in the order of nature.

This religiosity rejects the concept of an interventionist God, yet still sees holiness as vital to humanity. It should be noted that neither Einstein nor Buber found meaning in traditional Jewish ritual and prayer. Rabbi Mordecai Kaplan also rejected the concept of an interventionist God, but he created the foundation of Reconstructionist Judaism, which does include traditional ritual practice.

Thus, the tension between the Hebraic and Hellenistic ideas that Antigonos tried to resolve still remains. The challenge to those who accept the traditional view is to show how divine reward and punishment can be viable in the face of modern science and history. The challenge to those who believe in a non-interventionist God is to show how this belief can provide us with as powerful an inspiration and guidance as traditional religious beliefs have.

YOSE BEN YO'EZER:

Let your house be a meetinghouse for the wise;
Sit in the dust at their feet,
and drink in their words with thirst. (1:4)

יוֹסֵי בֶּן יוֹעֶזֶר אִישׁ צְרֵדָה וְיוֹסֵי בֶּן יוֹחָנָן אִישׁ יְרוּשָׁלַיִם קִבְּלוּ מֵהֶם. יוֹסֵי בֶּן
יוֹעֶזֶר אִישׁ צְרֵדָה אוֹמֵר: יְהִי בֵיתְךָ בֵּית וַעַד לַחֲכָמִים, וֶהֱוֵי מִתְאַבֵּק בַּעֲפַר
רַגְלֵיהֶם, וֶהֱוֵי שׁוֹתֶה בַצָּמָא אֶת דִּבְרֵיהֶם.

YOSE BEN YO'EZER urges the formation of a devoted and personal association with scholars. In the Sages' view, study of Torah will help the young form good moral character, and will help guide adults on the right path so that they resist the temptation to do wrong. Study of sacred texts is also, in the view of the Sages, a worthy goal in itself and brings us close to God. Thus, learning should be a lifelong commitment, which should affect our choice of who we listen to, associate with, and marry.

The Sages' ideal of a scholar, of "the wise," is not the same as the later Western concept of an intellectual. The Western ideal is of a person who becomes an expert in understanding some aspect of society, nature, or history. A concern with helping mankind is secondary to this expertise. The Sages, by contrast, were concerned with problems of ethics and law that are immediately applicable to bettering human relationships and society, as well as religious ritual. The goal of a Torah scholar is thus to attain practical wisdom for living.

MODERN LIFE

AS THE Sages' approach to ethics differs from the Western philosophical tradition that flows from Socrates, so too the reason we are to "sit in the dust at their feet" differs from the reasons for formal education today.

The Western philosophical tradition has mainly been a search for firm foundations for ethics—a way to single out which ethical principles are valid, and to justify them. Proposed principles include "the greatest happiness of the greatest number" (utilitarianism) or fundamentally equal respect for all persons (Kantian principles). While these efforts have shed valuable light on the connections between ethics, social welfare, and individual freedom, they have been rather sterile when it comes to personal guidance.

The approach of Western ethics failed because, in reality, ethics cannot be reduced to a single principle or to a few principles. Even such basic ethical goals as increasing happiness, reducing misery, and respecting individuals can and do come into conflict with one another. As Nobel Prize-winning economist Kenneth Arrow has shown, there is no unique way to resolve such conflicts; varying compromises affect different groups differently, and finding improved social solutions requires creativity.

Much of the substance of practical ethics is concerned with resolving conflicts of "right versus right," such as those between justice and peace, as well as "lesser evil" choices, where we need to decide between seriously flawed options. Western philosophy has only recently come to study subjects such as medical and business ethics. By contrast, such practical issues are a central focus of the Sages' efforts. Thus, while the tradition of the Sages is narrow compared to Western thought as a whole, in the area of applied ethics it is often up-to-date and sometimes ahead of our time.

Because of the failure of Western philosophical ethics to establish a firm foundation for ethical theory, many have concluded that ethics is simply a matter of personal or group preference—a view known as relativism (see 1:1B). However, this view is not sound. When people live by values of callousness, domination, and cruelty, it leads to societies full of poverty, suffering, and strife. When people live by the values of the Sages, it leads to societies with stable, loving families, prosperity, and peace. The religious viewpoint adds that our desire for a human world of love and peace is rooted in a cosmic purpose that transcends humanity.

Even one of the greatest critics of religion, the 20th-century English philosopher Bertrand Russell, toward the end of his long life said, "I find myself incapable of believing that all that is wrong with wanton cruelty is that I don't like it" (*Philosophy* 35, 1960).

The conviction that our preference for justice and kindness is also what God desires can give us the courage to look beyond ourselves to the welfare of others and to the future consequences of our actions— exactly what ethical values tell us to do. Religious beliefs and ethical values thus support each other. The Sages' vision of a society whose members are strengthened by study, practice, and religious faith thus has great power. The two traditions that have combined moral and intellectual education, Chinese and Jewish, are among the longest surviving, in spite of conquest by foreign powers.

Let your house be open wide;
Let the poor be members of your household;
And don't talk too much with the wife. (1:5)

יוֹסֵי בֶּן יוֹחָנָן אִישׁ יְרוּשָׁלַיִם אוֹמֵר: יְהִי בֵיתְךָ פָּתוּחַ לָרְוָחָה, וְיִהְיוּ עֲנִיִּים
בְּנֵי בֵיתֶךָ, וְאַל תַּרְבֶּה שִׂיחָה עִם הָאִשָּׁה. בְּאִשְׁתּוֹ אָמְרוּ, קַל וָחֹמֶר בְּאֵשֶׁת
חֲבֵרוֹ. מִכַּאן אָמְרוּ חֲכָמִים: כָּל הַמַּרְבֶּה שִׂיחָה עִם הָאִשָּׁה–גּוֹרֵם רָעָה
לְעַצְמוֹ, וּבוֹטֵל מִדִּבְרֵי תוֹרָה, וְסוֹפוֹ יוֹרֵשׁ גֵּיהִנֹּם.

THE HEBREW continues with a commentary: "This being said of one's own wife, so much more so of another's wife. Thus sages have said: He who talks a lot with the woman causes evil to himself, neglects the study of the Torah, and in the end will inherit Gehinnom." Gehinnom is the Rabbinic conception of Hell, though the nature of that hell and the length of one's stay there is unclear. The school of Hillel says that people are only condemned to stay in Gehinnom for a year, though the totally wicked are confined to remain there eternally (RH 17a–b).

Don't talk too much. "Woman" and "wife" are the same word in Hebrew. Yose ben Yoḥanan begins by commending hospitality and personal generosity to the poor, so the harsh final statement about women is all the more shocking. Traditional commentators soften this statement by interpreting "talk" as meaning "gossip." But if we ask what it is about wives and women as a class that should make us single them out as people we should not talk too much to, it is evident that this saying is disparaging to women. The argument that men lack the self-control to act properly—including engaging in regular Torah study—is a poor excuse for limiting the roles of women, and for not treating one's wife as a full and equal partner. Men can and should exert enough self-control to treat all women with respect.

The reality is that the Sages were all men, and their great wisdom is sometimes marred by narrow-minded remarks about women. These regrettable remarks are balanced to some degree by talmudic comments with the opposite tenor: "Your wife is short, so bend down to whisper to her [in seeking her counsel]" (BM 59a), and a man should "love his wife as himself and honor her more than himself" (YEV 62b).

Still, this mishnah is the most prominent of wrong-headed statements about women in the talmudic literature. There is a story concerning

24

this saying and a comment by the one woman highly respected in the Talmud as a scholar. This is Beruriah, the daughter of Ḥanania ben Teradion (see *Avot* 3:3) and wife of Rabbi Meir (see 4:12). Rabbi Yose the Galilean was once walking on a road when he encountered Beruriah, and he asked her: "By which road do we go to the city of Lydda?" She replied, "Galilean fool! Do not the sages say, 'Don't talk a lot with the woman?' You should have said, 'Whither Lydda?'" (ER 53b).

There may be a story behind the story. Divorce was rare among the Rabbis, but Rabbi Yose the Galilean divorced his wife, who was reputed to be a shrew. Beruriah would have known Rabbi Yose and his ex-wife, since Yose had been a student of Rabbi Akiva along with her own husband Rabbi Meir (see *Avot* 3:17–20). Beruriah was both sharp-tongued and brilliant, and may well have sympathized with the ex-wife. This exchange was evidently in public, and in asking by which way do *we* go to Lydda, Yose may have embarrassed Beruriah. Hence, in one erudite turn of phrase, she ridiculed both Rabbi Yose's taunting and the offensive saying from *Avot*.

Let your house be open wide. Hospitality—*hakhnasat oreḥim*—is one of the basic obligations that the talmudic Sages added to biblical commandments (SHAB 127a). Yose ben Yoḥanan added that we should personally take in the poor. In a world without social welfare institutions, such hospitality served a crucial moral role. It is easy to lose sight of the importance of such hospitality in our society, but recent economic crises serve as a reminder.

MODERN LIFE

IN MODERN marriages, couples regularly have to make decisions on their own roles, while each partner is presumed to have equal power in these decisions. In "companionate" marriages, then, regular discussion between husband and wife has become vitally important—contrary to what Yose ben Yoḥanan seems to advocate here. Indeed, modern marriage experts urge couples to set aside regular times for personal discussion. Egalitarian discussion of emotionally charged issues is, however, quite difficult. Over the past 50 years, psychologists have developed powerful techniques for overcoming the difficulties of discussing emotionally charged issues, opening the possibility for applying Jewish values to marriage in a more positive way than the unfortunate phrase here would suggest.

Choose for yourself a mentor;
Acquire for yourself a friend;
And judge every person in a favorable light. (1:6)

יְהוֹשֻׁעַ בֶּן פְּרַחְיָה וְנִתַּאי הָאַרְבֵּלִי קִבְּלוּ מֵהֶם. יְהוֹשֻׁעַ בֶּן פְּרַחְיָה אוֹמֵר:
עֲשֵׂה לְךָ רַב, וּקְנֵה לְךָ חָבֵר, וֶהֱוֵי דָן אֶת כָּל הָאָדָם לְכַף זְכוּת.

CHOOSE FOR *yourself a mentor. Rav*, translated here as "mentor," literally means "master," as in "master and disciple." This term later became the title for Jewish clergy.

Joseph Agassi, a philosopher from Jerusalem, once read a brilliant essay in the field he was studying in college. He sought out the author and said to him: "There is a saying in the Talmud, 'Choose a teacher, and acquire a friend,' I choose you as my teacher." The teacher said, "But this college doesn't grant a degree in this subject." He said, "Nonetheless, I have come to learn from you." The college eventually established the degree, and he earned it. This illustrates the point of Yehoshua ben Peraḥiah: it is the responsibility of the student who is beyond childhood to take the initiative to seek out a mentor.

Acquire for yourself a friend. This phrase is traditionally read as meaning that you need a study companion. The Sages felt strongly that peers are a critical ingredient in a true education. *Avot* 4:18 strongly reinforces this view by saying that "your fellow students will establish [Torah] as your possession." The concept here is that the goal of learning is a matter not just of memorizing facts, but also of absorbing a tradition and learning a way of thinking. This kind of education, which eventually transforms the student into the master of a tradition, requires a master and several apprentices, all of whom interact with one another.

The basic meaning of *ḥaver* is "associate." However "friend" in the fullest sense is probably what is meant here, as the emotional support of friends while doing challenging studies is vital. The most dramatic story illustrating the importance of friendship is the legend of Ḥoni the Circle Maker. He was a revered expert in *halakhah*, as well as a miracle worker. He fell asleep for 70 years, and when he awoke all whom he had known had died. He went to the *beit midrash* to discuss Torah, but people would not believe that he was Ḥoni, and they did not respect him as people had before. He then prayed for death and died. Hence, the Talmud says, "Companionship (*ḥevruta*) or death" (TA'AN 23a).

Judge every person in a favorable light. The Hebrew is literally, "Be judging every person to the pan of merit"—the pan of merit or innocence being one of the two pans in the scales of justice. A number of stories in *Avot de-Rabbi Natan* and the Talmud make clear what this means: we should try to construct interpretations of events that are favorable to the people involved and charitably interpret their intentions.

Does this rule mean that we always should judge everyone favorably? Maimonides wouldn't go so far. In his commentary on this mishnah, he distinguishes three cases: If we don't know a person's reputation, we should judge him or her favorably. When we know the person has a good reputation, we should give him or her the benefit of the doubt, even if an action of his or hers looks bad. However, if the person has a bad reputation, we should not trust him or her to do right, even if his or her actions look good.

This principle of judging charitably is so fundamental in Rabbinic Judaism that it is included in the list of things "the fruit of which one eats in this world and the principal remains in the world to come" (SHAB 127a). This means that we gain a reward in this world, and not only in the world to come—as is thought to be the time of reward for most good deeds.

Modern Life

THE PRINCIPLE of judging charitably has become still more important in modern life. In the modern world we have much more flexibility in defining our roles in the relationships of husband and wife, parent and child, and boss and subordinate. This flexibility opens up opportunities for more effective cooperation and better relationships, but it also means that the fundamental conditions of our relationships are open to change. This makes discussions of how responsibilities are to be divided and carried out emotionally charged for both parties.

We humans are nervous and cantankerous creatures, quick to become suspicious and to blame when anything goes wrong. This ever-present human tendency can and does easily sabotage relationships that could otherwise be happy and productive. Responding out of anxiety in this way has two damaging aspects. The first is that it renders our own thinking primitive and limited; instead of seeking better solutions, we begin thinking only in terms of dichotomies—fight or flight, friend or enemy, good or bad. The second damaging effect of suspicion is that attacking or criticizing the other person in a relationship raises his or her anxiety and defensiveness, so that he or she tends to return blame and to do the same kind of simplistic thinking, instead of problem-solving and seeking more effective ways to cooperate on common goals.

If we follow this mishnah, it breaks this negative spiral of fear, mistrust, and the ensuing communication breakdown. It first moves us to empathy, so even if our assessment of the other person in a relationship with us is not entirely favorable, it still opens the way to engaging in cooperative efforts to solve problems, instead of practicing mutual blame and recrimination.

Is the advice of this mishnah naïve? The Hebrew phrase here, *hevei dan*, literally "be judging," indicates that we should develop a habit of judging people in a favorable light, but not that we should ignore exceptions when there are real threats to our well-being. The mitzvah to "surely rebuke your neighbor"(*LEV 19:17*) obviously means that we must recognize wrong when we see it. Similarly, having the habit of judging others favorably in relationships implies that to protect ourselves we need to be particularly cautious in seeing that we associate as far as possible only with people of good character, as the next mishnah urges: "Do not fraternize with the wicked" (*Avot 1:7*).

This mishnah is an astonishingly rich and concise summary of what is needed for effective education, at least in preparation for the transition to an adult vocation. What cannot be gained by learning on one's own is a strong sense of the strengths and weaknesses in a particular field, the structure of its ideas and its problems. This can only be gained by discussion with a mentor who is in possession of the modern unwritten lore of the field, the "tacit knowledge," as philosopher Michael Polanyi called it. And only by critically assessing the knowledge, ideas, skills, and problems of the field with other young students will the field be vital and dynamic, and will it able to grow in the hands of the new generation.

The relationship between mentor and student can be highly rewarding for both sides. But it is also a fragile relationship, which can shatter into quarrels and recriminations, and is therefore difficult to manage. Relationships among students can also be compromised by rivalry. Perhaps, Yehoshua ben Peraḥiah includes the admonition to judge people in a favorable light in his saying because that is a key to keeping relationships positive, productive, and loving.

Keep away from a bad neighbor;
Do not fraternize with the wicked;
And do not despair about calamity. (1:7)

נִתַּאי הָאַרְבֵּלִי אוֹמֵר: הַרְחֵק מִשָּׁכֵן רָע, וְאַל תִּתְחַבֵּר לָרָשָׁע, וְאַל תִּתְיָאֵשׁ
מִן הַפּוּרְעָנוּת.

KEEP AWAY. We could approach a bad neighbor in hopes of improving relations with him or her, but here Nittai of Arbel warns us that more trouble will come of it.

Do not fraternize with the wicked. We may be tempted to associate with a person we know is of bad character because it seems we will benefit from the association. Obviously, the Sages would object. A more difficult issue arises when we feel we should be willing to associate with a troubled opponent to make that person better. A hero is "some say, [one] who makes of an enemy, a friend" (ARN 23). Perhaps, the conclusion to draw is that we should make the effort when we believe the enemy is not actually wicked, but misguided and redeemable.

In another interpretation, an early commentary reads "the wicked" as meaning the wicked within ourselves, so that "do not associate with the wicked" warns us to heed only the voice of our better nature.

Do not despair. This saying has a double meaning, as *puranut*, translated here as "calamity," can also mean "divine punishment." One meaning, then, is that we should not despair because we do not yet see the wicked suffering divine punishment. A second meaning is that we should also not despair because of the afflictions of disease and disaster that befall the innocent, including ourselves and those we love. Faith in divine judgment is a central but troubled belief espoused by the Sages. This issue, which we first encountered in 1:3, is the theme of the book of Job in the Bible, and is examined again and again from different angles throughout *Avot*.

The suffering of the innocent is still harder to understand and more difficult to bear than is the prospering of the wicked. Why and how to love a God who allows the suffering of the innocent is the most serious challenge to Jewish theology. Traditionally, some have tried to give reasons why God would visit afflictions on the seemingly innocent, including here in *Avot* (5:11). Job in the Bible and Rabbi Yannai here (4:19) humbly confess bafflement at this, but love God nonetheless. A new, intriguing idea explaining the presence of evil came from Rabbi Isaac Luria, 16th-century kabbalist, or Jewish mystic. Most Western mystics, following the ancient Greek philosopher Plotinus, say that God created the world through the "emanation" of God's self. Rabbi Luria said instead that God created the world through a process of self-limitation or withdrawal, *tzimtzum*. The world left behind after that process was a flawed one that allows evil—a world that it is our task to repair.

MODERN LIFE

OF THE many calamities that the Jewish people have experienced and survived, the Holocaust, which is in the memory of many living today, is the most distressing and troubling. The Holocaust caused many to "despair about calamity" and to abandon any role for spirituality in their lives. But many others did not despair, and still find holiness in the world and in their lives.

In response to the horror of the Holocaust, a number of thinkers have attempted to explain how a loving God can allow evil in the world, by appealing to the idea that God has limited powers. Supporters of this idea, which is also inherent in Luria's *tzimtzum* concept, include Mordecai Kaplan, the founder of Reconstructionism, and Rabbi Harold Kushner, author of *When Bad Things Happen to Good People*.

For this writer, the mystic visions of Luria, the naturalistic certainties of Kaplan, and the sympathetic interpretations of Kushner make assertions about the divine that are presumptuous, as they go beyond what we can possibly know. A theology of humility seems more convincing and more true. We can stand in awe before the beauty, majesty, and terror of nature; we can experience the mysterious link from one soul to another and to ourselves as part of a whole, experience oneness with nature and humanity, and glimpse a mystic sense of oneness with God. All these experiences of the transcendent, without creating a presumption that we understand God, can support our placing value on the enduring: a more just society, love, the treasure of learning, and insight into the mysteries of nature, society, and ourselves.

In any case, the decision not to despair, to embrace life, and to love the world and its Creator is the decision to be a religious person in the Jewish way. This embrace of life includes the effort, through performing ethical actions urged in *Avot*, to uplift life and to make it worth living.

While a judge, do not act as an advocate;
While the litigants stand before you, regard them both as
*   guilty;*
But when they leave, having accepted the judgment,
*   regard them both as innocent. (1:8)*

יְהוּדָה בֶּן טַבַּאי וְשִׁמְעוֹן בֶּן שָׁטַח קִבְּלוּ מֵהֶם. יְהוּדָה בֶּן טַבַּאי אוֹמֵר: אַל
תַּעַשׂ עַצְמְךָ כְּעוֹרְכֵי הַדַּיָּנִין, וּכְשֶׁיִּהְיוּ בַּעֲלֵי הַדִּין עוֹמְדִים לְפָנֶיךָ, יִהְיוּ
בְּעֵינֶיךָ כִּרְשָׁעִים, וּכְשֶׁנִּפְטָרִים מִלְּפָנֶיךָ, יִהְיוּ בְּעֵינֶיךָ כְּזַכָּאִין כְּשֶׁקִּבְּלוּ
עֲלֵיהֶם אֶת הַדִּין.

SHIMON BEN SHATAH:

Examine the witnesses thoroughly,
*   and be careful in your words,*
*   lest they learn from them to lie. (1:9)*

שִׁמְעוֹן בֶּן שָׁטַח אוֹמֵר: הֱוֵי מַרְבֶּה לַחֲקוֹר אֶת הָעֵדִים, וֶהֱוֵי זָהִיר בִּדְבָרֶיךָ,
שֶׁמָּא מִתּוֹכָם יִלְמְדוּ לְשַׁקֵּר.

HAVING GOOD laws and a just court system to enforce them were of the highest importance to the Sages. They included the establishment of law courts as among the seven "laws of the sons of Noah"—rules that God is said to have set for all nations, and which to the Sages were basic requirements of a civilized society. *Avot* is unusual for a text in the Talmud in leaving aside legal issues, and focusing only on general principles that should guide behavior. Yet these principles, though not laws themselves, provide an ethical foundation for the development of law.

This reverence for law and the concern for its just formulation and execution is one of the characteristic features of Judaism. Moses promulgated laws that replaced the arbitrary power of a pharaoh or king with just rules that applied to everyone equally. This was 700 years before the Athenian leader Pericles declared proudly that Athens was governed by equal justice, no matter a person's station in life.

The Sages accepted that the laws of Moses came directly from God on Mount Sinai, but they were also influenced by Greek ideas about legislation. They developed their own system for adapting the Mosaic laws to their time through discussions, debates, legal interpretations, and rulings by judges and scholars that are recorded in the Talmud.

Through this system, the Sages continued to pursue Moses' concern for justice, for the well-being of humanity, and in particular for justice in and the welfare of the Jewish community.

While a judge. This phrase is not in the Hebrew, but is clear from context. According to scholar Solomon Zeitlin, Shimon ben Shataḥ inaugurated the first systematic cross-examination of witnesses, a practice later taken up by the Romans, and then incorporated into European jurisprudence (*Rise and Fall of the Judean State* 1, 415).

While the litigants. The presumption of guilt sounds very odd to modern ears, but in context and in the Hebrew it makes sense. Here ben Tabbai and ben Shataḥ are speaking not of a criminal trial, but of litigants in a lawsuit. *Rasha,* here meaning "guilty" is also the word for "wicked." The import is that judges—who decide the cases—should not take what litigants say at face value, as they are biased in their own favor and may not be honest. Cross-examination and fact-checking are thus critical. *Zakha,* translated here as "innocent," also means "worthy," indicating that if the parties accept the judgment, both should be treated as upstanding citizens and not be stigmatized for having gone to court.

MODERN LIFE

UNTIL ABOUT 1800, Jews lived as resident aliens in largely self-governing communities, under talmudic law. When they began being accepted as full citizens in Western European societies, this situation changed radically. As Jews already accepted the principle "the law of the land is the law," civil and criminal law shifted to the hands of non-Jewish authorities. However, Jewish law has continued to be of interest from a number of angles. First, for Jews accepting the laws relating to religious ritual—such as celebrating Shabbat and the festivals and observing kashrut (dietary laws)—*halakhah* continues to be relevant and important. Some Jews following traditional practices also go to a *beit din,* a court of rabbinic law, to settle disputes. In Israel, people have the option of using religious courts to adjudicate disputes involving family law.

Finally, we should note that many issues discussed in the Talmud do not fall strictly into the category of "law" as the term is usually used in English. Many rules are not specific directives with punishments for their violation; they are rather ethical guidelines, or general guidelines for living. Such ethical and life guidance is the focus of *Avot.*

Love work,
Hate domination,
And do not become familiar with the authorities. (1:10)

שְׁמַעְיָה וְאַבְטַלְיוֹן קִבְּלוּ מֵהֶם. שְׁמַעְיָה אוֹמֵר: אֱהַב אֶת הַמְּלָאכָה, וּשְׂנָא
אֶת הָרַבָּנוּת, וְאַל תִּתְוַדַּע לָרָשׁוּת.

LOVE WORK. This is the first of several sayings in *Avot* praising the value of work. The Sages valued work as honorable and fulfilling, and the prosperity coming from it as good. But they did not sanctify work, as did the much later "Protestant ethic," which saw material success in work as an indication of being favored by God. For the Sages, the pinnacle of the week is the Sabbath, on which no work is done.

Hate domination. The Hebrew *rabbanut*, here "domination," is literally "the quality of being a master." Twentieth-century Rabbi Chaim Stern pointed out that this mishnah can be read as rejecting both sides of domination: we should hate dominating others, and we should not let ourselves be dominated. Abraham Lincoln captured the idea when he said, "As I would not be a slave, so I would not be a master." Another reading—also probably intended—is that we should be very hesitant to seek high office, and accept it only with great reluctance.

Do not become familiar with the authorities. All three of Shemaiah's sayings relate to career: love the work itself, not just its result; do not take pleasure in dominating others at work; and do not cozy up to governmental authorities in order to try to get ahead. Beginning in the time of Shemaiah, the Romans dominated the Judean state, and the Sages viewed the Roman governments as suspect, unreliable, and dangerous.

MODERN LIFE

THE PROTESTANT ethic was transformed in America by Benjamin Franklin and others. Hard work and productivity, instead of gaining us entry to heaven, would gain us worldly success. Thus, the Protestant ethic turned into what we can call the "Success ethic:" the equating of competitive success with self-worth and happiness. Indeed, in time, success became an idol that Americans worshipped. The great 19th-century American philosopher William James once called this idol the "bitch goddess Success." Einstein beautifully contrasted this worship of success with a Jewish view of work:

&❧ A successful man is he who receives a great deal from his fellow men, usually incomparably more than corresponds to his service. The value of a man, however, should be seen in what he gives and not in what he is able to receive. The most important motive for work in the school and in life is pleasure in work, pleasure in its result, and the knowledge of the value of the result to the community. (*Ideas and Opinions*, 62)

Under the influence of the "human potential movement" and in an environment of prosperity, in the 1960s, most young Americans started aspiring to work that would be not only remunerative, but fulfilling. This contrasts with the traditional view, which Maimonides expresses in his commentary on this mishnah: the reason we should love work is that we would otherwise shirk it, become destitute, and be led into earning through dishonest means. Perhaps supporting both views, industrialist and Jewish leader Aaron Feuerstein has argued that the "curses" in Genesis 3, our work "with the sweat of our brow" and our bearing and raising children, are actually blessings in which we most closely imitate God through creativity.

Hate domination. What constitutes improper domination? In equal relationships, the principle is pretty clear: divide responsibilities and rewards equally, and then there is no one being unfairly dominated. But many of our relationships are unequal—teacher and student, boss and subordinate, parent and child. In these, a standard for justice is that the person with authority or money not abuse his or her power. This means that he or she carry carries out his or her role according to the responsibilities entailed by the role of parent, teacher, or boss. If the person in authority neglects his or her duty to the other person as defined by his or her role, and uses his or her power for selfish gain, that is abuse of power. Abuse of power or "taking advantage" of another person is known in rabbinic parlance as *hona'at reah* (LEV 25:17). This phrase is most often used to describe taking advantage of others financially, but it applies more generally, as well.

To avoid being taken advantage of, of being unfairly dominated, the modern technique of "assertive" communication is invaluable. Assertiveness involves saying clearly and openly what you want—or don't want (see also *Avot* 1:14). This alone is powerful as it is highly correlated with good relationships.

O sages, be careful with your words;
For you may incur the penalty of exile,
  and be banished to a place of evil waters;
The disciples who come after you will drink of them and die,
  and the Name of Heaven be profaned. (1:11)

אַבְטַלְיוֹן אוֹמֵר: חֲכָמִים הִזָּהֲרוּ בְדִבְרֵיכֶם, שֶׁמָּא תָחוּבוּ חוֹבַת גָּלוּת וְתִגְלוּ
לִמְקוֹם מַיִם הָרָעִים, וְיִשְׁתּוּ הַתַּלְמִידִים הַבָּאִים אַחֲרֵיכֶם וְיָמוּתוּ, וְנִמְצָא
שֵׁם שָׁמַיִם מִתְחַלֵּל.

RABBI YEHUDAH:

Take care in talmud,
  for an error in talmud is as serious as intentional sin. (4:16)

רַבִּי יְהוּדָה אוֹמֵר: הֱוֵי זָהִיר בְּתַלְמוּד, שֶׁשִּׁגְגַת תַּלְמוּד עוֹלָה זָדוֹן.

TALMUD LITERALLY means "study," and here refers broadly to the whole process of studying, discussing, and teaching Jewish sacred literature, Torah. These sayings deal with the dangers of false beliefs and heresy.

The context of the first statement is the persecution of the Pharisees that took place under Jewish kings who sided with the Sadducees, the Pharisees' rivals in ancient Judea. Avtalion's predecessor, Yehudah ben Tabbai, had spent time in Alexandria, which may be the place of "evil waters," or heresy, as mentioned in the saying. The first saying indicates the special responsibility of leaders whose words will have large consequences.

The second saying is likely from Yehudah bar Ila'i, who lived a century and a half later. He was a leader in rebuilding Jewish learning after the Roman defeat of the Jewish Bar Kokhba rebellion. After the Roman triumph, the Emperor Hadrian led one of the worst slaughters of Jews before the Holocaust. When these persecutions relented, Yehudah ben Ila'i held a convention of scholars at Usha in the Galilee, and reestablished Jewish learning and the Sanhedrin, the Jewish high court. In these circumstances, he was acutely aware that he and his colleagues were securing Judaism and Jewish society for the future.

In tension with the defense of good and true beliefs are the dangers of dogmatism and fanaticism, in which mistaken beliefs that may be wrong are uncritically accepted and defended, and can even be used as license to do violence.

That errors in philosophy and law can indeed have grave consequences may be seen in the 20th century, when the adoption of Nazism and Bolshevism led to the suffering and death of millions of people. Ideas have consequences.

Modern Life

Two important modern ideas shed light on the issue of how to handle erroneous ideas. The first is the doctrine of tolerance, particularly religious tolerance, which arose in Holland, England, and the United States. This doctrine was created in reaction to exhaustion with religious wars in Europe. The second important modern idea is the model of scientific research: openness to criticism as a spur to creativity and the growth of knowledge. In science, dogmatism is banished and everything, no matter how fundamental, is open to criticism, revision, and improvement. This openness to criticism and collaborative effort has brought about some of the greatest advances in human history.

Measured against modern ideas of tolerance and of openness to criticism, Jewish tradition has both strengths and weaknesses. The Talmud is remarkably non-dogmatic. It records minority opinions and, as Menachem Fisch has argued in *Rational Rabbis*, is willing to reverse earlier rulings. Erroneous ideas are taken on openly, as part of a process of inquiry and judgment that is self-correcting.

Avot itself begins by stating that the whole tradition is sacred, but immediately adds that we should be slow and careful to judge—indicating that the truth is hard to ascertain, and errors are easy to commit, including in religious matters. However, in the Middle Ages, the mainstream tradition became more dogmatic in approach, with figures like Maimonides codifying rulings and beliefs as eternal, to be built upon, but never changed. Current Orthodoxy follows this approach.

It is important for a tradition to have boundaries in order to be robust and internally dynamic. But the historical record demonstrates that hostile relations with those whose views are antithetical to ours are not productive. The *birkat haminim*, the "blessing" that harshly condemns heretics, has been of no help in stopping rivals such as Christianity. In fact, the contact with different cultures, the ancient Greek in particular, resulted in a creative and productive new synthesis: Classical Judaism. It seems that both separation and interaction are engines of vitality for a tradition.

Be among the disciples of Aaron:
A lover of peace and pursuer of peace;
Love all fellow creatures,
And bring them near to the Torah. (1:12)

הִלֵּל וְשַׁמַּאי קִבְּלוּ מֵהֶם. הִלֵּל אוֹמֵר: הֱוֵי מִתַּלְמִידָיו שֶׁל אַהֲרֹן, אוֹהֵב שָׁלוֹם
וְרוֹדֵף שָׁלוֹם, אוֹהֵב אֶת הַבְּרִיּוֹת וּמְקָרְבָן לַתּוֹרָה.

A LOVER of peace. The Hebrew scriptures are very concerned with the wars necessary to establish and defend the Jewish state, but the emphasis of Judaism since Hillel's time has been on making peace. In 40 BCE, Herod, backed by the Romans, besieged Jerusalem. Leaders of the Pharisees, likely including Hillel, were said by Josephus to have urged the people to lay down their arms. For the sake of peace they welcomed Herod—whom they despised—into the city. Thus, the emphasis in the Talmud is on communal peace and peace between individuals.

Three generations later, in 65 CE, followers of Hillel continued to advocate peace, but were outvoted in a council on a day that the Palestinian Talmud (SHAB 17) says was as dark for the Jewish people as the day the Golden Calf was made. The rebellion against Rome went forward, resulting in the destruction of the Temple. As a result of this, and of the subsequent failure of the Bar Kokhba rebellion in 135 CE, the Jewish people did not have sovereignty over their own land for the next 1800 years.

After Hillel's time, peace became a central concern in Rabbinic Judaism, as reflected in this important text in the Mishnah:

&❧ These are the things of which a person enjoys the fruits in this world, and remain as a fund of merit for him for the world to come: honoring of mother and father, bestowing kindness, and making peace between one person and another; and Torah study leads to them all. (PE'AH 1:1)

In the Talmud, six more things are added to make an additional list: welcoming guests, visiting the sick, concentration in prayer, early attendance at the house of study, raising sons to learn Torah, and judging others in a favorable light (SHAB 127a). These two lists are reconciled by noting that the additional six are included under *gemilut ḥasadim*, "acts of kindness." A variation on these lists also appears in the siddur, the traditional prayer book.

In the generation after Hillel, Jesus of Nazareth took Hillel's message of love and peace a step further, saying in the Sermon on the Mount, "Resist not evil . . . If someone slaps you on the right cheek, turn and offer him your left . . . If a man in authority asks you to go one mile, go with him two . . . Love your enemies." W. H. Hudson, 19th-century naturalist and novelist, argued the contrary, that we have a moral obligation to strike back against the powerful who wrong us, because it is only the fear that the poor and weak may strike back that prevents the strong from totally oppressing and exploiting the weak. The Jewish Sages endorsed neither of these extremes, but advocated a middle position: we should pursue peace, but self-defense is also proper and appropriate. This policy means that each person and each country need to solve the difficult problem of how best to act to achieve both goals.

And bring them near to the Torah. The Jewish view toward seeking converts has varied greatly over history. When Ezra returned from the Babylonian exile, he ordered that intermarriages with non-Jews be broken up. The book of Ruth, by contrast, has the non-Jewish Ruth marry the Jew Boaz, and become an ancestor of King David. The Pharisees, of whom Hillel was a leader, had a very favorable view toward seeking and accepting converts, and did proselytize. According to historians, about 10 percent of the Roman world was Jewish at the time the Jewish state fell in 70 CE. After the fall of the Jewish state, Jews continued to accept converts as full Jews, but did not proselytize and warned potential converts of the difficulty of being a Jew in the condition of exile.

MODERN LIFE

IN THE late 20th century, Rabbi Alexander Schindler reversed the rabbinic reluctance to seek converts, and led the American Reform movement to begin "outreach" to non-Jews married to Reform Jews, and to those not affiliated with another religion. At the same time, he led the Reform movement to declare as Jews the children of a Jewish father and non-Jewish mother who are raised as Jews—thus contradicting the talmudic tradition that only those born to Jewish mothers or formal converts are to be considered Jewish. This latter decision was roundly condemned by more traditional Jewish denominations as splitting Judaism. Would Hillel, were he alive today, praise these efforts for bringing people near the Torah, or condemn them for dividing Judaism?

Promote your name—lose your name;
Fail to add—you diminish;
Fail to study—you deserve to die;
And exploit the crown—you perish. (1:13)

הוּא הָיָה אוֹמֵר: נְגִיד שְׁמָא אֲבַד שְׁמֵהּ, וּדְלָא מוֹסִיף יָסֵף, וּדְלָא יַלִּיף קְטָלָא
חַיָּב, וּדְאִשְׁתַּמֵּשׁ בְּתָגָא חֲלָף.

THESE SAYINGS are in Aramaic, the language common throughout the ancient Near East. It gradually displaced Hebrew as the spoken language of Jews, and was Hillel's native tongue, as he came from Babylonia, where it was spoken. The Gemara, the commentary part of the Talmud, is written in Aramaic.

Of Hillel, the Talmud says: "In ancient days when the Torah was forgotten from Israel, Ezra came up from Babylon and reestablished it. Then it was again forgotten until Hillel the Babylonian came up and reestablished it" (SUK 20a). Hillel is the central figure of *Avot* and was a seminal figure in the development of the Classical Judaism of the Mishnah and Talmud. Hillel put forward rules for interpreting the Torah so that it could be adapted to conditions in later times. He thus gave focus and direction to the whole enterprise of *talmud*, which explores the Torah and applies it to contemporary times.

Hillel was also personally renowned for patience, humility, devotion to learning, and seeking peace. The following story about Hillel includes all of these traits, as well as his belief in the primacy of ethics.

&❧ A certain heathen came to Shammai and said to him: "If you can teach me the whole Torah while I stand on one foot you can convert me to Judaism." Shammai drove him away with a builder's cubit [a ruler] which was in his hand. He went to Hillel and Hillel said to him, "What is hateful to you, do not do to your neighbor: That is the whole Torah. The rest is explanation: go, study." (SHAB 31a)

Hillel's formulation here of the "golden rule" is one of the earliest. Other formulations can be found in ancient Greek learning, in the sayings of Confucius, and in Christianity.

Promote your name. This saying can mean simply that with fame comes critics who will spoil your reputation. But here "promote" seems also to imply that the person acting improperly tries to inflate his or her accomplishments in order to impress others and advance his or her own cause.

Fail to add. This saying is traditionally interpreted: if you don't add to your own learning you will lose the learning you have. It can also be taken more broadly to mean that if a generation merely tries to preserve the heritage of its past, its level of culture decays. It must strive to add to its heritage and to make it relevant, in order just to sustain its strength.

Hillel himself "added." He effectively nullified the Torah law requiring cancellation of debts in the sabbatical year. This nullification was crucially important because people were reluctant to lend close to a sabbatical year and, by that era, commercial trading, which depends on credit, was vital to the economy. Hillel said that creditors could make a declaration to the court, called a *"prosbul,"* making the court the official creditor. Since the court was not a "neighbor or brother" (DEUT 15:2), the letter of the Torah law was not violated. Hillel acted decisively to preserve both the authority of the Torah and a strong economy.

Fail to study. This saying probably refers to the "death" of a person's reputation and influence. When people don't study, then their ideas and teachings become superficial, so their influence deserves to die out.

And exploit the crown. This admonition repeats, with even greater force, the warning of Hillel's teacher Shemaiah (*Avot* 1:10) not to try to exploit the power of the Roman government, Many did in fact die at the hands of the Romans, even before the wars with Rome.

MODERN LIFE

As THE next mishnah indicates, Hillel believed that some kind of self-assertion is legitimate, as opposed to the improper kind of self-promotion indicated in this mishnah. What kind of self-promotion is proper? What kind is wise? These are important questions in our age of mass media and social "networking" for career advancement. Obviously, being honest is necessary. But beyond that, these seem to be open questions.

Hillel's insistence that we try to add both to our own learning and— as I read him—to our heritage sets a dauntingly high standard. Yet, perhaps this is Hillel's point in using such extreme language. Without such seriousness of purpose and devotion to growing our traditions, and to making them vital today, they will weaken and fade away.

If I am not for myself, who is for me?
And when I am for myself, what am I?
And if not now, when? *(1:14)*

הוּא הָיָה אוֹמֵר: אִם אֵין אֲנִי לִי מִי לִי, וּכְשֶׁאֲנִי לְעַצְמִי מָה אֲנִי, וְאִם לֹא
עַכְשָׁו אֵימָתָי.

TODAY, HILLEL's famous three questions are usually taken rhetorically,
meaning: look out for yourself and stick up for yourself, or no one else
will; if you are only concerned for your own selfish interests, you are
unworthy; and now is the time to act. Medieval commentators also take
the questions rhetorically, but give a more pious interpretation: only I
can carry out my responsibility to do good, and receive the merits by
which God will judge me when I die. Maimonides adds psychological
insight: when a person is young, he or she acquires habits of doing right
or wrong—virtues and vices. Therefore, youths should do good deeds
now, and not wait until adulthood.

Hillel put these sayings in the form of questions, though, because, I
believe, he intended them to be taken not only rhetorically, but also to
actually be asked and answered when we face important decisions.

If I am not for myself, who is for me? This question not only implies
that it is legitimate to pursue your own interests, but also launches you
into thinking of the best way to carry out that pursuit. Your answer to,
"If I am not for myself—if I have to rely totally on others—who is for
me?" will also give you a shrewd idea of who your friends and allies are,
and who is not with you, or may even be actively opposed to your efforts.

When I am for myself, what am I? The common translation of this
saying as "If I am only for myself, what am I?" is misleading as it nar-
rows the question to being only a rhetorical one. Taken as a real question it asks, "What should be my role in this situation?" This is partly
a moral question: what do I owe to others and what do they owe to me?
And it is also a practical question: how should we define and share
responsibilities in a way that is most beneficial to both people in a
relationship?

If not now, when? This final question is the strategic question of timing—of when to problem-solve, when to decide, and when to act. What
matters are urgent? When should I postpone a decision or action?

What can I do now to improve my options later? What can I do now to protect myself if events undermine my plans?

Hillel's three questions encapsulate a philosophy of life that is a true synthesis of the ancient Hebrew and ancient Greek traditions—a synthesis at the heart of Classical Judaism. Greek sages, such as Plato and Aristotle, assume that everyone instinctively pursues his or her own personal happiness, and they try to show how wisdom can build a bridge to others, that it is in one's self-interest to serve others as well. This idea is known as "enlightened self-interest." The biblical Prophets start with the idea that God commands us to fulfill our obligations to society, and promises to reward us personally if we obey.

Hillel doesn't assume here that the gap between the self and society will be bridged by wisdom alone or by obedience to God's commandments alone. He indicates rather that each of us has a responsibility to build that bridge from both sides. We need to take the initiative to find courses of action that serve our own self-interest *and* the interests of others. Each of us needs to creatively address the problem of balancing our personal interests with our obligations to others. Each time we face an important life decision, the three questions launch us and guide us on this quest for balance.

This balanced approach to ethics—which actively harmonizes the interests of self and other, of the individual and society—is the hallmark of Rabbinic ethics. It is a contrast to both the "looking out for number one" ethics of Ayn Rand and the view of Calvin that self-denial is at the heart of being good and ethical. With his philosophy and principles for interpreting scripture, Hillel provided a coherent program for *talmud*, an active problem-solving effort on ethical and social issues that has continued and grown from generation to generation.

Modern Life

WHEN WE take Hillel's questions as ones to be answered when we face a decision, they raise practical issues that psychologists and experts on management have considered.

If I am not for myself, who is for me? Interpreted as a rhetorical question, this idea is supported by modern theories of "assertiveness." The idea is that there is a way to express our needs and wants to others in a manner that is neither aggressive and attacking, nor passive and withdrawing, by simply stating openly what we want or don't want. This is not a universally applicable method, because sometimes it is better to act without discussion. And sometimes it is wise not to be open about our wants and needs, particularly with people who are not trustworthy. But in many situations, this is a powerful technique, as it demonstrates respect for the other person, and opens the way to getting what you want, or to starting a discussion that can lead to a fair compromise. Interpreted instead as a question to be answered, "Who is for me?" is a question of who is an ally, and who an opponent. This is a key question in civil life, as gaining and keeping allies are usually the keys to winning.

When I am for myself, what am I? "What am I?" has us inquire into our duties in different roles in life. Confucius said, in a related idea, that the key to a good society is that "the father be a father, the son a son, the ruler a ruler," meaning that each person should fulfill his or her duty honestly and competently. Compared to ancient days, however, our roles are more fluid, and are more often negotiated by the people involved: boss and subordinate, parent and teenaged child, husband and wife.

In these fluid situations, as management experts have pointed out, role conflict and ambiguity are main sources of dysfunction in organizations and relationships, because they undermine cooperation and productivity. Asking the question "What am I?" is the first step to ethically and effectively resolving this issue of defining roles.

If not now, when? This question is a key question of strategy. Sometimes, such as in courtship, hesitation is disastrous, while other times acting too soon results in losing out. The question links to Ecclesiastes:

> A season is set for everything, a time to every experience under heaven: A time for being born and a time for dying ... A time for slaying and a time for healing ... A time for weeping and a time for laughing, A time for wailing and a time for dancing ... A time for embracing and a time for shunning embraces ... A time for silence and a time for speaking; A time for loving and a time for hating; A time for war and a time for peace. (ECCL 3:1–8)

Hillel is asking, "What time is it now? What action is appropriate?" In military strategy, two great principles are *initiative*—how to act now to increase the chances of success—and *security*—how to act now to prevent future disaster, or provide options in the event of a defeat. These principles are also of great value in career and life planning, and both involve timing. Hillel's last question sparks such strategic thinking.

Make your Torah a set priority;
Say little and do much;
And receive every person with a pleasant face. (1:15)

שַׁמַּאי אוֹמֵר: עֲשֵׂה תוֹרָתְךָ קֶבַע, אֱמוֹר מְעַט וַעֲשֵׂה הַרְבֵּה, וֶהֱוֵי מְקַבֵּל אֶת
כָּל הָאָדָם בְּסֵבֶר פָּנִים יָפוֹת.

MAKE YOUR Torah a set priority. This partly means that, in planning our week, we should set aside a regular time for study and not let the pressures of daily life push that aside. "Make," *aseh* in Hebrew, can also be read as "do," so that this phrase can also be interpreted as, "Do your Torah consistently," meaning that we should carry out the ethical and ritual commandments consistently.

Torah study was regarded by the Sages as so important that a much later talmudic Sage, Rava, included a version of Shammai's injunction as the second of six questions that every person is asked when he or she faces judgment in the world to come:

&❧ Did you deal honestly in business?
Did you fix times for Torah study?
Did you engage in procreation?
Did you hope for salvation?
Did you engage in critical discussion of wisdom?
Did you understand how to infer one thing from another? (SHAB 31a)

Torah study in the Sages' experience is morally, intellectually, and spiritually transformational. That's why it is a dominating theme in *Avot*. It is also interesting that both the devotion to study and to dialectics (critical discussion, inference) come from Greek tradition. This passage from Talmud dramatically illustrates how Hebraic and Greek traditions are the warp and woof of the fabric of Classical Judaism, which we read here in *Avot*.

Say little and do much. This phrase is traditionally interpreted as referring not to being a person of few words, but to being careful to promise little, and to do a great deal more than you promise. It applies to charitable giving, as well as promises in relationships. The opposite is the person who boasts about what he or she will do and doesn't deliver.

Receive every person with a pleasant face. In other parts of the Talmud, Shammai is compared unfavorably to Hillel: "A person should always be gentle like Hillel, not impatient like Shammai" (SHAB 30b). Yet, here it is Shammai who emphasizes the importance of beginning every interaction in an agreeable, affable manner.

Modern Life

THE IMPORTANCE to good relationships of starting off an interaction well has been confirmed in research observing the interactions of successful and unsuccessful married couples. Those who maintain a good relationship tend to begin potentially difficult discussions with a "soft start," as marriage researcher John Mordechai Gottman has put it. When one person reacts harshly, the ability of the other person to reframe the issue in a more soothing or less threatening way helps to maintain the relationship.

Those couples who start off harshly or escalate a dispute tend to do poorly in the marriage and end up divorced. Thus the proverbs, "The mouths of the wise say words that charm, but the lips of fools are their undoing" (ECCL 10:12) and "A soft answer turns away wrath, but a grievous word stirs up anger" (PROV 15:1), turn out to be of profound importance in human relations.

The second saying also identifies a crucial factor in relationships: what we promise and deliver to those with whom we have ongoing relationships. These often largely implicit promises make up the compact underlying a relationship, and influence whether and how that compact is fulfilled. Being careful not to overpromise insures that reasonable expectations are set, and that they are easy to fulfill or even surpass, leaving the other person content. Overpromising is likely to lead to discontent. Setting the right expectations, like starting off agreeably, is one of the secrets to good relationships. These sayings are thus deceptively simple: they seem restricted, but in fact contain far-reaching insights into human relationships.

Finally, the first saying, if we interpret it as, "Do your Torah consistently," refers to another crucial issue in relationships: carrying out the ethical obligations of each specific relationship to the other person, such as being parent, child, boss, subordinate, or friend. When the other person in the relationship, or we ourselves, feel unfairly treated, that kills joy, damages cooperation, and threatens the relationship.

Thus, taken together, Shammai's insights, like Hillel's, touch on issues fundamental to good human relations.

RABBAN GAMLIEL:

Choose for yourself a mentor;
Remove yourself from the doubtful;
And do not tithe by estimation excessively. (1:16)

רַבָּן גַּמְלִיאֵל הָיָה אוֹמֵר: עֲשֵׂה לְךָ רַב, וְהִסְתַּלֵּק מִן הַסָּפֵק, וְאַל תַּרְבֶּה
לְעַשֵּׂר אֲמָדוֹת.

RABBAN GAMLIEL was the son or the grandson—which is not clear—of
Hillel, and as heir to Hillel was head of the Jewish community in his
time. He was known for rulings that lessened the people's burdens, such
as his ruling that only one witness to the death of a woman's husband
was necessary to free her to remarry under Jewish law.

At first reading, this saying seems to be advocating a stringent ad-
herence to tradition and a quest for certainty. But a closer reading reveals that Rabban Gamliel may be advocating a more complex view.

Because of the final clause about tithing, it is fair to conclude, as did
Maimonides in his commentary, that these statements all concern the
process of making rulings on cases and laws that came before rabbis.

Choose for yourself a mentor. In this context, there are two implications of this injunction. The first is similar to that of the same words in
Avot 1:6: the student needs the experience of apprenticeship to one day
become a master. Being self-taught is not really an option. Apprenticeship is important particularly for learning Talmud, because what is to
be mastered is not simply a group of texts, but a way of thinking.
Hillel had introduced rules or techniques for interpreting a passage of
Jewish law and applying it to new situations. These rules cannot be applied mechanically, but rather creatively, and the only way to learn their
appropriate use is by trying to apply them and being corrected by a
master and fellow students.

A second implication of the saying, in this context, is that even after
we cease being formal students, we should continue to consult older,
more experienced masters on difficult issues. The evolution of *halakhah*
over the centuries thus has been a collaborative effort between younger
and older scholars.

Remove yourself from the doubtful. This saying probably means that
you should remove as much doubt as you can about the facts and law
before ruling on a case (cf. 1:1). But it can also mean to remove yourself

from doubtful cases—where the issue cannot be settled clearly, make no ruling, set no punishments. When we look at the way the Talmud later evolved, this is arguably a second, intended meaning. The Talmud reports conflicting views, and only goes on to report rulings when particular cases demand it. Clearly, Rabban Gamliel is advocating the careful and accurate understanding of issues before ruling. Where such a full understanding cannot be achieved, though, he may well be advocating leaving it to the future and to others to sort out the issue.

Do not tithe by estimation excessively. According to the Torah, farmers were required to "tithe," to give a tenth of their crop to the Temple. Rough estimation created problems, though. If one gave too little, the portion held back would be improper for his or her own use. Giving too much was not correct because depriving oneself is not right, and anything beyond the one-tenth portion would also be of questionable ritual fitness for Levites, who received the tithe. The point here, then, is that taking the time to measure properly, rather than using guesswork, is important.

MODERN LIFE

THE QUESTION of how to deal with doubt is an important issue in religion generally. The great American philosopher William James pointed out in his essay "The Will to Believe" that we have to make many decisions in life that involve our values, but both the basis of those values and the outcome of our decisions are surrounded with uncertainty. For often there is not, and even cannot be, deciding evidence. And among these difficult decisions are ones that are unavoidable.

The decision to trust or not trust one's wife or husband is not avoidable, so long as one stays married. And the quality of trust or suspicion will affect the relationship. Similarly, James argues, the decision of whether to have faith that it is better to live by such enduring values as truth, beauty, justice, and kindness is also unavoidable, and will affect our lives. This decision, along with a decision to see the roots of these values in the transcendent, is the decision to be religious. For James, uncertainty is evidently not a threat to religion, but rather calls it forth.

There are some figures in Judaism, as well as in other religions, who instead view doubt as a threat, and their solution is to insist that every aspect of their religion is certainly true, and beyond any revision. This outlook tends to lead to a withdrawal from the rest of society.

All my days I grew up among the sages, and
I have found nothing better for a person than silence;
And the main thing is not the learning, but the doing;
And all who speak too much bring on sin. (1:17)

שִׁמְעוֹן בְּנוֹ אוֹמֵר: כָּל יָמַי גָּדַלְתִּי בֵּין הַחֲכָמִים, וְלֹא מָצָאתִי לְגוּף טוֹב
מִשְּׁתִיקָה. וְלֹא הַמִּדְרָשׁ עִקָּר, אֶלָּא הַמַּעֲשֶׂה. וְכָל הַמַּרְבֶּה דְבָרִים מֵבִיא חֵטְא.

ALL MY days... Shimon, as son of Gamliel, Sage of the previous mishnah and great-grandson of Hillel, grew up surrounded by Torah scholars. Evidently, he had contact with many people who were brilliantly
debating the interpretation of Torah, but not putting it into practice.
This saying is a biting criticism of such behavior.

Not the learning, but the doing. "The learning" here translates "*midrash,*" which specifically refers to the study of Torah, but also means
the creative interpretation of Torah texts.

This warning note is sounded against the background of Rabbinic
tradition, which is almost obsessed with the importance of study. There
is a famous debate in the Talmud on the issue of which is greater: study
or deeds. At the beginning of the debate, Rabbi Tarfon held that deeds
are greater and Rabbi Akiva that study is greater. In the end, all concluded that "study is greater, for it leads to deeds" (KID 40b). This conclusion resolves the conflict by saying that the two are always in
harmony. However, Shimon ben Gamliel's saying contradicts this conclusion, as it clearly implies that there are learned people, including
those learned in Torah, who don't act properly. Unfortunately, this observation is often corroborated even today.

All who speak too much. This saying raises the question of what kind
of speech is too much and "brings on sin." The Sages called this speech
lashon ha-ra, "the bad tongue" or "the evil tongue." The current expression to "badmouth" somebody is similar. Maimonides, commenting on
this mishnah, points out that *lashon ha-ra* refers to speech that dispar-
ages others, even when it is true, and thus does not actually constitute
slander. Interestingly, a similar concept is found in Buddhist ethics.

Later Sages believed that *lashon ha-ra* is both an extremely common
and extremely grave sin. The Talmud says that the ancient Temple was
destroyed in the time of Shimon ben Gamliel partly because of *lashon*

ha-ra. A personal insult sparked a chain of events that led to the Roman attack on Jerusalem (GIT 55b). The Sages compared *lashon ha-ra* to an arrow: once shot, it cannot be taken back. Indeed, they indicated that the evil tongue can be more deadly than the sword because it can "speak in Rome and kill in Syria, speak in Syria and kill in Rome" (J PE'AH 1:1). Gossip that can cause strife between people is also directly prohibited by the Torah, as interpreted by the Rabbis (LEV 19:16).

Modern Life

IN THE late 19th century, Rabbi Israel Meir Kagan wrote an important book on *lashon ha-ra, Chofetz Chaim* (meaning "a seeker of life"—a name Kagan himself came to be called). His position essentially was that speaking *lashon ha-ra*—or even listening to it—is prohibited unless there is a compelling reason to allow it. Such compelling reasons include, for example, that you will prevent another person from being harmed by warning him or her against associating with a bad person.

Chofetz Chaim is generally extremely stringent about not engaging in or even listening to *lashon ha-ra.* For in his view, while *lashon ha-ra* is one of the most common of sins, it is also one of the most serious. Indeed, we can see today the grave harm the Sages warned about in many different cases, including the killing sprees of disturbed youths who have been bullied, and the terrorist attacks of 9/11, fueled by hateful rhetoric. And of course the power of gossip, true or false, to damage reputations is familiar to us all.

Still, one could argue that the rules concerning *lashon ha-ra* need to be rethought for contemporary life. Much of modern life is lived in large institutions, such as schools, corporations, and government organizations. In these, the issue of *lashon ha-ra* is important and difficult. On one hand, negative gossip sometimes does great damage, but on the other hand, negative gossip can often serve as a vital guide to career survival.

The Torah says not to take up an empty rumor (EX 23:1). But how certain do we need to be to convey information that might protect someone? And should there be different standards for how much certainty is needed for giving such information to one's spouse? To a trusted friend? It would seem that the nature of one's responsibilities to the other person, and knowing how responsible he or she is with information, might well make a difference as to whether it is ethical to pass on the information to him or her.

RABBAN SHIMON BEN GAMLIEL:

By three things is the world sustained:
by justice, by truth, and by peace. (1:18)

רַבָּן שִׁמְעוֹן בֶּן גַּמְלִיאֵל אוֹמֵר: עַל שְׁלֹשָׁה דְבָרִים הָעוֹלָם קַיָּם: עַל הָאֱמֶת, וְעַל
הַדִּין, וְעַל הַשָּׁלוֹם, שֶׁנֶּאֱמַר: "אֱמֶת וּמִשְׁפַּט שָׁלוֹם שִׁפְטוּ בְּשַׁעֲרֵיכֶם."

THE HEBREW in this mishnah concludes with a prooftext: "As it is said:
Execute a judgment of truth and peace in your gates" (*ZECH 8:16*).
Rabban Shimon ben Gamliel was the grandson of Shimon ben Gamliel,
author of the previous mishnah, and the father of Yehudah haNasi, who
compiled *Avot* and the whole Mishnah. The way to reconcile this saying and *Avot* 1:2—that the world "stands upon the Torah, worship and
acts of kindness"—is to say that those three are the purposes for which
God created the world, whereas justice, truth, and peace are the principles that sustain the world, and prevent it from collapsing.

The three values in this mishnah can be seen to promote the welfare
of humanity on two levels: the interpersonal and the social.

By justice, by truth. On the social level, a government that creates just
laws and courts that fairly administer them promote peace and harmony in society, or *yishuv ha-olam*, "the settlement of the world," as
Maimonides called it. In the biblical context, "truth" refers not simply
to the accuracy of statements, but also to the moral dimension of truth-
telling: honesty, keeping promises, and avoiding deceit. On the interpersonal level, truth is essential for trust and effective cooperation, while
lies destroy relationships from within. For example, experts who have
studied the damage that infidelity does to marriages say that the lying
does as much or more damage than the sexual betrayal.

For a whole society to be able both to know the real effects of governmental policies, and to give feedback to those in power and change
these policies, greatly helps sustain peace and prosperity, as philosopher
Karl Popper has pointed out. Democratic governments, which allow a
free press, debate, and voting to choose leaders, increase the power of
truth to change society for the better.

Peace. Strife and war are obviously destructive to society. Justice and
truth are important to sustaining peace, but they can sometimes come
into conflict with that goal. The Talmud has an interesting analysis of
such conflicts, and how to resolve them.

Justice vs. peace. When parties are in dispute, peace between them may be reached through a settlement that both sides can agree on, rather than through a strictly just solution that leaves one party feeling injured and angry. In *Sanhedrin* (6b), the Rabbis debate as to when mediation and compromise are appropriate, and when a legal judgment is called for. Rabbi Eliezer, son of Rabbi Yose the Galilean, argues that arbitration should be forbidden because justice should always rule. In a memorable phrase he said, "Let justice pierce through the mountain"—meaning always to strive for strict justice, whatever the obstacle or cost.

Rabbi Yehudah ben Korha takes the opposite side. Referring to the same prooftext as Rabban Shimon ben Gamliel here, he argues that when people turn to courts of law, no peace results, and where there is already peace, people don't turn to courts: "What is that kind of justice in which peace abides—we must say: arbitration." The report of the debate identifies the "pierce the mountain" view with Moses, and the priority on peace with his brother Aaron. The decision at the end of the discussion is that offering mediation as an alternative to court is always meritorious. But the question of the point at which to stop offering mediation is left unresolved.

Truth vs. peace. Sometimes the truth can offend and set people against one another. The Talmud identifies two areas in particular in which truth can be compromised. One of these is in the tactful shading of the truth for the sake of good manners.

The question is raised, "How does one dance [and sing] before the bride? The school of Shammai says: 'the bride as she is.' The school of Hillel says: 'Beautiful and graceful bride.'" Against the school of Shammai, the school of Hillel maintained that "changing" of words is proper even if the bride is lame or blind, and in spite of the Torah passage, "Keep far from false words" (EX 23:7). Thus, the Sages concluded, "One should always try to get along well with people" (KET 17a).

A second area of conflict between truth and peace concerns peace in the home, *shelom bayit.* When God tells Sarah that she will bear a child with Abraham, she laughs, saying, "my husband so old." But God then reports Sarah's words to Abraham as "old as I am" (GEN 18:12–13), which will not offend Abraham. Sarah had also said to God that she is "withered." Still, God changed what Sarah actually said. The Sages thus conclude that words can be "changed" for the sake of family peace (BM 87a).

M<small>ODERN</small> L<small>IFE</small>

J<small>USTICE VS. TRUTH.</small> English jurist William Blackstone, influenced by Abraham's argument with God on behalf of the innocent of Sodom (G<small>EN</small> 23), said, "Better that ten guilty persons escape than that one innocent suffer." In America, this principle has led to the establishment of many rules for protecting defendants, rules that have limited a jury's access to the truth. In fact, prominent lawyer Alan Dershowitz has written, "The American justice system is built on a foundation of not telling the whole entire truth" (*The Best Defense*). After a number of infamous trials in which the seemingly guilty have gone free, many Americans feel the right balance between justice and truth has not been struck in their legal system.

Truth vs. peace. Interestingly, the idea that it is sometimes ethically preferable to shade the truth is not accepted in traditional Christianity: St. Augustine, St. Thomas Aquinas, and philosopher Immanuel Kant all absolutely prohibit lying—even to save a life, which is antithetical to the Jewish point of view. The permitted examples in Jewish tradition of situations in which lying is permitted seem to be at the extremes: when the most grave danger is present or when the lies told are the most inconsequential polite "white lies." For lighter cases, a measure of the acceptability of lying is to ask: if you were in the other person's place, would you approve of being lied to?

Justice vs. peace. The study of when and how to mediate and negotiate has made great strides in the past 50 years, with new techniques for those working in fields of international diplomacy, business, labor, divorce mediation, and education. The techniques that have been developed are valuable aids to creating both peace and justice in the world.

Justice. Despite important progress on negotiation and mediation, psychology has had a blind spot in on the issue of the impact of justice, or fairness, in relationships. We all know that when one person or both people in a relationship feel the relationship is basically unfair, or that one side is not fulfilling his or her responsibilities, it causes great strain, and threatens the relationship. What impact do societal standards of justice have on marriage relationships? How important is justice, as compared to compassion and kindness? These, and many similar questions have yet to be researched and answered.

Chapter Two

Which is the right path that you should choose for yourself?
One that is admirable in your eyes,
And admirable in the eyes of others. (2:1A)

רַבִּי אוֹמֵר: אֵיזוֹ הִיא דֶרֶךְ יְשָׁרָה שֶׁיָּבוֹר לוֹ הָאָדָם? כָּל שֶׁהִיא תִּפְאֶרֶת
לְעוֹשֶׂיהָ וְתִפְאֶרֶת לוֹ מִן הָאָדָם.

"RABBI" LITERALLY means "my master." The person referred to here simply as "Rabbi"—as he was referred to by his students—is Yehudah ha-Nasi, direct descendant of Hillel, and the chief representative or *"Nasi"* of the Jewish community under the Romans. Yehudah haNasi edited the final, definitive version of the Mishnah, including *Avot*. He was revered by his contemporaries. One said: "Not since the days of Moses were learning and high office combined in one person until Rabbi" (GIT 59a).

Which is the right path? Yashar, here translated as "right," literally means "straight," and also has the connotation of honesty and integrity. All of Yehudah haNasi's sayings in this mishnah address situations in which the ethically right choice is not obvious to us, and where we face temptations.

One that is admirable. Tiferet, or "admirable," comes from the root meaning "to decorate," and is variously translated as "splendid," "beautiful," and by extension, "honorable." As commentator Rabbi Shimon ben Tzemaḥ (c. 1400) points out, Yehudah haNasi has given us a two-part test here to help us judge whether a course of action is ethical; the action needs to pass both parts. For example, an action may seem appealing and admirable from one's own point of view—making money on a certain venture and helping one's family with it, for example. But if the story of the venture were made public, and people viewed it as unsavory or unethical, the venture would fail the second test.

The action may fail in the opposite way: it may appeal to other people, but violate one's own conscience. A course of action by a politician, such as an appeal to fear and hatred, may be highly approved of by the majority of his or her constituents, yet the politician may know that in the long run it is bad for the country, and that it violates his or her own conscience. On a family level, a child may be very happy that a parent indulges his or her bad behavior, but the parent knows on some level that such indulgence may teach the child to be selfish and inconsiderate.

Underlying Yehudah haNasi's saying is the idea that, although gaining a correct understanding of situations may often be difficult, the moral sense is the common heritage of all humanity. A similar idea is behind a later saying in *Avot* by Ḥanina ben Dosa:

     If the spirit of your fellow man finds you pleasing, the spirit of the Holy One finds you pleasing. If the spirit of your fellow man does not find you pleasing, the spirit of the Holy One does not find you pleasing. (*Avot* 3:13)

However, the idea that being popular or "cool" or pleasing to others is always right is not Jewish. Rabbi Joseph Hertz, Chief Rabbi of the British Empire in the early 20th century, pointed out that the prophets were quite willing to say what was not pleasing or popular, but was morally right. Ḥanina ben Dosa clearly indicates, though, that being crabby and disagreeable is not a sign of merit, and pleasing people in some respect is desirable. His phrase "the spirit of your fellow man" probably indicates that the aspect of other people that we should strive to please is their better nature—the *yetzer ha-tov*—and not their baser instincts—the *yetzer ha-ra* (avarice, lust, and the desire to dominate).

Modern Life

YEHUDAH HANASI's starting point is very different from the "if it feels good do it" standard, which has been promoted in our time as "liberated." His premise is that there is a straight path, a path of integrity that we should do our utmost to follow. Following an ethical path has been commanded by God, and is emotionally rewarding, as well as spiritually fulfilling. In this mishnah, Rabbi gives us a mental process that will help us keep on that path.

Disillusionment with the "if it feels good" approach is vividly expressed in the song lyric of Cheryl Crow: "If it makes you happy/It can't be that bad/If it makes you happy/Then why the hell are you so sad?" Indeed, the Sages say that craving for pleasure can "drive a person from the world" (4:28).

One that is admirable. Some have formulated a modern version of the second part of Rabbi's test this way: If your actions were on the front page of the newspaper tomorrow, how would you feel? And looking at more recent technologies, the question could be posed all too realistically: If you checked your social media account and found word of your actions being spread all over the Internet, how would you feel?

RABBI:

Be as careful with a minor commandment as with a major
one, for you do not know the rewards of the commandments.
Weigh the losses in doing the right thing against the gains,
and the gains in committing a sin against the losses.
Reflect on three things and you will not come into the grip of
sin: know that above you are an eye that sees, an ear
that hears, and all your deeds written in a book. (2:1B)

וֶהֱוֵי זָהִיר בְּמִצְוָה קַלָּה כְּבַחֲמוּרָה, שֶׁאֵין אַתָּה יוֹדֵעַ מַתַּן שְׂכָרָן שֶׁל מִצְוֹת.
וֶהֱוֵי מְחַשֵּׁב הֶפְסֵד מִצְוָה כְּנֶגֶד שְׂכָרָהּ, וּשְׂכַר עֲבֵרָה כְּנֶגֶד הֶפְסֵדָהּ. הִסְתַּכֵּל
בִּשְׁלֹשָׁה דְבָרִים, וְאֵין אַתָּה בָא לִידֵי עֲבֵרָה. דַּע מַה לְמַעְלָה מִמְּךָ, עַיִן רוֹאָה,
וְאֹזֶן שׁוֹמַעַת, וְכָל מַעֲשֶׂיךָ בַּסֵּפֶר נִכְתָּבִים.

BE AS *careful with a minor commandment.* Whereas the first part of *Avot*
2:1 is a guide to choosing the right path, these next three parts concern
our motivation to keep to that path. In the Torah, punishments are laid
out for violating negative commandments, but the rewards of following positive ones are often not clear. Here "Rabbi," Yehudah haNasi,
seems to be assuring us that God will give great rewards, whether in
this life or the next.

Weigh the losses in doing the right thing against the gains. "Doing the
right thing" here is the translation of *mitzvah*, also "commandment."
Because Yehudah haNasi is speaking of losses and gains that we can
reckon, in this sentence he seems to be referring to benefits and losses
in this life, and is urging us to think more deeply of long-term consequences when we face temptation, consequences which can motivate us
to do the right thing. If it is obvious that we will have to sustain a loss
to do the right thing, then an understanding of the long-term benefits
to ourselves and others may keep us on the right path. And if it is obvious that we can gain something by doing wrong, an understanding of
the long-term pain that we will cause others and suffer ourselves may
again keep us on the right path.

Reflect on three things. In this unforgettable metaphor, Yehudah ha-
Nasi expresses the core Rabbinic doctrine of individual providence:
the idea that God is watching over each of us, can intervene in our
lives accordingly, and will judge us each for our deeds both in this life

and the next. It is interesting that in an earlier generation, Akavia ben Mahalalel, less confident of his listeners' faith, expressed this warning in more threatening terms:

• Reflect upon three things and you will not come into the grip of sin. Know where you came from, where you are going, and before whom you must give account. Where you came from: a fetid drop. Where you are going: to a place of dust, worm, and maggot. And before whom you must give account: the Supreme King of kings, the Holy One, blessed be He. (*Avot* 3:1; cf. *Avot* 4:29)

MODERN LIFE

WEIGH THE losses. What are the benefits and risks of acting as a mentsh— a caring, responsible person? Living as a mentsh promotes strong, loving personal relationships. Though there is no guarantee of success, as relationships take two, being selfish and devious is almost certain to destroy trust. Thus, in personal relationships, we have very strong motivation for at least appearing to be caring and to have integrity.

Unscrupulous, ruthless people do sometimes get ahead in business, but at the cost of harming their relationships and reducing respect and love from others. With courage and creativity, the honest can succeed in business, as the case of Aaron Feuerstein illustrates (see 2:6b). Being ethical does not mean being naïve, and an ethical person needs to be just as shrewd a strategist as an unethical person in order to succeed.

Thus in weighing losses and gains, it is important to explore ethical strategies for achieving our goals. Indeed, the commitment to living according to the ethical mitzvot (commandments) means that we focus on ethical options when we look for ways to further our goals and solve our problems. When we are tempted by obvious unethical paths—usually having to do with sex or money—Rabbi's reminder is to recall why we take the ethical path, and the gains we reap from doing so.

Reflect upon three things. In a sermon, a modern rabbi told the story of a wedding where another rabbi leaned over and said softly, "Lovely wedding, pity the bride is so ugly." Unfortunately, a videotape caught the comment, to the mortification of the offending rabbi. The day after hearing the story, a child heard her mother losing her temper and said, "The tape is always running." Whether or not we can accept reward and punishment in an afterlife, Rabbi Akiva's unforgettable image of an eye that sees will make us think twice and modify our actions.

RABBAN GAMLIEL, SON OF RABBI YEHUDAH HANASI:

> *Excellent is the study of Torah along with worldly*
> *activities, for toil in both causes sin to be forgotten.*
> *All Torah unaccompanied by labor ends*
> *in idleness and causes sin.*
> *Let all who work with the community work with them*
> *for the sake of Heaven.*
> *Then the merit of their ancestors will aid them, and*
> *their righteousness will endure forever.*
> *"And upon you, I will bestow a great reward,*
> *as if you had accomplished it." (2:2)*

רַבָּן גַּמְלִיאֵל בְּנוֹ שֶׁל רַבִּי יְהוּדָה הַנָּשִׂיא אוֹמֵר: יָפֶה תַלְמוּד תּוֹרָה עִם דֶּרֶךְ אֶרֶץ, שֶׁיְּגִיעַת שְׁנֵיהֶם מַשְׁכַּחַת עָוֹן, וְכָל תּוֹרָה שֶׁאֵין עִמָּהּ מְלָאכָה סוֹפָהּ בְּטֵלָה וְגוֹרֶרֶת עָוֹן. וְכָל הָעוֹסְקִים עִם הַצִּבּוּר, יִהְיוּ עוֹסְקִים עִמָּהֶם לְשֵׁם שָׁמַיִם, שֶׁזְּכוּת אֲבוֹתָם מְסַיַּעְתָּם, וְצִדְקָתָם עוֹמֶדֶת לָעַד, וְאַתֶּם מַעֲלֶה אֲנִי עֲלֵיכֶם שָׂכָר הַרְבֵּה כְּאִלּוּ עֲשִׂיתֶם.

EXCELLENT IS *the study. Derekh eretz,* "worldly activities," is literally "way of the land." Its meaning here is engagement in the world, including earning a living.

This first saying is a classic formulation meant to resolve the tension between study and work in rabbinic values. On one hand, worldly work is regarded as honorable and necessary—though not as sacred, as it is in the Protestant ethic. For example (cf. 1:10), the commandment to rest on the Sabbath begins, "Six days shall you labor" (EX 20:9), and Yehudah haNasi interpreted this clause as a commandment to work on the first six days, as we are commanded to rest on the seventh. It is also said that he who doesn't teach his son a trade teaches him to be a gangster (KID 29a). On the other hand, work is also regarded as onerous, a punishment for Adam's sin (KID 82b). Study of Torah is regarded as one of the highest priorities in life, as we see throughout *Avot,* and one Sage (Nehori, KID 82a) said he would teach his son only Torah. The resolution is that devotion to both work and Torah study is needed.

Rabban Gamliel, in saying that "toil in both causes sin to be forgotten," rejects Torah study without a way to earn a livelihood. Maimonides, commenting on this mishnah, says that without an occupation, a person will become desperate and turn to sinful means to earn a livelihood.

Let all who work. Scholars were community leaders, and the second half of this mishnah continues by giving guidelines for leadership. Leaders should work "for the sake of Heaven"—that is, unselfishly serve the community. If they serve the community this way, their work will be aided by "the merit of their ancestors," and God will reward them even if they cannot accomplish all they strive for.

Modern Life

Torah with worldly activities. This phrase, *Torah im derekh eretz* in Hebrew, was adopted by Rabbi Samson Raphael Hirsh in the mid-19th century as the motto for the "neo-Orthodox" movement. It means being committed to full engagement with both Torah and modern life. And it seems that today, Jewish day schools, whether communal, Conservative, or Reform, have been dedicated to a similar ideal.

However, outside this context, this ideal is facing big challenges. Religious education in non-Orthodox Judaism in the U.S. has mainly taken place in supplementary religious schools, and these have not succeeded in making most Jews into the lifelong students of Torah that Rabban Gamliel advocates. In Israel, secular Jewish education has not taught the rabbinic tradition, the bulk of Torah. And among the ultra-Orthodox, the *haredim*, many boys are trained only for Torah study, so that many are unprepared to earn a livelihood outside the religious community. This has created a problematic situation in which Torah scholars, good or bad, become wards of the state. This *haredi* practice seems to be a direct violation of this mishnah, and what it warns against.

Let all who work with. This mishnah raises the issue of the best way to structure organized Jewish religion, and the proper activities of lay leadership. (On professional leadership, see *Avot* 4:7.) The ideal of working "for the sake of Heaven" means that individuals set aside their personal agendas, and work for the benefit of the whole community. But as Rabbi Edwin Friedman pointed out, people tend to see the synagogue as a quasi-family, and to bring in and act out issues that existed in their original family. How can lay leadership stay on track in acting "for the sake of Heaven," while avoiding personal agendas and quarrels? Perhaps one key is in the first part of the mishnah: studying Torah and applying it to the issues that boards face.

RABBAN GAMLIEL:

> *Be wary of the authorities, for they befriend a person*
> *   only for their own advantage.*
> *They appear as friend when it suits them, but do not*
> *   stand by a man in his hour of need. (2:3)*

הֱווּ זְהִירִין בָּרָשׁוּת, שֶׁאֵין מְקָרְבִין לוֹ לָאָדָם אֶלָּא לְצֹרֶךְ עַצְמָן, נִרְאִין
כְּאוֹהֲבִין בִּשְׁעַת הֲנָאָתָן, וְאֵין עוֹמְדִין לוֹ לָאָדָם בִּשְׁעַת דָּחֳקוֹ.

RABBI ḤANINA, DEPUTY HIGH PRIEST:

> *Pray for the welfare of the regime;*
> *But for fear of it people would swallow one another*
> *   alive. (3:2)*

רַבִּי חֲנִינָא סְגַן הַכֹּהֲנִים אוֹמֵר: הֱוֵי מִתְפַּלֵּל בִּשְׁלוֹמָהּ שֶׁל מַלְכוּת, שֶׁאִלְמָלֵא
מוֹרָאָהּ, אִישׁ אֶת רֵעֵהוּ חַיִּים בְּלָעוֹ.

THESE TWO contrasting sayings reflect Rabbinic attitudes toward an oppressive Roman government. In general, the Rabbis were—with good reason—very wary of the Roman authorities, and tried to build a strong Jewish community life while avoiding them. But Rabbi Ḥanina here strikingly says that even a bad government is better than no government at all, for without it people, including Jews, would descend into barbarism.

Both of these *mishnayot* reflect the attitude of Jewish leaders who stood apart from government. Through much of the period the Rabbis in *Avot* lived, the Jewish people were not masters in their own house. And this became even more true subsequently, until the reestablishment of the Jewish state in modern times. As a result, the Jewish Sages focused on interpersonal and communal issues, but not on issues of political power and organization.

The state as it existed in biblical times had a monarchy from the rule of King Saul until the Babylonian exile, and again Judea had a monarchy under the Hasmonean kings, from 164 BCE until the fall of the Second Temple in 70 CE. The management of the Jewish state under monarchy suffered from many of the same grievous ills as other monarchies, with, according to the assessment in the TANAKH, many bad kings and only a few good ones. After the Jewish state fell, aside from praying for its reestablishment there was little focus on issues of state.

As a result, though the Torah itself contains discussion of the organization of the state, this discussion largely ceases in Rabbinic Judaism.

Modern Life

Two CHANGES in modern times radically changed the relationship of Jews to the state. For most of the time from the fall of the Temple in 70 CE to 1800, Jews lived as largely self-governing foreigners within states. And they stayed in places they didn't own at the sufferance of the local ruler. In this situation, talmudic law administered by rabbis was strong, but it did not concern itself with regulation of the non-Jewish state.

This situation changed radically when, under the influence of the Enlightenment, Western European states began to offer Jews full citizenship, beginning around 1800. One reaction to this new opportunity was the creation of Reform Judaism. A key part of Reform theology was to reject the idea of a national messiah who would restore the Jews to Zion, and to replace that idea with the aspiration for a "Messianic Age," in which all peoples would live together in peace in a just world. And it was the responsibility of every Jew to work toward this world, as did the prophets of old. But now the concern was not with the Jews as a nation, but rather with all of humanity.

The new theology restored the prophetic search for justice within the state, and so gave a rationale for involvement in the politics of the states in which Jews were now citizens. At the same time, because they rejected the idea of a messiah who would restore the monarchy of King David, Reform Jews were free to pursue new political ideas, so long as they could be seen as furthering general Jewish values such as justice and peace.

As a reaction against the theological innovations of Reform Judaism, neo-Orthodoxy was established to preserve talmudic law (halakhah) while still being engaged in modern society. Later, a middle way, Conservative Judaism, also advocated engagement. The Reform movement has remained the most active in social reform, at least in America.

In Eastern Europe, which remained under the old system of treating Jews as foreign residents governed largely by themselves well into the 20th century, the story was very different. Orthodox groups, which by then had split into traditional and Ḥasidic, still followed the traditional path of avoiding all but necessary contact with the government. More than that, the attitude had turned into a kind of quietism: an effort to avoid trouble by practicing avoidance of and passivity toward state authorities. This passivity became fatal after the rise of Hitler. Orthodox Rabbi Irving "Yitz" Greenberg writes:

> Orthodox Judaism taught passivity ... Zusya Friedman, spokesman for Agudas Yisroel [the Union of traditional Orthodox and Ḥassidim] in 1942 said, "God has always made miracles. We are in danger. This, again, means God will save us with miracles. Anybody who resorts to force will only bring upon us the wrath of the Nazis and they will destroy us even more. And so it is prohibited in the Jewish law to talk and think in terms of armed resistance." (*Jews and Judaism in the 21st Century*, E. Feinstein, ed., 49.)

Facing economic hardship and oppressive governments, many Jews in Eastern Europe rebelled against the passivity of their rabbis, and abandoned Jewish religion for secular Socialism, either in a universalist form, or in the form of political Zionism—advocacy of creating a state for Jews. Fleeing hardship, a third of the Jewish population left Eastern Europe, most for America or the Land of Israel, then Palestine. Jews, partly through international sympathy and partly through the force of arms, won their own state in 1948, and adopted a liberal democratic government. Ninety percent of those remaining in Eastern Europe were murdered in the Holocaust.

In the face of discriminatory and often oppressive governments for 1900 years, it did make sense for the Jewish community to work around political powers. But now, in liberal democracies, Jews have an opportunity to influence events, so they have a responsibility to fulfill Jewish values in the political sphere. Thus, our relations with political authorities are more similar to what they were before the fall of the Temple than they are to relations with the state during rabbinic dominance, from 70 to 1800.

The politics of the ancient period were, however, represented by two antiquated models of the state. One model found in the TANAKH is of a decentralized tribal society, which worked poorly under the Judges. The other is monarchy, which, as noted earlier, had a sorry record resembling that of other, non-Jewish monarchies.

People have argued that Jewish tradition supports diverse political philosophies, from Socialism to free-market libertarianism. The reality is that Rabbinic Judaism does not pronounce on these issues, and we are left to our own creative efforts to decide how best to apply the heritage from both the Torah and the Rabbis to the political issues of our day.

Do His will as if it were your will, so that
  He may do your will as His will.
Nullify your will before His will, so that
  He may nullify the will of others before your will. (2:4)

הוּא הָיָה אוֹמֵר: עֲשֵׂה רְצוֹנוֹ כִּרְצוֹנֶךָ, כְּדֵי שֶׁיַּעֲשֶׂה רְצוֹנְךָ כִּרְצוֹנוֹ. בַּטֵּל
רְצוֹנְךָ מִפְּנֵי רְצוֹנוֹ, כְּדֵי שֶׁיְּבַטֵּל רְצוֹן אֲחֵרִים מִפְּנֵי רְצוֹנֶךָ.

THIS MISHNAH could be read as a simple promise that if you obey God, God will in return give you whatever you want and defeat all who oppose you. Rabban Gamliel probably had a deeper, more complex idea in mind. The saying implies that when you devote yourself to being wholly pure in your motives, you profoundly change yourself and the world you live in.

Do His will. This phrase can also be translated, "make His will as yours," since *oseh* means both "make" and "do." Here, the identification of the self with God serves the characteristic Jewish focus on ethical action, on following mitzvot, God's commandments. By making our will as God's will, we ask for nothing that God does not want for us, and so, Rabban Gamliel seems to say, we will not be disappointed.

Nullify your will. This second saying has some resonance with the Taoist idea of the power of "nonaction." According to this concept, the forces of nature are so powerful that if you try to go against them you will be crushed. If you go along with them, or "go with the flow," then you will conquer opposition effortlessly. Rabban Gamliel's idea may be that when we act with purity of purpose, our actions are so in harmony with the one who rules the world, we will triumph over all foes. However, because Judaism believes in actively working against evil, Rabban Gamliel probably had a more activist view in mind. One interpretation of his mishnah is that our personal good will influences others to change for the better, so the ill will of others will not touch us. Another is that when our will is pure, God will take our side, as in ancient days with Moses and King David, and help us defeat our enemies.

MODERN LIFE

EXTREME HUMILITY is part of the logic of mysticism, and later mystics have seen the nullifying of the will that this mishnah advocates as part of mystical practice. All varieties of mysticism have in common the idea that there is an underlying unity in the world that is not obvious to everyday perception. Mystical experience is the experience of that oneness—the oneness of our selves with others, with nature, with God. If we are to merge with God, the separate self has to, in some sense, disappear—a core idea in Buddhism, and in Kabbalah.

The religiosity of the Sages has similarities to that in the TANAKH, and also to that of the medieval mystics, but it is also different from both in important ways. In the TANAKH, the emphasis is on the love and awe of God, and on obeying God's commandments. There is no call for people to be close to God or to experience God's presence. Indeed, in a world in which most people believed in many gods, the action of supernatural forces in the world was generally unquestioned. In the TANAKH, though, those with a *direct* experience of God are described as seers and prophets, special people who experience God's word through visions, or through ecstatic experiences. They do not seek God; God chooses them, and they reluctantly agree to be messengers of God's words.

The practice of prophecy ended a generation after the destruction of the First Temple in 586 BCE. According to the Sages, God no longer communicated with humanity through the *ruah hakodesh*, the Holy Spirit, as God had done with the prophets. Furthermore, the Sages specifically rejected any *bat kol*, or "voice from heaven," as an authority for deciding matters of *halakhah*. Instead, in an important turning point in Jewish history, they insisted on logical analysis of the texts, and a majority vote would decide what interpretation or conclusion was to be law (ED 7:7; see *Rational Rabbis* by Menachem Fisch for extensive discussion of this event).

This shift from direct divine guidance to indirect guidance through the study of sacred texts had great benefits: it unified Judaism and made it adaptable to new conditions. This was vital, as disunity was then a constant threat. For many competing religious beliefs were then swirling in the Middle East—both in Judea, where there were many sects deemed heretical by Rabbinic standards, and outside Judea, where many pagan religions existed. There regularly arose leaders who claimed divine inspiration for their views. In this situation, charismatic individuals could disrupt the fragile community, struggling to survive, with claims of new visions directly from God. In place of the reliance on charismatic visionaries, the new reliance on discussing texts and voting on rulings created a social process that draws on the wisdom of many people. Because of the rules for interpreting Torah, and the possibility for new laws to mend social problems, the system could also respond to new conditions. The Rabbinic system was rational, humane, and adaptive.

Though direct instructions from the divine were not accepted, experience of the transcendent was held to be commonplace, in the form known as *Shekhinah*, the dwelling or Presence of God in the world. As we see here in *Avot* (3:3), the sanctifying Presence is said to rest upon two people when they discuss Torah. Even though the Presence is everywhere, likened to light shining throughout the world, it especially rests upon, for example, 10 people praying, upon a husband and wife when they are worthy, and upon those giving charity to the poor.

Not content with this feeling of the Presence, four of the Sages of *Avot* are said to have engaged in esoteric speculation, "entering the garden" (ḤAG 14b). But only one, Akiva, came out whole. Mystical speculation in Rabbinic Judaism thus had a reputation of being both seductive and dangerous. The Sages reject withdrawal from family and the world that a wholehearted mysticism demands (*Avot* 2:2, 2:5). The goal in life for the Sages of the Talmud was not seeking to unite oneself with God, but rather reverence and following God's commandments through prayer, Torah study, and good deeds (1:2).

In the Middle Ages, the full mysticism of the *Zohar* came into Judaism: the world is one and all within God, and thus the world of appearance is to some degree unreal—a doctrine alien to both the Torah and the Sages. The allure of mysticism is that it promises knowledge and rapture beyond ordinary life. The key weakness of mysticism is that the gap between the vision of the world as one and the reality of a varied and changing world cannot be bridged in any logical way. As a result, the conclusions drawn by mystics are sometimes fantastic and arbitrary; they can inspire great insights, but also false and damaging ideas. And this in fact happened with the false prophesy of Shabbatai Tzvi and the licentiousness of the Frankists.

Traditionally, in Judaism, the world is not an illusion, but a gift; and the self is not a burden, but a blessing. And our proper relation to the world is not to escape it, but to embrace its reality, including the reality of the living God who sustains it. Today, mysticism is seen as deep. But for this writer, the Sages' pursuit of holiness through engagement with love and work is the deeper wisdom, and the greater challenge.

HILLEL:

Do not separate yourself from the community.
Do not trust yourself until the day of your death.
Do not judge your comrade until you have come into his place.
Do not say a thing that should not be heard,
  for in the end it will be heard.
Do not say: "When I am free, I will study";
  perhaps you will never be free. (2:5)

הִלֵּל אוֹמֵר: אַל תִּפְרוֹשׁ מִן הַצִּבּוּר, וְאַל תַּאֲמִין בְּעַצְמְךָ עַד יוֹם מוֹתְךָ, וְאַל
תָּדִין אֶת חֲבֵרְךָ עַד שֶׁתַּגִּיעַ לִמְקוֹמוֹ, וְאַל תֹּאמַר דָּבָר שֶׁאִי אֶפְשָׁר לִשְׁמֹעַ,
שֶׁסּוֹפוֹ לְהִשָּׁמַע, וְאַל תֹּאמַר לִכְשֶׁאֶפָּנֶה אֶשְׁנֶה, שֶׁמָּא לֹא תִפָּנֶה.

Do NOT separate yourself. This saying is probably in opposition to the monastic cults that existed in Judaism in the days of Hillel, called "Essenes" by the ancient historian Josephus. The good and pious life is to be lived in the family and the community, not as a religious hermit or monk or nun. *Tzibur,* translated here as "community," can also be translated as "public," and thus refers to civil society generally, not only to the Jewish community.

Do not trust yourself. Ma'amin, translated here as "trust," is the word also used for trust or belief in God. This is a warning not to think that you are beyond temptation, and not to expose yourself to temptations to do wrong. It may also be an admonition against being too sure of the correctness of your own views. Einstein wrote admiringly of the "half humble, half skeptical" attitude of the older scientist he most admired, Hendrik Lorentz. That phrase captures the attitude that this mishnah commends to us.

Do not judge your comrade. Ḥaver, here translated as "comrade," can also mean "friend" or "colleague." One interpretation of this saying is that we should not make judgments at all. For how can anyone ever fully put himself or herself in the place of another person? This would be a misinterpretation, however. For Hillel, in fact, acted as a judge, and we have already read the injunction to be careful in judging in *Avot* (1:1b). What is Hillel asking us to do, then? He is saying that when it is appropriate for us to judge another person, we should try to imagine ourselves in his or her place, and see the situation through his or her

66

eyes, and only then come to a judgment. Ideally, this involves actually listening to the other person's account of events.

Do not say. "Should not be heard"—literally "cannot be heard"—and *lishmoah,* "heard," imply a degree of influence on the person listening. This saying is probably a warning against esoteric traditions, such as mystical traditions, in which "secret knowledge" is passed on from masters to acolytes. If it is improper to say publicly, then don't say it privately. The principle applies to many other types of harmful speech, as well.

Modern Life

PSYCHOLOGICAL RESEARCH has confirmed that the ability to imagine ourselves in another person's situation is a key to developing compassionate feelings for others. A revealing example of failure to have compassion is the case of men who beat their wives to control them. They lack a sympathetic understanding of the suffering they are causing. And, interestingly, they themselves were often cruelly beaten as children, but did not see their own suffering as abusive. In other words, without making a conscious decision about it, they have accepted the viewpoint of the abusive parent who lacked compassion for them. Psychologist Steven Stosny has found that, remarkably, when taught to put themselves in the place of others, abusive husbands actually are able to learn compassion and stop their abuse. Sympathetic understanding creates a transformative experience.

Hillel's injunction indicates that judging others fairly is difficult and something that we should be reluctant to attempt. However, there are circumstances in which it is important to make judgments of others' characters: rebuking to prevent wrong, in keeping with the Torah's commandment (LEV 19:17); avoiding association with the wicked (*Avot* 1:7); protecting ourselves from harm; and doing our duty as a judge or juror in a court of law.

Why are failures of empathy so widespread? Psychologist Alfred Adler observed that when we divide "us" and "them," and label "them" as "enemy," we dangerously excuse ourselves from having compassion. Stosney has similarly noted that anger drives out compassion. When we are in the grip of anger, we think of fight or flight, not of trying to understand the other person, or even of how best to serve our own goals and fulfill our obligations. The combination of unchecked alienation and anger causes a great deal of human folly and cruelty.

HILLEL:

> *The crude do not fear sin,*
> > *and the ignorant cannot be models of piety.*
> *The bashful do not learn,*
> > *and the short-tempered cannot teach.*
> *And not all who succeed in business are wise.* (2:6A)

הוּא הָיָה אוֹמֵר: אֵין בּוּר יְרֵא חֵטְא, וְלֹא עַם הָאָרֶץ חָסִיד, וְלֹא הַבַּיְשָׁן לָמֵד,
וְלֹא כָּל הַקַּפְּדָן מְלַמֵּד, וְלֹא כָּל הַמַּרְבֶּה בִסְחוֹרָה מַחְכִּים.

HILLEL'S SAYINGS here are vivid expressions of the rabbinic belief that learning and cultivation are important to developing good moral character, and to making a complete and admirable human being.

The crude do not fear sin. The Hebrew word here for a crude person, *boor*, comes from the term for a field that lays uncultivated, with weeds and briars growing in it. The person who has not been brought up with proper adult examples and teaching lacks sensitivity and understanding. Not understanding or feeling the harm that will be done by a sin, he or she may not feel any inhibition from committing it.

The ignorant cannot be models of piety. This phrase, "*Am ha-aretz* is not a *hasid*," uses two special Rabbinic terms. *Am ha-aretz,* literally "the folk of the land," came to mean an ignoramus. Here, the ignorance alluded to is probably a lack of familiarity with the sacred texts, either because of illiteracy or lack of study. A *hasid* is literally a person of loving-kind-ness, *hesed,* but the term came to mean, in Rabbinic language, a devout person, a model of piety in the observance of religious ritual and in consistent, overflowing kindness to others.

Having sounded the signal importance of learning to develop character, Hillel next pinpoints the most common failings of teachers, students, and the general public in their efforts to increase wisdom.

The bashful do not learn. Generally, being sensitive to shame, *baishan* in Hebrew, is praised by the Rabbis—but not in the pursuit of learning. The student must be bold, and not hesitate to ask questions or make mistakes. Otherwise, he or she will not be truly engaged and learn. Because children in a large class are most concerned about looking foolish in the eyes of their classmates, this is still a common failing of students today, even in their college years.

The short-tempered cannot teach. According to Hillel, impatient, censorious teachers cannot succeed in teaching students. A wise educator, Dr. Albert Mamary, said, "You can threaten and punish children into doing a lot of things, but learning is not one of them." If a student must come forward eagerly to learn well, then teachers must do everything to see that students are not intimidated from coming forward. Because teachers possess greater knowledge and power, being short-tempered and overbearing are their easiest and most serious failings.

And not all who succeed. If being timid and short-tempered are the typical failings of students and teachers, respectively, then the typical failing of the general public is to give too much credibility to the "rich and famous." According to a Yiddish saying, "If you have money, men think you wise, handsome, and able to sing like a bird" (*Leo Rosten's Treasury of Jewish Quotations,* 370). Hillel warns us that while some successful businessmen may be wise, others are not.

MODERN LIFE

THE CRUDE do not fear sin. Modern psychological studies have found that many neglected and abused children respond by emotionally numbing themselves, and in the process are in danger of growing up not feeling the suffering of others. They are thus at much greater risk of acting callously in their relations with others, and unfortunately of passing on abuse or neglect to the next generation.

The ignorant cannot be models. The idea that education will improve a person's character is challenged by the existence of educated murderers and tyrants. Really, how important is education in building character? It is important to note that Torah study combines intellectual, moral, and spiritual education. This is supposed to take place within a community that, at least in principle, is practicing the values it preaches.

Maimonides wrote that if a person is brought up with a good example, and he or she does good deeds while young, doing good deeds will become a habit. Then, doing Torah study will reinforce that good character, and keep a person on the right path. But if one acted badly when young, Torah study will not have the same grip over him or her, and he or she will be more easily led astray by temptation. Torah study, then, while no guarantee of good behavior, does strengthen and direct a core of good character first established by example and practice when young.

HILLEL:

In a place where there is no person to make a difference,
strive to be that person. *(2:6B)*

וּבְמָקוֹם שֶׁאֵין אֲנָשִׁים הִשְׁתַּדֵּל לִהְיוֹת אִישׁ.

THIS SAYING translates literally to: "In a place where there are no people, strive to be a person." What is meant by "person" is a real human being in the fullest sense: a caring, capable, and responsible person—a person who knows the right thing to do, and does it. Such a person came to be called in Yiddish a "mentsh." Aaron Feuerstein translates this mishnah using the Yiddish term: "In a place where there isn't a mentsh, then it's up to you to be that mentsh." In Feuerstein's reading, Hillel is saying: in a place where there is no one else who is taking responsibility to do what should be done, you yourself should step up, take responsibility, and strive to do what needs to be done.

MODERN LIFE

MR. FEUERSTEIN himself was called "number-one mentsh of the U.S.A." by former U.S. Secretary of Labor Robert Reich because of his kindness and loyalty to his workers after a devastating fire burned down his textile factory, Malden Mills. The fire happened on his 75th birthday, but Feuerstein decided not only to rebuild, but also to keep paying all his workers—about 2000 people—until the factory could be rebuilt. This kind of courage to do the right thing in difficult circumstances is clearly what Hillel was urging. In fact, Feuerstein says that this mishnah, which his own father quoted regularly, encouraged him in his hour of crisis to take the very risky but compassionate path.

Consciously following the philosophy of balancing interests implicit in Hillel's earlier three questions (1:14), Feuerstein has tried throughout his career to combine two goals: making a profit and doing good—in other words, making money and being a mentsh.

Are material success and ethical conduct compatible? Feuerstein acknowledges that ruthless, callous people do sometimes succeed materially. But he argues that long-term success is best built on an ethical foundation. When you maintain concern for the people you work with and for the community, and try to serve their needs, you build the kind of relationships that benefit you in the long run.

In Feuerstein's case, this actually turned out to be so. During the fire, 27 of his workers, hearing of Feuerstein's commitment and knowing his steadfast loyalty, stayed in one burning factory building and fought the fire alongside the firemen, saving the machinery from destruction. This enabled the factory to continue producing enough for the business to survive until the rest of the factory could be rebuilt, and full production restored. Thus, the trust and loyalty built through treating employees with fairness and consideration over 50 years actually saved the business during a crisis.

Feuerstein has pointed out that combining material success and being a mentsh is not easy, but requires courage and creativity. At the moment of crisis when he learned of the fire, he says that along with this mishnah of Hillel, he also thought of a line in Shakespeare's *King Lear:* "I have full cause of weeping; but this heart shall break into a hundred thousand flaws, or e'er I weep" (scene 4, line 197). Crying and depression leads to inaction, whereas courage and action are needed in the hour of crisis. Feuerstein adds: "That night I knew I had to be creative, because on my creativity would depend the chances of coming through."

When I pointed out to Mr. Feuerstein that the decision to keep the factory open, and the decision to pay the employees were separate, he replied that in his mind "they were all one." This illustrates a feature of the Jewish ethical approach to decision making. In general, ethical decision making is not a matter of searching for all options, scrupulous and unscrupulous, and only then applying ethical values to choose. It is rather one of conducting the search process within a framework of ethical principles. This creative process is wholly devoted to finding ethical actions that best solve the problem.

In this case, Feuerstein was also following the Jewish injunction going back to Hillel (1:14) to find a course of action that serves both one's own interest *and* the interests of the other people involved. His creative solution was the idea of wetting down his factory's machinery to save enough equipment to stay in business until the factory could be rebuilt. And because of his faithfulness to his employees, they willingly helped.

It is also interesting that both taking an ethical approach and focusing on quality go together with a long-term perspective. When labor costs went up and textile factories left New England, Feuerstein decided he could stay and compete through innovation and quality of product, rather than trying to compete simply on price. Finally, it is encouraging to see that Feuerstein's confidence that he was doing the right thing gave him not only courage, but great joy in his work.

HILLEL:

Hillel saw a lone skull floating in the water. He spoke to it:
Because you drowned others, you were drowned;
And in the end those who drowned you will be drowned. (2:7)

אַף הוּא רָאָה גֻּלְגֹּלֶת אַחַת שֶׁצָּפָה עַל פְּנֵי הַמָּיִם, אָמַר לָהּ: עַל דְּאַטֵּפְתְּ
אַטְּפוּךְ, וְסוֹף מְטַיְּפָיִךְ יְטוּפוּן.

THIS UNFORGETTABLE scenario exemplifies the cycle of violence trig-
gered by acts of vengeance and bolsters the Torah's prohibition against
vengeance (LEV 19:18). In the Talmud, this saying of Hillel's is paired
with another: "To a place that I love, there my feet take me: if you come
into my house, I will come into your house; if you won't come into my
house, I will not come into your house" (SUK 53a). Together, these two
sayings of Hillel vividly portray the way the reciprocity of human relations causes actions to reverberate through the whole social fabric:
respect and cooperation beget respect and cooperation; violence begets
violence. Efforts at vengeance rebound to hit back at the vengeful person, in a vicious cycle, while respect and cooperation rebound to bring
respect and help from others in a positive, virtuous cycle.

This mishnah of Hillel is an effort to counteract the temptation to
vengeance by reminding us of the unintended consequences of our actions. Many critiques of hatred and anger and of the pleasure of vengeance run throughout the Rabbinic literature. For example, in *Avot*
4:24, a Sage, Shmuel HaKatan, quotes Proverbs 24:17–18: "If your enemy
falls, do not exult; if he trips, let your heart not rejoice, lest the Lord
see it and be displeased, and avert His wrath from him [and on to you]."

At the same time, the Talmud recognizes the rights to redress wrongs
and to self-defense. How do we distinguish just redress or self-defense
from vengeance? Justice is first of all distinguished by the use of courts
of law and a legal process to try and judge a case. This shift from individual vengeance to social judgment helps to break the cycle of violence.
Violent self-defense is only allowed in the case of an immediate threat
of bodily harm, which cannot be stopped by any court.

Courts are fundamental to a civilized society, because of the shift
away from individual vengeance. The Rabbis included courts in the basic "Noahide Laws," laws that the Sages argued, on the basis of passages in Genesis, were given by God to humanity before the time of Noah,
and so apply to any society for it to be considered minimally civilized.

This mishnah strongly rejects vengeance as futile and self-defeating, but a startling passage in the Talmud seems to directly conflict with it, and raises issues that are still with us today. Seemingly contradicting Hillel's saying, Rabbi Yoḥanan said, "Any scholar who does not avenge himself and bear a grudge like a snake is no scholar" (YOM 22b–23a). This passage also seems to contradict the commandments against vengeance and bearing a grudge (LEV 19:18). The context of this passage is a discussion of why King Saul was punished by God. Saul was punished, it is said, because he was publicly insulted by King Naḥash of Ammon (whose name means "snake" and who is portrayed as ruthless) and failed to respond. King Naḥash took this failure to respond as a sign of weakness and attacked a group of Israelites whom King Saul then had to go to war to defend (1 SAM 10:27–11:2). Here, surprisingly, it is not the first Jewish king, Saul, but the "snake" Naḥash who acted vengefully, who is taken as the model to follow.

The Talmud resolves the contradiction between Rabbi Yoḥanan's saying and Leviticus 19:18 by saying that the prohibition against vengeance and holding grudges applies to anything involving goods or money. But the case of a public insult to a Jewish leader is different. The leader should indeed first try to reconcile with the adversary. But if this fails, he or she should counter the insult or attack. The principle, it seems, is that a leader cannot function without respect and, when publicly disrespected, must respond to retain leadership.

MODERN LIFE

MORE TYPICALLY, the Talmud praises those who "are insulted but do not insult, who hear themselves reproached but do not reply" (YOM 23). This is in tension with the idea that leaders should not ignore insults, and allow respect for them to be undermined. Today many people face the question of resolving this tension as they are in leadership situations. This includes teachers, parents, and business managers. For example, in competitive situations, such as manufacturing, there is a danger that maligning a company's product will kill its profits. And politicians running for office, and not yet in a position of authority, may lose because of insults aimed at them by opponents. On the other hand, replying to insults is often counter-productive, and leads to a cycle of further anger and insult, just as Hillel warns in this mishnah. This issue is a difficult one where it seems more work is needed to specify the best guidelines.

More flesh, more worms;
more wealth, more worry;
more wives, more witchcraft;
more maidservants, more lechery;
more manservants, more robbery.

More Torah, more life;
more study, more wisdom;
more counsel, more understanding;
more charity, more peace. (2:8A)

הוּא הָיָה אוֹמֵר: מַרְבֶּה בָשָׂר–מַרְבֶּה רִמָּה, מַרְבֶּה נְכָסִים–מַרְבֶּה דְאָגָה,
מַרְבֶּה נָשִׁים–מַרְבֶּה כְשָׁפִים, מַרְבֶּה שְׁפָחוֹת–מַרְבֶּה זִמָּה, מַרְבֶּה עֲבָדִים–
מַרְבֶּה גָזֵל, מַרְבֶּה תוֹרָה–מַרְבֶּה חַיִּים, מַרְבֶּה יְשִׁיבָה–מַרְבֶּה חָכְמָה, מַרְבֶּה
עֵצָה–מַרְבֶּה תְבוּנָה, מַרְבֶּה צְדָקָה–מַרְבֶּה שָׁלוֹם.

MORE FLESH, *more worms.* Hillel's stinging indictment of a life devoted to pursuing wealth, social status, and sensual pleasure. In Hillel's time, polygamy and slavery still existed. According to traditional interpreters, there was so much strife among "co-wives" in a polygamous marriage that some resorted to magic (forbidden by the Torah) to try to influence events in their favor. In Roman times, maidservants and manservants were often slaves. With the extreme powerlessness of slaves, masters were tempted to sexually exploit female slaves and to brutalize male slaves. Female slaves were tempted to curry favor sexually, while male slaves were tempted to get back at their masters through thievery.

While Hillel and other Sages are critical of a life of indulgence and the pursuit of status, it is important to note that they do not support a religion of self-denial or, in other words, of asceticism. The Talmud, in fact, puts strict limits on self-denial and forbids self-harm.

More Torah, more life. The Sages' view of the good life, in four words. By "more Torah," Hillel means both a life lived according to Torah and Torah study itself. As opposed to the false appeal of a life focused on the pursuit of wealth and status, the life of Torah is uniquely fulfilling, both in one's relationships with other people, and in one's relationship to God. Of course, in the context of Rabbinic Judaism, this phrase also alludes to the afterlife: a life of good deeds will win you a place in the world to come.

More study, more wisdom. The Hebrew *yeshiva*, "study," literally means "sitting," and also is the name of schools for higher education in Talmud. Here, Hillel asserts the power of formal education, and in particular formal education in Torah, to raise humanity to a higher level.

More charity, more peace. Tzedakah, which in the Bible means "righteousness," acquired the additional meaning of "charity" in the Rabbinic period. Charity is, in the eyes of the Rabbis, obligatory and a form of righteous action. Hillel here uses the double meaning of *tzedakah* to deliver a powerful message: doing the right thing will increase peace, while wrongdoing increases strife. But to strengthen the groups and communities we are part of, we need to go beyond practicing strict justice and act with charity, including giving money to help others.

MODERN LIFE

MORE COUNSEL, more understanding. Pride and a desire to protect our status create strong psychological barriers to seeking and taking advice. For example, many brilliant leaders have failed because of their unwillingness to seek and listen to counsel from subordinates. Management expert W. Edwards Deming helped many corporations to strengthen themselves by teaching their managers to seek and listen to advice, including critical comments, from subordinates. Seeking counsel from superiors is also difficult because people have a natural resistance to being dominated. For example, many teens, eager to become more independent, ignore good advice from parents to their own detriment. While it requires a strong stomach to hear criticism, the willingness to seek and listen to counsel is a secret source of great strength.

More charity, more peace. The Jewish rule in relationships is not to insist on everything you are entitled to. The Talmud says, "A father should not insist on his rights," and, "A father should honor his wife and children more than his means allow" (HUL 84b). Rabbi Chaim Stern has said, "Marriage is not a matter of give and take, but give and give." Husbands and wives should not be regularly calculating if they are getting their due, but give with trust that their giving will be returned. The underlying idea here is that a certain generosity of spirit is key to peaceful, cooperative, and loving relationships (see *Avot* 2:13).

HILLEL:

If you gain a good name, you gain for yourself.
If you gain knowledge of Torah,
*   you gain for yourself life in the world to come. (2:8B)*

קָנָה שֵׁם טוֹב–קָנָה לְעַצְמוֹ, קָנָה לוֹ דִּבְרֵי תוֹרָה–קָנָה לוֹ חַיֵּי הָעוֹלָם הַבָּא.

RABBI SHIMON:

There are three crowns:
The crown of Torah, the crown of priesthood,
*   and the crown of royalty;*
But the crown of a good name is above them all. (4:17)

רַבִּי שִׁמְעוֹן אוֹמֵר: שְׁלֹשָׁה כְתָרִים הֵן: כֶּתֶר תּוֹרָה, וְכֶתֶר כְּהֻנָּה, וְכֶתֶר מַלְכוּת,
וְכֶתֶר שֵׁם טוֹב עוֹלֶה עַל גַּבֵּיהֶן.

IF YOU gain a good name. The point of Hillel's first sentence is that a person who does good deeds, and so gains a good reputation, benefits himself as well as others. The Talmud tells an illustrative story (BB 11a): King Monobaz, who had converted to Judaism, distributed his royal stockpiles during hard times. His brothers came to him and said, "Your father saved and added to the treasures of his fathers, and you are squandering them." Part of his answer was, "My fathers gathered for others and I have gathered for myself." His meaning was that his ancestors, apparently building wealth for themselves, had in fact benefited their heirs; and while apparently doing good just for others, he was in fact benefiting himself in both this world and the world to come.

If you gain knowledge of Torah. What, beyond a good name, does a person gain by knowledge of Torah that merits life in the world to come? One interpretation is that through knowledge of Torah, a person consistently knows the right thing to do. Thus, regardless of whether or not anyone else knows about his or her good deeds, the person gains a place in heaven. Another interpretation is that in studying Torah, God's universal plan, one gets a taste of eternity while in this life.

There are three crowns. Ancient priests, as well as kings, wore a crown. The "crown of Torah" refers to the figurative crown of learning, knowledge of Torah. It may also refer literally to the crowns placed on the staves of Torah scrolls.

76

A good name is above them all. This phrase can be interpreted two ways. One interpretation is that having a good name is more valuable than being a king, priest, or Torah scholar. The second is that without a good name, one cannot be a good king, priest, or scholar. In order to be effective in any of these roles, one needs a reputation as a person who does good deeds.

MODERN LIFE

ONE OF the ways that those who gain a good name benefit personally is in their feelings about themselves. Research shows that our feelings about ourselves are influenced by our expectations of how we will be treated by others. These feelings are actually quite complex, and some are more within our power to change than others.

One level of feelings about ourselves is our basic sense of *self-worth,* which is largely determined by our philosophy. If we believe that we are made "in the image of God" (GEN 1:27), we will believe in our personal worth largely independent of the outside world. On a second level, we have *self-respect* when we believe that we deserve respect from others. This feeling is won through ethical conduct: when we treat others with justice and kindness, we know we deserve respect in return. A third level, *self-esteem,* comes from being esteemed by others for our usefulness. It is garnered by developing our characters and acquiring work skills, thus strengthening our abilities to serve others.

All three of these levels are sustained by Jewish beliefs and values: being made in the image of God, treating others with respect, and serving others through skills we acquire.

A fourth level, not supported by Jewish values, is a feeling of *glory* or ego, in which we rejoice in being looked up to by others. This is won by gaining admiration from others for good looks, money, power, etc. As Mark Twain once said, "Man will do many things to get himself loved; he will do all things to get himself envied." We have the least control over this last level, and it makes our personalities very tense and fragile. Any setback to the goal of personal superiority will be crushing because we have made our approval of ourselves dependent on it. This hazard of pursuing glory is recognized in the Talmud: Rabbi Alexandri says, "The least wind will trouble a man who has haughtiness of spirit" (SOT 5a).

Thus, having self-approval rooted in Jewish values provides a much stronger foundation for maintaining joy in life even in the face of disappointments.

*If you have learned much Torah, do not flatter yourself,
because for this you were created. (2:9)*

רַבָּן יוֹחָנָן בֶּן זַכַּאי קִבֵּל מֵהִלֵּל וּמִשַּׁמַּאי, הוּא הָיָה אוֹמֵר: אִם לָמַדְתָּ תּוֹרָה
הַרְבֵּה, אַל תַּחֲזִיק טוֹבָה לְעַצְמְךָ, כִּי לְכַךְ נוֹצָרְתָּ.

*Rabban Yoḥanan ben Zakkai had five students . . . (2:10)
He used to recount their praises:
Eliezer ben Hyrcanus is a plastered cistern
    which does not lose a drop;
Yehoshua ben Hanania—happy is she who bore him;
Yose, the priest, is a pious man;
Shimon ben Netanel fears sin; and
Elazar ben Arach is an ever-flowing fountain. (2:11)*

חֲמִשָּׁה תַלְמִידִים הָיוּ לוֹ לְרַבָּן יוֹחָנָן בֶּן זַכַּאי, וְאֵלוּ הֵן: רַבִּי אֱלִיעֶזֶר בֶּן
הוֹרְקָנוֹס, רַבִּי יְהוֹשֻׁעַ בֶּן חֲנַנְיָא, רַבִּי יוֹסֵי הַכֹּהֵן, רַבִּי שִׁמְעוֹן בֶּן נְתַנְאֵל,
וְרַבִּי אֶלְעָזָר בֶּן עֲרָךְ.

הוּא הָיָה מוֹנֶה שְׁבָחָם: אֱלִיעֶזֶר בֶּן הוֹרְקָנוֹס–בּוֹר סוּד שֶׁאֵינוֹ מְאַבֵּד טִפָּה,
יְהוֹשֻׁעַ בֶּן חֲנַנְיָה–אַשְׁרֵי יוֹלַדְתּוֹ, יוֹסֵי הַכֹּהֵן–חָסִיד, שִׁמְעוֹן בֶּן נְתַנְאֵל–יְרֵא
חֵטְא, אֶלְעָזָר בֶּן עֲרָךְ–כְּמַעְיָן הַמִּתְגַּבֵּר.

הוּא הָיָה אוֹמֵר: אִם יִהְיוּ כָּל חַכְמֵי יִשְׂרָאֵל בְּכַף מֹאזְנַיִם, וֶאֱלִיעֶזֶר בֶּן
הוֹרְקָנוֹס בְּכַף שְׁנִיָּה, מַכְרִיעַ אֶת כֻּלָּם. אַבָּא שָׁאוּל אוֹמֵר מִשְּׁמוֹ: אִם יִהְיוּ
כָּל חַכְמֵי יִשְׂרָאֵל בְּכַף מֹאזְנַיִם, וֶאֱלִיעֶזֶר בֶּן הוֹרְקָנוֹס אַף עִמָּהֶם, וְאֶלְעָזָר
בֶּן עֲרָךְ בְּכַף שְׁנִיָּה, מַכְרִיעַ אֶת כֻּלָּם.

THE FULL text here introduces Yoḥanan ben Zakkai by saying that he "received from Hillel and Shammai," and concludes with further praise of two of the students: "He used to say: if all the sages of Israel were in one pan of the scales and Eliezer ben Hyrcanus in the other pan, he would outweigh them all. Abba Shaul said in his name: If all the sages of Israel were in one pan of the scales, and Rabbi Eliezer ben Hyrcanus also with them, and Rabbi Elazar ben Arach in the other pan, he would outweigh them all" (2:12).

Yoḥanan ben Zakkai, the youngest student of Hillel, played a pivotal role in the history of Judaism, because he was the leader at the time the Temple was destroyed in the year 70 CE. Then an old man, he was trapped in the Roman siege of Jerusalem, and at risk of being slaughtered. His students Rabbi Eliezer ben Hyrcanus and Rabbi Yehoshua ben Ḥanania brought him out through the Jewish Zealot lines in a coffin, saying their old teacher had died, and Jewish law required his burial within 24 hours outside the walls of Jerusalem. The Zealots, who had backed the war and whom Yoḥanan ben Zakkai had opposed, were not then letting any Jews flee besieged Jerusalem, but the ruse, permitted under Jewish law to save a life, succeeded and they escaped. Ben Zakkai and his two students immediately went to see the Roman general Vespasian. Vespasian, who knew that ben Zakkai had opposed the rebellion against Rome, then asked what he could do for him. Instead of asking for treasure, ben Zakkai said: "Give me Yavneh and its sages." Learning would save Judaism.

Having been granted the freedom to study and promulgate Torah, the elderly ben Zakkai knew that the future of Judaism depended upon the wisdom of his students. To put it another way, he knew that the future of Judaism depended on his success as a teacher. Judging by his students, he must be counted as one of the great teachers in history. In these *mishnayot* and the next two he gives implicit lessons on how to be a great teacher.

If you have learned. This saying is directed toward teachers and fledgling scholars: if your gift is for scholarship, do not be haughty and overbearing, but accept that you were given the gift of intellect to serve others with it.

Recount their praises. Yoḥanan ben Zakkai not only understood the unique gifts of each of his outstanding students, but also publicly praised them. (On the specific praises, see below, 2:15–19.) The next mishnah continues the lesson-by-example on being a great teacher. First, Yoḥanan ben Zakkai does not restrict students to book learning, but tells them to go out into the world and learn in ways that will enrich their learning from texts. Finally, when he assesses his students' answers, he does judge them, but with wonderful tact and appreciation.

MODERN LIFE

IN THE modern world, these qualities still hold as markers of excellence in teachers: an attitude of service to students, warm appreciation and praise for students, engagement of students with the real world, and tactful judgment of students' efforts.

Yoḥanan ben Zakkai:

He said to his students: Go out and see
* which is the good path that a person should stick to.*
Rabbi Eliezer said, a good eye;
Rabbi Yehoshua said, a good friend;
Rabbi Yose said, a good neighbor;
Rabbi Shimon said, one who foresees consequences.
Rabbi Elazar said, a good heart.
He said to them: From among your sayings, I recognize that of
Elazar ben Arach, for within his words yours are included. (2:13)

אָמַר לָהֶם: צְאוּ וּרְאוּ אֵיזוֹ הִיא דֶּרֶךְ טוֹבָה שֶׁיִּדְבַּק בָּהּ הָאָדָם. רַבִּי אֱלִיעֶזֶר
אוֹמֵר: עַיִן טוֹבָה. רַבִּי יְהוֹשֻׁעַ אוֹמֵר: חָבֵר טוֹב. רַבִּי יוֹסֵי אוֹמֵר: שָׁכֵן טוֹב.
רַבִּי שִׁמְעוֹן אוֹמֵר: הָרוֹאֶה אֶת הַנּוֹלָד. רַבִּי אֶלְעָזָר אוֹמֵר: לֵב טוֹב. אָמַר
לָהֶם: רוֹאֶה אֲנִי אֶת דִּבְרֵי אֶלְעָזָר בֶּן עֲרָךְ מִדִּבְרֵיכֶם, שֶׁבִּכְלַל דְּבָרָיו דִּבְרֵיכֶם:

He said to them: Go out and see which is the bad path
* that a person should stay far from.*
Rabbi Eliezer said, a bad eye;
Rabbi Yehoshua said, a bad friend;
Rabbi Yose said, a bad neighbor;
Rabbi Shimon said, one who borrows and doesn't repay.
Rabbi Elazar said, a bad heart.
He said to them: From among your sayings, I recognize that of
Elazar ben Arach, for within his words yours are included. (2:14)

אָמַר לָהֶם: צְאוּ וּרְאוּ אֵיזוֹ הִיא דֶּרֶךְ רָעָה שֶׁיִּתְרַחֵק מִמֶּנָּה הָאָדָם. רַבִּי
אֱלִיעֶזֶר אוֹמֵר: עַיִן רָעָה. רַבִּי יְהוֹשֻׁעַ אוֹמֵר: חָבֵר רָע. רַבִּי יוֹסֵי אוֹמֵר: שָׁכֵן
רָע. רַבִּי שִׁמְעוֹן אוֹמֵר: הַלֹּוֶה וְאֵינוֹ מְשַׁלֵּם, אֶחָד הַלֹּוֶה מִן הָאָדָם כְּלֹוֶה מִן
הַמָּקוֹם, שֶׁנֶּאֱמַר: "לֹוֶה רָשָׁע וְלֹא יְשַׁלֵּם, וְצַדִּיק חוֹנֵן וְנוֹתֵן". רַבִּי אֶלְעָזָר
אוֹמֵר: לֵב רָע. אָמַר לָהֶם: רוֹאֶה אֲנִי אֶת דִּבְרֵי אֶלְעָזָר בֶּן עֲרָךְ מִדִּבְרֵיכֶם,
שֶׁבִּכְלַל דְּבָרָיו דִּבְרֵיכֶם.

The Hebrew includes a prooftext: "One who borrows from man is as one who borrows from God—as it is said: The wicked man borrows and does not repay; the righteous is generous and keeps giving" (PS 37:21).

80

A good eye. A "good eye" means a generous, open nature, a person who enjoys giving and doing things for others. A "bad eye" means a grasping, possessive, envious, and jealous nature. The superstitious version of *ayin ha-ra,* "the evil eye," prevalent in later literature, is related but different: this is the supposed power of an eye filled with envy or hatred to magically harm others by glaring at them.

A good friend. To be a good friend or colleague is more complex than having an attitude of generosity and benevolence—a "good eye." Good personal relationships also require that each person have an understanding of the other, and balance his or her own interests with those of the other person.

A good neighbor. Being a good neighbor is more general. As we can't choose our neighbors, this is a question of being a good citizen, and of fulfilling legal obligations and communal responsibilities.

One who foresees consequences. Rabbi Shimon's description of the "right path" adds the time. From the corresponding "bad path"—one who borrows and does not repay—we can see the meaning: we should be aware of the longer-term consequences of our actions, and take these into account when making decisions.

A good heart. In the era of the Sages, the heart was also viewed as the seat of understanding, so a good heart includes both understanding and good intentions. In other words, a person with a good heart both wants to do the right thing and understands what that is. Yoḥanan ben Zakkai sees this quality as including all of the others: being generous, being a good friend, being a good citizen, and having foresight.

MODERN LIFE

ONE WHO foresees consequences. Modern life offers us many more opportunities than were available in traditional societies. We have many more career opportunities, more influence over our future paths through life, and the opportunity to choose our own mates.

When we have the prospect of realizing these opportunities, our lives become an exciting adventure. However, with the opportunities also come risks of failure, loss, and rejection. And if we feel those risks are getting the better of us, then we can be plagued by anxiety, depression, or chronic anger, depending on how our fears are directed. The duality of opportunity and risk is like a double-edged sword of Damocles hanging over us, making our lives emotionally challenging, even while they are materially much more comfortable than those of our ancestors.

The difficulty of dealing with these opportunities and their attendant risks is that the future always remains uncertain. The wry Yiddish proverb says: *a mentsh tracht, und Gott lacht,* "A person plans, and God laughs." Our knowledge of the future and our control over it are partial and shaky at best. And yet what we do will, in all likelihood, influence our future. Because we have only partial knowledge and control, we can never make that double-edged sword of opportunity and risk vanish.

Fortunately, we do have a way of dealing with these anxieties effectively, in spite of continuing risks. When we come to a decision on how to deal with a plan or policy that we are satisfied is best, we feel a sense of relief, and can let go of continual worry. That sense of relief, which I think all of us can identify with, I call "making peace with the future."

To make peace with the future requires us to to foresee consequences, as Rabbi Shimon ben Netanel advises. We can avoid looking at the long-term consequences of our actions by drifting and not making any decisions on long-term issues, or by doing the opposite and making impulsive decisions. Both of these forms of evasion have a high cost, though. Avoiding long-term decisions leads to constant anxiety, depression, or anger—and we are likely to drift into crises without having resources to help us out. Impulsive decisions can keep anxiety at bay, but only by denying the reality of risks. Then, because those decisions are not well-informed, they are likely to land us in a mess.

The task of making peace with the future often requires the courage to examine long-term consequences of our actions, the creativity to devise strategies that serve our future and that of others, and the discipline to carry our plans through. Thus "foreseeing consequences" has become a central and challenging task of modern life.

That the Sages believe in planning reflects their characteristic commitment to this life. By contrast, Buddhism, a religion of detachment, views seeking things for yourself, for your future, as "craving," the source of all suffering (see *Avot* 4:1c). Yet the powerful Buddhist technique for "letting go" of concern about the future can still be used when we have a plan of action for our future. For then we can focus on carrying out the tasks of the day, enjoying the moment, and letting go of worries, knowing we are doing our best, and that the rest is in the hands of God.

Let the honor of your colleague be as dear to you as your own;
Do not be easy to anger;
And repent one day before your death. (2:15A)

הֵם אָמְרוּ שְׁלֹשָׁה דְבָרִים: רַבִּי אֱלִיעֶזֶר אוֹמֵר: יְהִי כְבוֹד חֲבֵרְךָ חָבִיב עָלֶיךָ
כְּשֶׁלָּךְ, וְאַל תְּהִי נוֹחַ לִכְעוֹס, וְשׁוּב יוֹם אֶחָד לִפְנֵי מִיתָתְךָ.

Let the honor. In Hebrew, "honor" and "respect" are a single word, *kavod*. The importance of honor, in the sense of protecting or building the reputation of a person, has unfortunately been neglected in our time as superficial or hypocritical. In Chinese tradition, by contrast, the evocative phrase for showing respect is to "give face," which is seen as centrally important to good human relations. While the main focus of Rabbinic thinking about personal relationships is on right and wrong, we see here, and in many other passages in *Avot*, the view that good manners—ritually showing respect—are also vital to good relationships.

Rabbi Eliezer's bitter experience with colleagues, which we will examine in conjunction with the next mishnah, probably inspired his inclusion of this heartfelt plea.

Do not be easy to anger. The Book of Proverbs and the Rabbinic literature are both full of warnings about the dangers of anger and its devastating impact on relationships. Maimonides, who urges that we should absolutely minimize feelings of anger (MT, *Hilkhot Deot 2:3*), nevertheless feels it is sometimes important to appear angry, so that those around us know we are serious about an issue. He therefore recommends, paradoxically, that we occasionally display anger, but not when we actually feel it.

Repent one day before your death. The idea here is that since you don't know when you will die, you should repent every day. Repentance means that you should admit guilt where you have done wrong, apologize, make amends to those you have wronged, and refrain from doing wrong again. According to the Rabbis, a test of true repentance is when a person is in the same situation as when he or she sinned and does not sin again. Repentance is also part of the process of atonement, of moving back closer to God after one has been estranged through sin. Because the "return" (the literal meaning of *teshuvah*) is not only a return to goodness, but also a return closer to God, repentance is a vital concern of Jewish mystics.

MODERN LIFE

ALL OF our negative emotions are a reaction to pain, or to the fear of pain. Guilt is a feeling of pain at causing others harm; shame is a feeling of humiliation in the eyes of others. Anger is a feeling of fear and hostility in reaction to injury or to the threat of pain inflicted by another; jealousy is a feeling of pain over being deprived of one we love or over the threat of that deprivation; envy is a feeling of pain and hostility at a perceived rival's well-being.

On these negative emotions, Jewish tradition has been pro-guilt and anti-anger, but in modern times, the fashion has been the other way around. Negative feelings toward oneself, such as guilt and shame, are to be totally avoided, whereas negative feelings toward others are often considered "healthy."

A sounder view is that all negative emotions are valuable as "trigger signals" that tell us when we face an important problem, but are extremely dangerous when we become fixated on them. Unfortunately, we humans do have the tendency to become fixated on such emotions, and then have a simpleminded "fight, flight, or freeze" reaction that ends up hurting us or others. The key is to become unstuck, and to do thoughtful problem solving, and to find more productive solutions to the problems that face us, solutions that help both ourselves and others.

Do not be easy to anger. In current times, under the influence of Freud, many accept a "pneumatic" theory of anger: anger is a fixed quantity that has to come out in some way. In this view, focusing on and expressing anger provides a healthy release, and repressing anger only results in it coming out in other ways that are more harmful to the individual's psyche.

Research now seems in fact to confirm the traditional view that holding onto anger only exacerbates it and its destructive consequences. Today, there are many anger management programs, which aim at teaching people to deal more productively with the causes of their anger. One of the most interesting views, from psychologist Steven Stosny, is that compassion and anger are conflicting emotions. The effort to understand another person and to empathize with his or her feelings dissipates anger, and enables us to resolve problems more effectively.

Warm yourself at the fire of the wise,
*   but be careful of their glowing coals, lest you be burned;*
For their bite is the bite of a jackal,
*   their sting is the sting of a scorpion,*
*   their hiss is the hiss of a serpent,*
*   and all their words are like burning coals. (2:15B)*

וֶהֱוֵי מִתְחַמֵּם כְּנֶגֶד אוּרָן שֶׁל חֲכָמִים, וֶהֱוֵי זָהִיר בְּגַחַלְתָּן שֶׁלֹּא תִכָּוֶה,
שֶׁנְּשִׁיכָתָן נְשִׁיכַת שׁוּעָל, וַעֲקִיצָתָן עֲקִיצַת עַקְרָב, וּלְחִישָׁתָן לְחִישַׁת שָׂרָף,
וְכָל דִּבְרֵיהֶם כְּגַחֲלֵי אֵשׁ.

WHEN YOHANAN BEN ZAKKAI praised his student Rabbi Eliezer as "a plastered cistern which does not lose a drop (2:11)," he was alluding to Eliezer's phenomenal memory. Rabbi Eliezer was an extraordinarily brilliant man with a conservative and inflexible outlook. He tended toward the more restrictive interpretations of tradition that Shammai had advocated, rather than toward Hillel's freer interpretations, which were more accommodating to humanitarian needs.

Rabbi Eliezer's differences in outlook with other Rabbis came to a head in one of the most momentous disputes in the history of Judaism. As is often the case, the spark that started this major quarrel was a relatively minor issue—debate as to whether a type of oven was *kasher*, ritually fit for use. The real dispute, though, was over the proper standard for interpreting tradition. Were divine inspiration and the authority of past Sages to be the proper basis for a decision? Or was the standard rational argument, taking into account both the letter of the sacred texts and the needs of humanity, to be the basis? Rabbi Eliezer was on the side of authority and divine inspiration. Rabbi Yehoshua ben Hanania— his old comrade in the daring rescue of Yohanan ben Zakkai—was on the other side of the argument: first, reasoning based on the texts, and then a vote by the Sages should decide issues of *halakhah*.

According to a legend in the Talmud (BM 59b), after Rabbi Eliezer failed to convince his colleagues with arguments based on texts, he said, "If the *halakhah* agrees with me, let this carob tree prove it!" And the tree, roots and all, moved 100 cubits. The others replied that a tree didn't prove anything. So in a second miracle, a stream ran backward. Again, this was rejected as valid proof of Eliezer's argument. In a third miracle, the walls of the *beit midrash* (place of Torah study) began to bend in at Rabbi Eliezer's request. But when Rabbi Yehoshua ben Ḥanania rebuked the walls because they were not a proper source of proof, they ceased bending in out of respect for him. Finally, a voice from heaven rang out that the *halakhah* was in accordance with Rabbi Eliezer.

Rabbi Yehoshua replied by quoting Deuteronomy 30:12: "It is not in the heavens"—the "it" being God's instructions, the Torah. He was arguing that because God's word has already been fully revealed, the majority rule should decide on its interpretation, with no new divine intervention being sought or accepted.

Not only did the majority accept the view of Rabbi Yehoshua ben Ḥanania, but Rabban Gamliel II (grandson of the first Rabban Gamliel), then *Nasi* (representative of the Jews to the Romans), imposed a ban forbidding Rabbi Eliezer to teach or argue his views. Rabban Gamliel evidently felt that if Rabbi Eliezer continued to advocate his views, it could split the Jewish community, which was then struggling to survive in the wake of the Temple's destruction. Rabbi Eliezer, who loved Torah as much as life, was deeply embittered over being cut off from colleagues and students.

The tragedy was even more poignant because Rabbi Eliezer was married to Rabban Gamliel's sister. The story is told that Rabbi Eliezer's wife forbade him from bending down in private prayer, for fear that he would pray for the destruction of her brother. As his connection with God was so intimate, she feared that if he prayed for harm to her brother, the curse would be fulfilled.

The Talmud evidently agrees with the majority decision, but not with the ban on Eliezer, as the whole discussion is presented in the context of demonstrating the evils of using one's power to take advantage of others. As Rabbi Eliezer lay dying, his old friend Yehoshua ben Ḥanania clung to him, in tears, crying out, "The ban is annulled! The ban is annulled! *Rabbi! Rabbi!*" (literally, "My Master! My Master!"). Many of Rabbi Eliezer's rulings were reinstated after his death, but the standards of judgment in the Talmud still follow those of Yehoshua ben Ḥanania.

MODERN LIFE

ANYONE WHO has witnessed scholars' quarrels will instantly recognize the mixed feelings of admiration and bitterness in Rabbi Eliezer's warning here—a warning that reflects his personal ordeal.

The evil eye, the evil inclination, and hatred of humanity drive a person from the world. *(2:16)*

רַבִּי יְהוֹשֻׁעַ אוֹמֵר: עַיִן הָרָע, וְיֵצֶר הָרָע, וְשִׂנְאַת הַבְּרִיּוֹת, מוֹצִיאִין אֶת הָאָדָם מִן הָעוֹלָם.

RABBI YEHOSHUA BEN HANANIA's answer to Yoḥanan ben Zakkai's question of the right path was: "a good friend" (2:13). Rabbi Yehoshua's "three things" here reflect this concern with friendship. So, too, did his life. Like his friend Rabbi Eliezer, he had a serious clash with the *Nasi*, Rabban Gamliel, but his behavior and its result were very different from Rabbi Eliezer's.

A witness testified about the appearance of the new moon in a way contrary to the known science at that time. Rabbi Yehoshua rejected the witness, whom Rabban Gamliel had accepted. This caused a disagreement about the timing of Rosh Hashanah, the start of the Jewish year, and hence about the whole religious calendar. At issue was also whether scientific calculation or the authority of the *Nasi* would determine the calendar for Judea and Diaspora Jewry.

To assert his authority publicly, Rabban Gamliel ordered Rabbi Yehoshua to appear before him on the day that would have been Yom Kippur, the Day of Atonement, with his staff and his money—which would have been a desecration of that most holy day. Believing that Rabban Gamliel was wrong, but that the court led by him had the authority to decide the matter, Rabbi Yehoshua extremely reluctantly but dutifully showed up. The story continues: "Rabban Gamliel rose and kissed him on his head and said to him: come in peace my teacher [Rabbi] and my student—my teacher in wisdom and my student because you have accepted my decision" (RH 25a).

However, friction between the two continued and escalated. On one occasion, someone had asked Rabbi Yehoshua whether evening prayers were obligatory, and he said "no." When the same person asked Rabban Gamliel, he said "yes." Hearing of the disagreement, Rabban Gamliel then had the person ask about evening prayers publicly in the *beit midrash* when Rabbi Yehoshua was present, and repeated that evening prayers are obligatory.

Intending to confront Rabbi Yehoshua, Rabban Gamliel then asked, "Are there any who dispute this?" Yehoshua, accepting Rabban Gamliel's authority, said "no," avoiding the confrontation. Not letting go, Rabban Gamliel told Rabbi Yehoshua to stand up and asked others in the assembly to testify as to whether Rabbi Yehoshua had contradicted him earlier. Yehoshua tried to defuse the situation by replying with a joke, but Gamliel continued to press, embarrassing Yehoshua. At this point, knowing well the earlier conflicts between the two, the assembly rebelled and voted to depose Gamliel as *Nasi* because he embarrassed Rabbi Yehoshua in public—a grave sin in Rabbinic ethics.

In Rabban Gamliel's place, they installed the young Rabbi Elazar ben Azariah (BER 27b). Rabbi Yehoshua, friend to so many, had been backed by his friends. And when Rabban Gamliel apologized, he was partially reinstated to his position at Rabbi Yehoshua's insistence. Rabbi Elazar ben Azariah, Rabbi Yehoshua, and Rabban Gamliel later came together to make journeys to Rome to represent the Jewish community.

Rabbi Yehoshua was reputed to be very ugly physically, but his teacher Yoḥanan ben Zakkai rightly said, "Happy is she who bore him." What wonderful praise—might we all deserve such a compliment!

The evil eye. The bad or evil eye (bad and evil are the same word, *ra*, in Hebrew) here means a possessive, envious nature. It causes strife with others and so distances a person from others' company.

The evil inclination. Here we meet with the important Rabbinic concept of the *yetzer ha-ra*, the bad or evil inclination. In reconciling two biblical passages, the Sages came to the conclusion that all humans have both good and bad inclinations, and the God-given power to choose between them. The *yetzer ha-ra* often refers to sexual desire, but also to any potentially destructive urge such as rivalry or anger. The Rabbis recognized, though, that the *yetzer ha-ra* also has a positive side:

&❧ But for the *yetzer ha-ra* no man would build a house, take a wife and beget children. Thus said Solomon (ECCL 4:4): "All labor and all excelling in work, that is from a man's rivalry with his neighbor." (GEN RAB 9:7)

Rabbi Yehoshua's saying warns us that if we let these passions lead us in a destructive direction, we will cut ourselves off from society. So too, general hatred of people will lead to isolation. Yehoshua seems to have been remarkably free of the vices he condemns: envy, rivalry, and malice. His life is an inspiring model of what this freedom from envy, rivalry, and malice can do when it is joined together with a gift for friendship.

MODERN LIFE

THE STORY of the relations between these leaders of the new post-Temple, Classical Judaism illustrates both the great power and the great difficulty of sustaining a critical tradition, and making it thrive.

For the sake of improving ideas and finding the truth, maximum clarity and sharp criticism are invaluable. Progress emerges from clashes between views, as people develop their views and make their cases as strongly as possible for them (see *Avot* 5:20). If people "acknowledge the truth" (5:10), and are willing to admit errors, new insights will be gained.

Talmudic tradition prizes criticism, and even views it as a great compliment. There is the story of a sage whose friend and companion in Talmud Torah had died, and who was driven to despair by his students because they would only agree with him, and not dispute his views. In modern times, as Karl Popper pointed out, criticism has been an engine for the growth of knowledge in science, where contending views are judged through observation and experiment.

However, I think it fair to say that most people find distress, not joy, in arguing for the sake of finding the truth. If we look at rules of politeness, they do not promote clarity. Where the search for truth requires pointed questions and precise description of facts, politeness requires open questions that don't put people on the spot and avoidance of disclosing potentially embarrassing facts.

The story here of Gamliel, Eliezer, and Yehoshua dramatically illustrates how disputes, even among those committed to respectful debate can tear people apart. Yet for all the conflict, the overall message is that their devotion to working "for the sake of Heaven" ultimately kept them together, and laid the foundation for the survival of Judaism. Rabbi Eliezer was excluded, but that was because he wouldn't respect rational debate and majority rule. Rabban Gamliel and Rabbi Yehoshua, despite their personal conflict, resolved their differences by voting and through Rabban Gamliel's apology. The institutions for unified discussion and resolution survived, and everyone worked together for the community.

Through all of this, Rabbi Yehoshua was a role model because he possessed qualities that were the opposite of those he warned against in his mishnah: he was without jealousy and avoided rivalries, remaining a friend to all. If we are to realize and sustain precious learning communities like those of the Sages, Rabbi Yehoshua is a model who shows us the way.

RABBI YOSE:

Let the money of your associate be as dear to you
as your own. (2:17A)

רַבִּי יוֹסֵי אוֹמֵר: יְהִי מָמוֹן חֲבֵרְךָ חָבִיב עָלֶיךָ כְּשֶׁלָּךְ.

RABBI ELAZAR BEN SHAMMUA:

Let the honor of your student be as dear to you as your own;
Let the honor of your colleague be as your reverence for your
teacher;
And let your reverence for your teacher
be as your reverence for Heaven. (4:15)

רַבִּי אֶלְעָזָר בֶּן שַׁמּוּעַ אוֹמֵר: יְהִי כְבוֹד תַּלְמִידְךָ חָבִיב עָלֶיךָ כְּשֶׁלָּךְ, וּכְבוֹד
חֲבֵרְךָ כְּמוֹרָא רַבָּךְ, וּמוֹרָא רַבָּךְ כְּמוֹרָא שָׁמָיִם.

RABBI ISHMAEL:

Be deferential to your seniors, affable to your juniors
and receive every person with joy. (3:16)

רַבִּי יִשְׁמָעֵאל אוֹמֵר: הֱוֵי קַל לְרֹאשׁ, וְנוֹחַ לְתִשְׁחֹרֶת, וֶהֱוֵי מְקַבֵּל אֶת כָּל
הָאָדָם בְּשִׂמְחָה.

LET THE money. Rabbi Yose, when asked about the right path had answered, "A good neighbor"(2:13). And his first saying concerns a basic
social responsibility: being honest with other people's money. A wit
once said: "Most people are pretty honest—except when it comes to
money and sex." Of course, these are the parts of life where adults are
most tempted to be dishonest. Yose is thus giving us a way of viewing
our situation that will help us to resist temptation, a viewpoint that can
counterbalance the emotions we feel at the moment of temptation.

Let the honor of your student. This expands on Rabbi Eliezer's saying
"Let the honor of your colleague be as dear to you as your own," (2:15)
by applying it to an unequal relationship. In modern times, there has
been a passion for equality, but the fact that many important relationships are unequal—parent and child, teacher and student, boss and subordinate—tends to be overlooked. As a result of this neglect, people are
often unclear about what is just in unequal relationships.

Because students typically know much less and have less power than
their teachers, some teachers are tempted to take advantage of their
power and treat students disrespectfully. Rabbi Elazar ben Shammua

warns teachers against this. Yehudah haNasi indicated the respect students deserve in this expression of his appreciation for his students:

> From my teachers, I learned much Torah; from my fellow students, still more; and from my own students, the most of all. (MAK 10a)

Rabbi Elazar says that teachers shouldn't only be honored, but revered. This implies a deference to their authority in their role.

Be deferential. Rabbi Ishmael similarly distinguishes between what behaviors are appropriate toward people with whom you have different relationships. While some difference in behavior is appropriate, *all* people, no matter the relationship, should be received or welcomed joyfully. This admonition is stronger than Shammai's injunction to receive everyone "with a pleasant face" (*Avot* 1:15) and implies a warm and inviting attitude toward all people.

MODERN LIFE

How CAN unequal relationships be fair or just? The basic principle, as noted in connection with *Avot* 1:10, is that a person cannot be given a responsibility without the authority to carry it out. For example, a teacher must be able to keep order in his or her class to carry out the responsibility to teach, and so needs the authority to do so. If an unequal relationship is set up fairly, where the differences in roles are justified by the benefits of the relationship, the person with more power acts fairly by fulfilling his or her responsibilities. The person can also be unfair by exploiting his or her power beyond what is justified in the role or by failing to carry out the appropriate responsibilities. People who are subordinate can also be unfair by failing to fulfill their responsibilities. For example, teachers can show favoritism in grading, and students can disrupt a class and prevent others from learning.

The final two *mishnayot* here are about manners, rather than issues of justice. But once roles have been set, in order for a person to function in a role, appropriate manners are vital—as is noted in *Avot* 3:21. For example, students must be willing to defer to their teacher's reasonable requirements for order in the classroom. And the teacher needs to show respect for students by being patient with their errors and being willing to help them again and again, without putting them down.

Rabbi Ishmael goes much further in advocating an attitude not just of respect but of real warmth toward others—a high standard, and when we see it realized, we treasure it.

RABBI YOSE:

> *Prepare yourself to study Torah,*
> *for it isn't yours by inheritance.*
> *And let all you do be for the sake of Heaven. (2:17B)*

וְהַתְקֵן עַצְמְךָ לִלְמוֹד תּוֹרָה, שֶׁאֵינָהּ יְרֻשָּׁה לָךְ, וְכָל מַעֲשֶׂיךָ יִהְיוּ לְשֵׁם שָׁמָיִם.

SINCE HIS teacher Yoḥanan ben Zakkai praised Rabbi Yose as a pious man, a *ḥasid*, it is interesting to see what Rabbi Yose's concept of piety is in his three sayings. As noted before, *ḥasid* has the double meaning of a kind person and a devout person. Rabbi Yose's sayings reflect this concept—a wedding of religious devotion and good human relations. His first saying (2:17A) in effect says that honesty with others' money is the first duty of a pious person—a refreshing idea!

Prepare yourself. A second aspect of piety is devotion to learning Torah. Again, Rabbi Yose has a wonderful eye for the fundamental: no one inherits knowledge, so each person and each new generation has to work for it. Thus, we have to arrange our time and our activities so that regular study is a part of them.

Let all you do be for the sake of Heaven. Everything in life, Rabbi Yose tells us, can be done with the intent to follow God's commandments, and such a conscious intention will affect every aspect of our lives. Taken outside the context of Rabbinic ethics, this saying could be misread as urging the life of an ascetic: self-denial, isolation, and singular devotion to prayer and meditation. In the Rabbinic context, though, following the commandments means working to earn a living, marrying, raising children, being involved in the community, and pursuing justice. Thus, Rabbi Yose is urging, first of all, that when we interact with another person, we should always be mindful of the ethical principles of Judaism and put these principles above any selfish desires. Then our lives will be uplifted with a sense of holiness.

The concept of doing everything "for the sake of Heaven" includes not only our daily interaction with others, but also choices that affect primarily ourselves. In *Leviticus Rabbah* (34:3), Hillel is asked where he is going, and he says, "To carry out a commandment." When asked, "Which one?" he answers that he is going to the bath house to wash, and on another occasion to the toilet. "How are these commandments?" his companions ask. Hillel refers to the statement that man is made in the image of God (GEN 9:6), the implication being that care for one's body is a sacred duty.

Maimonides devotes Chapter 5 of his introduction to *Avot*—the *Eight Chapters*—to acting "for the sake of Heaven." He says that in order to do all things for Heaven's sake, we should follow a "middle path" of moderation, as Aristotle and other Greek philosophers advocated. We should enjoy pleasures that promote and preserve our physical and mental health, but not seek pleasure beyond these purposes. Maimonides says,

> There may be occasions when a person will seek to eat sweet foods as a therapeutic approach—e.g., he has lost desire for food, and it is necessary to arouse such a craving by eating sweet and tastily seasoned foods. Similarly, if a person is overcome by melancholy, he should endeavor to purge himself of it by listening to songs and music, strolling through gardens and magnificent buildings, and frequenting attractive works of art. (trans., Rabbi E. Touger)

Maimonides' purely health-oriented view of pleasure arguably goes further in the ascetic direction than does the Sages'. One Sage, Rav, said, "A man will have to give reckoning and account for everything that his eye saw and he did not eat" (P. KID 4:9, 66d), and, "My son, if you have the means, treat yourself well" (ER 54a). Still, Maimonides' overall message—that one should strike a healthy balance between pursuing pleasure and practicing restraint for the sake of better serving God—is a beautiful synthesis of Rabbinic and Aristotelian ethics.

MODERN LIFE

FOR THE sake of Heaven. Ḥasidism, which began in the 1700s, placed a renewed emphasis on experiencing the sacred in everyday actions. The goal of this was not only that our everyday actions would be instrumental to serving God, but also that we would experience holiness in our daily actions and personal relationships, by giving our actions a sacred intention—doing them "for the sake of Heaven." In the 20th century, Martin Buber celebrated this aspect of Ḥasidism and urged its adoption as a part of modern life. The philosophy in which he cast this was, however, a romantic one, relying mainly on feeling. Buber himself was in fact devoted to Torah and Ḥasidic lore, and it is hard to see how most people could regularly achieve this heightened experience of holiness without some kind of study, ritual practice, and social support.

Rabbi Shimon said:

Be mindful in the reciting of the Shema and of the Tefillah.
And when you pray, make your prayer not a set task, but
  a plea for compassion and grace before the Blessed Presence.
And do not be wicked in your own eyes. (2:18)

רַבִּי שִׁמְעוֹן אוֹמֵר: הֱוֵי זָהִיר בִּקְרִיאַת שְׁמַע וּבִתְפִלָּה, וּכְשֶׁאַתָּה מִתְפַּלֵּל,
אַל תַּעַשׂ תְּפִלָּתְךָ קֶבַע, אֶלָּא רַחֲמִים וְתַחֲנוּנִים לִפְנֵי הַמָּקוֹם, שֶׁנֶּאֱמַר:
"כִּי־חַנּוּן וְרַחוּם הוּא אֶרֶךְ אַפַּיִם וְרַב־חֶסֶד וְנִחָם עַל־הָרָעָה." וְאַל תְּהִי
רָשָׁע בִּפְנֵי עַצְמֶךָ.

BE MINDFUL. After the destruction of the Temple, the immediate problem Yoḥanan ben Zakkai and his students faced was what would substitute for sacrifices in the Temple, which were believed to cleanse people
of sin. They ruled that prayer and good deeds could equally cleanse
people of sin. Building on existing practice in the synagogues, they put
in place the basics of the traditional Jewish prayer service. The basic
parts of daily prayer are the *Shema* and the *Tefillah*. The *Shema*, "hearken," is a declaration of faith beginning, "Hearken O Israel: Yhvh our
God, Yhvh is One" (*DEUT 6:4*). (Here the four roman letters stand for
yod-hey-vav-hey, the sacred name of God, which is not pronounced;
"Adonai" or "Lord" is substituted.) The *Tefillah*, which literally means
"prayer," is a series of prayers of praise, petition, and thanks.

And when you pray. When the Rabbis established regular prayers,
the danger of perfunctory recitation of the prayer arose. Here, Rabbi
Shimon is alerting us to the need to concentrate spiritually and to maintain the prayers as a fresh and sincere petition. Originally, the *Tefillah*
included private petitions whose content could vary. Eventually, the
form became fixed and known as the *Shemoneh Esrei,* or *Amidah.* The
problem is that fixed, repeated prayer can become spiritually empty.
However, the absence of a fixed practice may result in neglect of prayer
and hence a lack of inspiration.

The final phrase, "the Blessed Presence," is a translation of *hamakom*.
The Rabbis used this word, literally "the place," to refer to God, alluding to God's quality of being present at all places and times. After this
statement on how to pray, the Hebrew has a prooftext: "For He is gracious and compassionate, slow to anger, abounding in kindness, and re-
nouncing punishment . . ." (JOEL 2:13).

And do not be wicked. The turmoil that led to the separation of Judaism and Christianity also occurred after the fall of the Temple, and involved Rabban Gamliel of Yavneh and the students of Yoḥanan ben Zakkai. This saying is likely a warning to reject Saint Paul's doctrine of original sin (c. 50 CE). According to Paul's interpretation of Genesis, human beings are born with a stain of sin, inherited from Adam, that can only be removed by God's intervention. Without that special intervention, all are condemned to eternal damnation. Furthermore, Paul wrote that this intervention is only possible through the belief in God's son, Jesus of Nazareth, whom God sent to earth to save humanity from original sin. Thus, God only saves from damnation those who accept Jesus.

We should note that the Rabbinic concept of the evil inclination, *yetzer ha-ra,* is fundamentally different from "original sin," as all adults have the ability to choose freely between the *yetzer ha-ra* and *yetzer ha-tov,* between a good and bad path in life. In the logic of Rabbinic Judaism, there is no original sin that interferes with free choice (*Avot* 3:19), and thus there is no need for divine intervention. No savior other than God is needed. In addition, the claim that God has a divine son appearing on earth seemed to the Rabbis to be giving God the nature and behavior of the Greek gods—much as claiming that God has a brother or wife would—and so violating the *Shema.* In the beginning of his mishnah, Rabbi Shimon warns us to be mindful of the meaning of the *Shema* as we recite it. In this mishnah, then, Rabbi Shimon puts his finger on two fundamental theological issues where Christianity and Judaism parted ways.

Another layer of meaning in this saying is a moral warning: we should not see ourselves as hopelessly corrupt, so that we then give up on moral improvement, and feel free to commit any sin whatsoever.

MODERN LIFE

ONE OF the key advantages of set prayers is the establishment of communal prayer, an innovation taken up by Christianity and Islam. This enables a heightened spiritual experience that transcends selfish concerns and strongly promotes a community. However, outside Orthodoxy, Jews are not as drawn to communal prayer as in ages past. This decline is likely due to waning belief in an interventionist God who can hear and answer our prayers. The challenge to non-Orthodox Jewish denominations, then, is to make prayer services spiritually fulfilling.

RABBI ELAZAR:

> *Be diligent in studying Torah,*
>   *and know what to answer to an Epicurean.*
> *Know before whom you toil, and that your Employer*
>   *can be trusted to pay you the wages for your labor. (2:19)*

רַבִּי אֶלְעָזָר אוֹמֵר: הֱוֵי שָׁקוּד לִלְמוֹד תּוֹרָה, וְדַע מַה שֶׁתָּשִׁיב לְאֶפִּיקוֹרוֹס,
וְדַע לִפְנֵי מִי אַתָּה עָמֵל, וּמִי הוּא בַּעַל מְלַאכְתְּךָ, שֶׁיְּשַׁלֶּם לְךָ שְׂכַר פְּעֻלָּתֶךָ.

RABBI ELAZAR was called an "ever-flowing fountain" of learning by his teacher Yohanan ben Zakkai (2:11). The meaning of this is that he always gained and communicated fresh insights and wisdom.

Know what to answer. Rabbi Elazar, in referring to followers of the Greek philosopher Epicurus, was clearly indicating that Jews should be familiar with other belief systems. His first saying, though, makes clear that one's biggest effort should be in the study of Torah. Thus non-Jewish beliefs will not "enter into your heart," as Maimonides puts it in his commentary to *Avot*.

Why did Rabbi Elazar think it was important to be able to answer the philosophy of Epicurus, as opposed to other rival belief systems? First, in his day, the polytheism and idol worship of the Greco-Roman world had little appeal to those living in Judea, and hence was seen as not worth criticizing. In fact, large numbers of non-Jews in the Roman Empire were attracted to Judaism, and followed some of its practices. A second belief system, the high-minded Greek philosophy of Stoicism shared with Judaism a belief in a world governed by providence, God's plan and influence. It did not have its own system of worship, but it accepted idol worship.

By contrast, Epicureans believed that the world, including human beings, consists solely of "atoms and the void." The world is devoid of purpose, lacking any spiritual dimension, and human affairs are only governed by human will and chance. The proper aim of humanity is pleasure, the greatest pleasures being in friendship and a simple life.

While Epicurus was an amiable personality, his philosophy was in direct conflict with Rabbinic beliefs. To deny that the world is governed by a purpose and a plan is to deny God. Such denial was referred to by the Rabbis as the belief that there is "no judgment and no judge," and was firmly rejected. Against this view, Rabbi Elazar's final statement asserts the belief in divine judgment.

MODERN LIFE

EPICUREANISM LARGELY died out in antiquity, but in the Renaissance it was revived. Isaac Newton's mechanical explanation of the rotation of the planets lent new prestige to the ancient idea that the world consists of "atoms and the void." The success of the atomic theory of chemistry was another triumph of mechanical explanation.

In the 19th century, Auguste Comte reintroduced Epicureanism in a new form as part of Positivism. According to Comte, everything not provable by a mechanistic explanation is to be rejected, including all traditional religions. Positivism was given a boost by Darwin's theory of evolution, which opened up the possibility that human purpose had evolved by accident from chaos. Thus, Epicureanism under a new name gradually became the main rival to traditional religions.

What to answer to a Positivist or Epicurean? First of all, the idea that human purpose can be explained away mechanically is itself an unproven project, a faith, and so fails by the Positivist's own standards.

Second, the project of explaining everything away scientifically is inherently impossible. Because of the nature of explanation in science, science cannot reduce to nothing the mysteries of time, change, and diversity. Scientific explanations and predictions are not prophesies, but logical deductions from theories that must be explicitly stated in language. For example, Newton's law, "F=ma," equates force, mass, and acceleration in a specific relationship. And acceleration involves terms for time and distance, or in other words, space. Where does force come from? Where do mass, space, time, and the scientific law itself come from? Every scientific explanation must relate several variables, and we can always ask "Why?" about those. Science cannot logically derive this variety of variables from oneness: explanation involves deduction of one statement from another, and all statements relate several variables (subject and predicate). So there is a limit. Diversity and change cannot be reduced to oneness, or nothing, and so be explained away by science.

Albert Einstein was well aware of the vast unknown, the mystery behind the basic formulas of physics. As noted earlier (1:3), he wrote: "A knowledge of the existence of something we cannot penetrate, our perceptions of the profoundest reason and most radiant beauty, which only in their most primitive forms are accessible to our minds—it is this knowledge and this emotion that constitute true religiosity." And he said that in the sense of his being in awe of this beautiful mystery, he was "deeply religious." Einstein recognized that, as Rabbi Abraham Joshua Heschel put it, science cannot answer the "ultimate questions" of why there is time, why there is diversity, why there is a world rather than nothing, and why indeed there are laws of nature.

Einstein's religiosity reveals how a sense of the transcendent can motivate us to love and appreciate nature. However, it is not enough to answer an Epicurean on other aspects of traditional religiosity, namely that God asks us to be ethical, and can give us comfort in distress. Einstein was led to reject traditional Jewish religion after reading the Positivists, and he made very clear that he rejected any notion of a God with will or intention. And he said that his religious feeling had nothing to do with ethics. However, after the rise of Hitler, he changed and came to see that religion offered the strongest hope of sustaining ethical values, and preventing the decay of humanity into barbarism. But he never reconciled this with his more Positivist side.

That same awe that Einstein felt about the inanimate world of nature can, I believe, be extended to include the world of the living and of humanity. And when we broaden the scope of our appreciation of the world, we can bring in some more of the traditional aspects of religiosity. Indeed, Einstein himself found the most mysterious and amazing thing is that we humans can understand the laws of nature. But because of his focus on the inanimate world of physics, he never integrated human consciousness into his philosophy.

Once we accept that the living world and human consciousness are part of nature, this same sense of awe enables us to see a richer sacredness in the world, including in ethical conduct. In the natural world, we see a pressure for evolution toward complexity and organization that goes against increasing chaos, against entropy. DNA is far more complex than any other chemical, and the human brain has more connections than there are stars in the Milky Way. Somehow this leads to a central consciousness and control, and our consciousness includes goals and intentionality.

The mystery of human consciousness partly is the mystery of the *now*. Einstein was a strict determinist, believing the world is like an already-recorded film, with everything set. But this does not, and cannot explain why we are experiencing this part of history, *now*. Nor does it explain our intentionality, the fact that we act now for the sake of future purposes. Neither the "now" nor intentionality, it seems, can be reduced to nothing, eliminated by scientific explanation. Rather, they seem part of the fundamental mysteries of creation, and so intimately linked to whatever created and sustains us.

If intentionality is indeed part of nature, then it would partly explain the drive for complexity, and that we ourselves hunger to move to the next step, to a more harmonious, productive, and joyous existence in human society. In other words, the drive to live by high ethical standards, which would create such an existence, is rooted deep in creation, and so inspired by the Creator. Considerations like this led Abraham Joshua Heschel to argue that God is not the impassive, non-intentional God of Einstein, or the "unmoved mover" of Aristotle, but rather the "most moved mover," the God of the Prophets who wants humanity to do justice, love kindness, and walk humbly with God. Heschel did say that God cannot be thought of as a person, as human, but is more than human, and mysteriously entwined with our feelings and our purposes.

The mystery of consciousness and intention also comes to the fore when we try to understand human history. Karl Popper argued against reductionism, saying that new ideas, such as the invention of the airplane, have a causal impact on history that cannot be reduced to the motion of atoms. There is a kind of "downward causation" in which the most complex elements, such as the ideas of how to build a functioning airplane, end up causing the least complex, bolts and screws (atoms included) to be moved as people learn the new ideas and build new airplanes. The ideas change the objects, rather than the other way around.

Heschel similarly argued that the new moral ideas of the Prophets, ideas of social justice, were unique innovations that changed history in a way that the causal interaction of matter and motion cannot by itself account for. All these considerations are arguments for the presence of the transcendent in our lives, in our awareness of the moment, and in our desire for a better world. These arguments are suggestive, rather than conclusive, but they do show that science as we know it has not even begun to address these issues, is ultimately limited, and will never be able to fully address them.

Most atheists today argue for a commitment to some kind of ethical system, so the question becomes: how is the experience of the transcendent important to ethics, and to other positive attitudes of the religious, such as awe and gratitude for life, beauty, love, and nature? Here, atheism dismisses the importance of the transcendent. Banishing any credence that our ethical feelings of awe have roots in something beyond us is not only dogmatic, but also leaves us with no inspiration or guidance on these critical issues of meaning and value when evidence is inconclusive. When we attend to these religious feelings, they can enrich our lives with feelings of awe, gratitude, generosity, and love.

There is also the issue of moral courage. Ethical values ask us to think of more than our individual wants and needs of the moment. As William James pointed out (see 1:16), we must make important life decisions even when we cannot have proof as to their consequences, or a knowledge of what is best to do. A sense of being part of or responding to a divinity that transcends individuals and time can support ethical values and offer us guidance. Thus, when we are tempted to take a short-term, apparently easier way, religious belief can give us the courage to take an ethical path. Epicureanism and Positivism give us no guidance and support, but Torah and Talmud, and the sense of God's Presence do.

The difficulty with religious feelings, though, is that feelings of connection to the transcendent do not in themselves give specific, reliable guidance. That different religions have such different beliefs shows that lack of clarity and specificity (see 2:4). Religious feelings have, alas, been used to motivate violence, war, and aggression.

Atheists have been recently arguing that this bloody record of religious war and fanaticism is the essence of religion. This identification of religion and fanaticism is, however, refuted by recent history: atheistic Communist movements have at times been as fanatic as the worst religious fanatics, and killed just as many or more people. The problem is fanaticism, and not religion or the lack of it.

Because terrible things have been done in the name of religion, it is clear that what is important is not just whether a person is religious, but what that person's religion consists of. The Judaism of the Sages in fact supports the most humane and cooperative values. And the principle of relying on past sacred texts and voting helps to block fanatic aberrations.

Finally, can we also find the comfort that religion traditionally offers the suffering? If we reject reward and punishment, as many in the modern era do, we cannot offer the same comfort that everything will work out for us in our heavenly reward. But we can, even without the traditional interventionist God, have the comfort of seeing that we are part of something larger than ourselves, something that will survive our egos even after we perish.

The day is short and the work much; the workers are lazy and the wages high; and the Master of the house presses. (2:20)

רַבִּי טַרְפוֹן אוֹמֵר: הַיּוֹם קָצֵר, וְהַמְּלָאכָה מְרֻבָּה, וְהַפּוֹעֲלִים עֲצֵלִים, וְהַשָּׂכָר הַרְבֵּה, וּבַעַל הַבַּיִת דּוֹחֵק:

You are not obliged to complete the work,
    but you are not free to neglect it;
If you have learned much Torah,
    you will be given much reward;
Your Employer is trustworthy
    and will pay you the reward for your labor.
And know that the granting of rewards to the righteous
    is in the time to come. (2:21)

הוּא הָיָה אוֹמֵר: לֹא עָלֶיךָ הַמְּלָאכָה לִגְמוֹר וְלֹא אַתָּה בֶן חוֹרִין לְהִבָּטֵל מִמֶּנָּה; אִם לָמַדְתָּ תּוֹרָה הַרְבֵּה, נוֹתְנִין לְךָ שָׂכָר הַרְבֵּה; וְנֶאֱמָן הוּא בַּעַל מְלַאכְתְּךָ, שֶׁיְּשַׁלֶּם לְךָ שְׂכַר פְּעֻלָּתֶךָ. וְדַע שֶׁמַּתַּן שְׂכָרָן שֶׁל צַדִּיקִים לֶעָתִיד לָבוֹא.

RABBI TARFON takes Rabbi Elazar's metaphor of employer and worker from the previous mishnah and extends it.

You are not obliged to complete the work. This refers no doubt to Torah study, but no less to ethical relationships and the pursuit of social justice. Rabbi Tarfon here distills the realism and pragmatism of Jewish ethics and law into a phrase. An interesting contrast is the "Sermon on the Mount," in which Jesus of Nazareth systematically criticizes the Rabbis for the moderate demands of their ethical mandates, and—perhaps because of his stated belief that the world would soon end—advocates a standard of extreme self-sacrifice. Many Christians have subsequently taken Jesus' words as stating idealized goals rather than practical demands. However, this leaves a big gap between aspiration and the question of actual practice.

One of the distinctive features of Classical Judaism, including *Avot* itself, has been its effort to define principles for living that are high-minded but also realistic. And the consequences of living by those principles are worked out in detail within the context of work, marriage, and family. Some of the sayings in *Avot*, such as "Nullify your will before

His will" (2:4) and "Let all you do be for the sake of Heaven" (2:17) are admittedly also idealized goals. However, subsequent sages and scholars have tried to define their demands in a realistic way. For example, we have discussed how Maimonides includes pleasures for the health of body and mind as a part of directing all our actions "for the sake of Heaven."

Know that the granting of rewards. After so many were martyred at the time of the eventually successful uprisings that led to the rededication of the Temple (now celebrated at Hanukkah), there was a change in emphasis to rewards in an afterlife. The concept of the afterlife as the primary place where once receives reward became firmly entrenched doctrine after the terrible persecutions by Hadrian.

The loss of faith by the great scholar Elisha ben Avuya is an example of the problem to which the concept of the afterlife was a solution. According to one version of the story in the Jerusalem Talmud (P HAG 2:1, 77b–c), ben Avuya saw a man gathering eggs from a nest at the top of a palm tree. The man let the mother bird go, as commanded in the Torah, but upon coming down, he fell and died. The Torah explicitly promises rewards for letting a mother bird go, so this incident seems to directly contradict the Torah.

The story goes on to say that Elisha ben Avuya's son-in-law Rabbi Ya'akov had preached that all rewards promised in the Torah are properly understood as being in the world to come, and that had Elisha accepted this, he would have never abandoned Judaism. Rabbi Ya'akov's view became the accepted view, and is advocated in this mishnah.

MODERN LIFE

You ARE not obliged to complete the work. A related story from the midrash is that the Emperor Hadrian saw a 100-year-old man planting fig trees and asked him, "Do you ever hope to eat of them?" And he replied, "If I am worthy I shall eat, and if not, then as my forebears have worked for me so I will work for my children" (LEV RAB 25:5).

These religious directives of Rabbi Tarfon address a key social problem: the tension between what directly and immediately benefits an individual, and the requirements of a cooperative, peaceful, and productive society. The way religion addresses this problem is worth looking at more closely because, as philosopher E.A. Burtt pointed out, all of the "Great Religions" of the world were developed to address it. The great religions shifted from concern with using the divine to control nature—the focus of animist and polytheistic religions—to spiritually based ethics that would strengthen social harmony.

Theft provides the simplest example of tension between individual and social interests. The ideal situation from the individual's point of view would be one in which all other people in the world would respect property rights, while he or she alone could just take whatever he or she wants. But if every individual becomes a thief, then society becomes insecure, with widespread violence over property. So for the sake of a society that serves individuals better, societies have to constrain individuals by setting up laws, courts, and police.

Generally, lawmaking is an ongoing enterprise of modifying the social framework so that people can serve their individual interests, but in a way that promotes the interests of society at large. The Sages were, of course, devoted to creative development of such a legal framework.

Many issues, though, are beyond the scope of law. For instance, issues of kindness and fairness in family relationships and in the workplace are too subtle to be included in the law. Negatively, people can be cruel and dishonest, deceptive and destructive, in ways that the law cannot reach. Therefore, more than law and law enforcement are needed to promote both a long-term perspective—such as this mishnah urges—and a devotion to interests of others beyond oneself.

All acts of kindness, of devoted work for the community, are "written in a book," as Rabbi Akiva said (*Avot* 2:1b), and will be rewarded in the next life. And those who are cruel and selfish will be punished. Thus, the Sages' vision strongly supported a cooperative community life, imbued with kindness, peace, love, and holiness.

These assurances of reward and punishment, though, are in tension with Antigonos' injunction not to work for rewards (1:3), and even more so with those devoted Jews who reject the concept of reward and punishment in an afterlife. No matter which belief one follows, his or her motivation must come from being a person of integrity, from a sense that he or she is doing God's will, and from finding acts of kindness and of justice spiritually uplifting. Thus, the kind of personal, emotional connection to the transcendent experienced by the prophets, the mystics, and modern thinkers like Einstein, Buber, and Heschel has become still more important.

Chapter Three

When two people sit together and exchange no words of Torah,
this is "a meeting of scoffers."
When two people sit together and exchange words of Torah,
the Divine Presence rests between them. (3:3)

רַרְבִּי חֲנִינָא בֶּן תְּרַדְיוֹן אוֹמֵר: שְׁנַיִם שֶׁיּוֹשְׁבִין וְאֵין בֵּינֵיהֶם דִּבְרֵי תוֹרָה הֲרֵי
זֶה מוֹשַׁב לֵצִים. שֶׁנֶּאֱמַר: "וּבְמוֹשַׁב לֵצִים לֹא יָשָׁב." אֲבָל שְׁנַיִם שֶׁיּוֹשְׁבִין
וְיֵשׁ בֵּינֵיהֶם דִּבְרֵי תוֹרָה, שְׁכִינָה שְׁרוּיָה בֵּינֵיהֶם. שֶׁנֶּאֱמַר: "אָז נִדְבְּרוּ יִרְאֵי
יְיָ אִישׁ אֶל־רֵעֵהוּ, וַיַּקְשֵׁב יְיָ וַיִּשְׁמָע, וַיִּכָּתֵב סֵפֶר זִכָּרוֹן לְפָנָיו לְיִרְאֵי יְיָ
וּלְחשְׁבֵי שְׁמוֹ" . אֵין לִי אֶלָּא שְׁנַיִם, מִנַּיִן אֲפִלּוּ אֶחָד שֶׁיּוֹשֵׁב וְעוֹסֵק בַּתּוֹרָה
שֶׁהַקָּדוֹשׁ־בָּרוּךְ־הוּא קוֹבֵעַ לוֹ שָׂכָר? שֶׁנֶּאֱמַר: "יֵשֵׁב בָּדָד כִּי וְיִדֹּם כִּי נָטַל עָלָיו."

THE FULL text includes the reference for the first sentence: "Happy is
the man who ... does not sit in a meeting of scoffers" (PS 1:1), and continues with a commentary arguing that a reward also comes to even one
person who studies Torah. Sayings from Rabbi Shimon and Rabbi
Ḥalafta ben Dosa of Kefar Ḥanania express similar ideas (see the end
of this book for the full texts):

🍃 If three people eat at a table and say there no words of Torah, it is as if they
eat from offerings to idols. But if three people eat at a table and say there
words of Torah, it is as if they eat at the table of the Lord. (*Avot* 3:4)

🍃 If ten people sit and occupy themselves with Torah, the Divine Presence
rests among them. (*Avot* 3:7)

These sayings offer one concrete example of directing one's actions
"for the sake of Heaven." They also etch a sharp dividing line between
a religious and a secular approach to life. If you want to follow the religious path, then when you talk with others, and when you sit to eat,
you will still have the divine instructions on how to live—Torah—in
your thoughts. And as you speak you will apply these directives consciously to what you say daily, and refer to them explicitly from time
to time.

Torah is traditionally studied in pairs, *ḥevruta*, so that each person
sharpens and corrects the other's understanding. In sitting to eat, reciting the blessings before and after the meal are one way of fulfilling the
saying of Rabbi Shimon. But the intention in these sayings is more
general, and involves a conscious engagement with the sacred tradition
and application of it to what we say in all conversations.

Rabbi Ḥanania ben Teradion was the father of Beruriah, the only outstanding female scholar noted in the Talmud (see the commentary to *Avot* 1:5), and father-in-law to Rabbi Meir (see 4:12). How deeply he believed in the words of his mishnah may be seen from the way he lived his life. He constantly spoke of Torah in his home, as we can see from the fact that his daughter became an outstanding scholar.

Rabbi Ḥanania ben Teradion's last day also testifies dramatically to his devotion to discussing Torah. After the wicked emperor Hadrian had forbidden teaching Torah, ben Teradion continued to study and teach. Roman soldiers caught him with a Torah scroll, and arrested him along with Rabbi Elazar ben Perata. He predicted that Elazar would survive because he had both practiced acts of kindness, *gemilut ḥasadim,* and mastered Torah. Ben Teradion thought he would not win a place in the world to come, because he had only occupied himself with Torah. (As the Talmud tells the story [AZ 17b–18a], Rabbi Ḥanania ben Teradion still won a place in the world to come because of an act of charity.)

The Romans wrapped Ḥanania ben Teradion in the Torah scroll, and burnt him and the Torah together at the stake. When asked what he was seeing as the flames rose, he said, "The parchments are being burned but the letters are soaring on high." When told to open his mouth and breathe in the flames so that he would die more quickly and reduce his suffering, he said, "Better that He who gave take away, and no person injure himself."

The Divine Presence rests . . . The *Shekhinah,* or Divine Presence, is the Rabbinic term for God's influence on earth. It is likened to a radiance, a light, which infuses those on whom it rests.

MODERN LIFE

MUCH OF human interaction consists of talking. In our era, concern with whether our speech is uplifting is generally absent. Speech has noticeably coarsened over the past 50 years, as can be tracked in popular culture. The idea has become that being brutal and profane is somehow brave and honest, whereas in reality it is cheap and disrespects the dignity of the individual. Moralizing is now regarded as presumptuous—even for parents to urge their children to be considerate, or for the state to urge citizens to be public-spirited. Done the wrong way, nothing is more irritating than moralizing, but done the right way, it uplifts. Practicing more of this beautiful ideal of the Sages would be a welcome change.

RABBI ḤANINA BEN ḤAKHINAI:

He who wakes in the night, or goes about on the road alone,
and turns his heart to idle matters,
puts himself in mortal danger. (3:5)

רַבִּי חֲנִינָא בֶּן חֲכִינַאי אוֹמֵר: הַנֵּעוֹר בַּלַּיְלָה, וְהַמְהַלֵּךְ בַּדֶּרֶךְ יְחִידִי, וּמְפַנֶּה
לִבּוֹ לְבַטָּלָה, הֲרֵי זֶה מִתְחַיֵּב בְּנַפְשׁוֹ.

RABBI YA'AKOV:

If a person is walking by the way reviewing his Torah, and
ceases, and says "How beautiful is this tree! How beautiful
is this field!" Scripture regards him as in mortal danger. (3:9)

רַבִּי יַעֲקֹב אוֹמֵר: הַמְהַלֵּךְ בַּדֶּרֶךְ וְשׁוֹנֶה, וּמַפְסִיק מִמִּשְׁנָתוֹ וְאוֹמֵר: מַה נָּאֶה
אִילָן זֶה, מַה נָּאֶה נִיר זֶה, מַעֲלֶה עָלָיו הַכָּתוּב כְּאִלּוּ מִתְחַיֵּב בְּנַפְשׁוֹ.

RABBI DOSTAI BAR YANAI:

A person who forgets one word of his study, the scripture
regards him as in mortal danger ... One is not in mortal
danger unless he sits and drives the words from his heart. (3:10)

רַרְבִּי דוֹסְתָּאי בַּר יַנַּאי מִשּׁוּם רַבִּי מֵאִיר אוֹמֵר: כָּל הַשּׁוֹכֵחַ דָּבָר אֶחָד
מִמִּשְׁנָתוֹ, מַעֲלֶה עָלָיו הַכָּתוּב כְּאִלּוּ מִתְחַיֵּב בְּנַפְשׁוֹ, שֶׁנֶּאֱמַר: "רַק הִשָּׁמֶר
לְךָ וּשְׁמֹר נַפְשְׁךָ מְאֹד פֶּן־תִּשְׁכַּח אֶת־הַדְּבָרִים אֲשֶׁר־רָאוּ עֵינֶיךָ." יָכוֹל אֲפִלּוּ
תָקְפָה עָלָיו מִשְׁנָתוֹ? תַּלְמוּד לוֹמַר: "וּפֶן־יָסוּרוּ מִלְּבָבְךָ כֹּל יְמֵי חַיֶּיךָ," הָא
אֵינוֹ מִתְחַיֵּב בְּנַפְשׁוֹ עַד שֶׁיֵּשֵׁב וִיסִירֵם מִלִּבּוֹ.

He who wakes. A person awake at night and one alone on the road both feel freer from social constraints. (The concerns here seem to be mainly about men, so I have kept the male gender in translation.) While the sense of God's commands might still keep them on the right path, the temptation for them to negate the covenant and violate the commandments, including the prohibition on adultery, is greater.

How beautiful. The Sages were in favor of savoring the beauty of God's world—there is a blessing upon seeing a beautiful sight. The warning here is not to worship beauty instead of God. Worship of beauty puts no demands on us, whereas God's commandments do.

A Person who forgets. The full text of this saying includes a commentary discussing the passage alluded to in the phrase "scripture regards him":

> 🙾 Only, take you care, take exceeding care for your self, lest you forget the things your eyes saw, lest you turn aside in your heart all the days of your life. (*DEUT 4:9*)

The commentary explains: if you read only the first part of the passage, you might think that when people try to learn something, and can't, they become endangered. The final phrase shows that only a willful forgetting of Torah endangers a person.

The full passage of the Torah prooftext (DEUT 4) gives us an understanding of what all three of these sayings are about. Moses stands before the assembled Israelites and urges them to stay true to the covenant they made at Sinai: the agreement to obey the Ten Commandments and the other divine laws. Moses reminds them of the thousands who had betrayed the covenant by worshipping the fertility god Baal-Peor through the ritual orgies of the pagan religion. All the betrayers had died by plague or in civil war, but those who stayed true to the covenant with God lived. Hence the "mortal danger" referred to in this saying.

Then, the warning not to forget the covenant follows. The Sages read it as referring to the words of Torah, rather than to the actual witnessing of the covenant. The Sages see every generation of Jews as having been spiritually present at Sinai; each generation renews the covenant through Torah study, prayer, and good deeds. The Sages also hold that reward and punishment happen in the world to come, and not only in this world, as with Moses. Even with these changes, the core point is the same: it is easy to ignore the covenant, but breaking it then leads to ethical violations that put a person's life at risk.

MODERN LIFE

THESE THREE warnings of mortal danger are a rebuke to the idea that the purpose of religion is only about feeling good. In our day, the advocates of "New Age" religion are concerned with how mystical or spiritual practices can help people feel better. But noticeably absent is any demand on people from the divine, either for ethical action or for study. Martin Buber was of the opinion that a God who makes no demands on us is not worth our attention. My impression is that New Age spirituality asks little and delivers little. The more demanding spirituality of the Sages asks much, and delivers much.

Rabbi Nehunia ben Hakanah:

All who accept the yoke of the Torah are relieved of the yoke
of the government and the yoke of worldly affairs.
All who cast off the yoke of Torah, the yoke of the government
and the yoke of worldly affairs is put upon them. (3:6)

רַבִּי נְחוּנְיָא בֶּן הַקָּנָה אוֹמֵר: כָּל הַמְקַבֵּל עָלָיו עוֹל תּוֹרָה, מַעֲבִירִין מִמֶּנּוּ
עוֹל מַלְכוּת וְעוֹל דֶּרֶךְ אֶרֶץ, וְכָל הַפּוֹרֵק מִמֶּנּוּ עוֹל תּוֹרָה, נוֹתְנִין עָלָיו עוֹל
מַלְכוּת וְעוֹל דֶּרֶךְ אֶרֶץ.

THIS MISHNAH personalizes a seeming paradox that is already at the heart of the account of the Exodus in the Torah. Moses tells Pharaoh that God has said: "Send out My people that they may serve Me" (EX 9:1). The freeing of the Hebrews from bondage is only the beginning of the story. Liberation is followed by the Hebrews receiving the Ten Commandments, then going to the Promised Land to live by those commandments. Humanity should not live free of rules, but be bound by just rules. We can be a help and a joy to one another, or we can be oppressors and predators. The constraints of law—given in the Ten Commandments and the laws that follow in Exodus—enable society to give people desirable options and the freedom to choose between them without coercion.

This connection between moral laws and freedom is brought out in a Rabbinic commentary on the Ten Commandments. The Torah writes that the commandments were "graven" on the tablets (EX 32:16). The Talmud says, "Read not *harut*, graven, but *herut*, freedom" (ER 54a). (The Torah is written with consonants only, leaving some words open to alternate readings.) The commandments, rules for living, give us freedom.

This mishnah applies this idea personally. It says that we don't have a choice between absolute freedom and constraint, but between constraints. If we choose to take on the constraints and demands of the Torah, we will be freed from demands of the government and from worldly worries. If we throw off the constraints of Torah, we will be bound by the government and by worldly demands.

The yoke of the government. The constraints that government places on people, aside from taxes, affect them directly only when they break the law. By following the Torah, a person will be honest and not fall afoul of the law. In Rabbi Nehunia ben Hakanah's time, the government was Roman. The Romans did not conscript Jews into their army, so conscription was not an issue. Unfortunately some governments, including at times the Roman government, intervened capriciously in the Jewish community, and not in accordance with just laws. Some thought that to be protected from this kind of intervention would require divine action against the government. But no miraculous rescue happened, and the Romans martyred Rabbi Akiva and others of his generation.

The yoke of worldly affairs. The lifting of this yoke probably represents a lifting of worry about the pressures of making a living, and about what will happen in life to us and those we love. Part of the concept here is that, if we are devoted to Torah, garnering riches and status are not our top priorities in life. If these things, the "way of the world," are our top priority, then there is no end to the burden, no lifting of the "yoke" we have placed on ourselves.

The traditional Jewish way of dealing with worry about what will happen to us is to do what is required of us in these ways: earning a living, caring for those we love, doing our share for a more just world, and then, trusting in God to take care of the rest. This traditional trust in God, in Hebrew *bitaḥon*, or "security," is illustrated in the following story about Hillel:

> ﷯ Once Hillel was coming from a journey, and he heard a great cry in the city. And he said: I am confident that this does not come from my house. Of him scripture says (PS 112:7): "He is not afraid of evil tidings; his heart is firm, trusting in God." (BER 60a)

MODERN LIFE

SOME KIND of trust or acceptance of what life will bring is necessary for a degree of peace of mind in this world. In the story about Hillel, it doesn't say that his home was protected. Rather, it says that he did not anticipate or worry that the problems were in his house. His policy seems to be the one central in Stoic philosophy, of letting go of worry about what is beyond our power to control. When facing an imminent threat, it is the rare person who can maintain his or her equanimity. When facing threats that are not so imminent, though, we can all handle them, providing we meet two challenges. The first is finding a relatively good plan to deal with long-term risk, what I have called "making peace with the future" (see *Avot* 2:13). The second is making peace with our own consciences by doing the right thing, even when it is difficult.

111

Give Him of what is His,
for you and yours are His. (3:8)

רַבִּי אֶלְעָזָר אִישׁ בַּרְתּוֹתָא אוֹמֵר: תֶּן לוֹ מִשֶּׁלוֹ, שֶׁאַתָּה וְשֶׁלְּךָ שֶׁלוֹ, וְכֵן בְּדָוִד
הוּא אוֹמֵר: "כִּי־מִמְּךָ הַכֹּל וּמִיָּדְךָ נָתַנּוּ לָךְ."

THIS MISHNAH includes this prooftext from King David: "... but all is from You, and it is Your gift that we have given to You" (I CHRON 29:14). In the translation, I have kept the male pronoun of the Hebrew original because the wordplay between "His" and "yours" works better as poetry. There is no implication, however, that God has masculine traits.

This saying sums up the Jewish view that reverence for God requires a person to be charitable. The Jewish view of charity has been extremely influential on the rest of the world, but some of its features—that charity is obligatory, and that it involves society, and not just individuals—remain distinctive.

That charity is a duty, rather than simply an expression of a caring heart, is indicated by the Rabbinic use of the word *tzedakah*—which in the Bible means "righteousness"—to mean "charity." In the Torah, farmers are required to give a tenth of their crop, a "tithe," along with other charitable donations. After the destruction of the Temple, the Sages regarded one-tenth of one's income as a "middling" amount to give to charity, but put an upper limit on charity of 20 percent of one's income, so that a person would not become impoverished (KET 50a).

Maimonides notes (MT, *Hilchot Matanot Ani'im* 10.1, 7–14) that God singled out Abraham for the covenant so that he would teach his offspring to do *tzedakah* and *mishpat*—righteousness and justice under law (GEN 18:19). Reading *tzedakah* in the Rabbinic way as "charity," Maimonides says that Jews, being bound by the covenant of Abraham, have a special responsibility to be charitable. He then describes "eight levels" of charity, from the most to the least worthy:

1. The donor gives the needy person a present or loan, or makes a partnership with him, or finds him a job "in order to strengthen his hand until he need no longer beg from people."
2. The donor gives without knowing the recipient, and the donor is also unknown to the recipient—such as in gifts through a tzedakah box: "One should not put into the box unless he knows the one responsible for the box is faithful and wise and a proper leader like Rabbi Ḥanania ben Teradion."
3. The donor knows the recipient, but the recipient does not know the donor. This option is advisable if those collecting tzedakah are not trustworthy.

4. The donor doesn't know the recipient, but the recipient knows the giver.
5. The donor gives before being asked.
6. The donor gives after being asked.
7. The donor gives gladly and with a smile.
8. The donor gives unwillingly.

Jewish communities have had many charitable organizations over the centuries that have constituted a social welfare network. These have included institutions to collect money for the dowries of poor brides, for the education of poor boys, and for redeeming captives. Beginning in the 19th century, some governments began to take responsibility for social welfare. Jewish communities continued to support their people, and also contributed to the settlement of British Palestine and then the modern Jewish state of Israel.

The vigorous tradition of giving charity is, along with universal education for boys, one of the key features of Judaism that has been responsible for its survival.

MODERN LIFE

IN MODERN society, governments have taken over some social welfare functions, but other functions have remained dependent on private donations.

An important question is: in this situation, which social problems should be left to the private sector to deal with, and which should be handled as matters of public welfare? The United States has lagged behind other wealthy industrial countries in providing a "safety net" for the poor.

However, the U.S. can be rightly proud of having developed a large nonprofit sector, supported by charity, that does good works. This tradition of charity, and the resulting obligation that many rich people in the U.S. feel to contribute heavily, is a remarkable feature of American society, not shared by most others. Looking at societies around the world, one of the great influences on whether a country is rich or poor depends on the attitudes of the rich toward both government policy and charity.

Another question is: given the existence of tax-supported welfare, what obligations remain for individuals to give charity? And how should Jews divide their giving between Jewish and non-Jewish causes? Many Jewish philanthropists have given generously to both.

All whose fear of sin comes before their wisdom,
their wisdom will live on.
All whose wisdom comes before their fear of sin,
their wisdom will not live on. (3:11)
All whose deeds are greater than their wisdom,
their wisdom will live on.
All whose wisdom is greater than their deeds,
their wisdom will not live on. (3:12)

רַבִּי חֲנִינָא בֶּן דּוֹסָא אוֹמֵר: כָּל שֶׁיִּרְאַת חֶטְאוֹ קוֹדֶמֶת לְחָכְמָתוֹ, חָכְמָתוֹ
מִתְקַיֶּמֶת. וְכָל שֶׁחָכְמָתוֹ קוֹדֶמֶת לְיִרְאַת חֶטְאוֹ, אֵין חָכְמָתוֹ מִתְקַיֶּמֶת:
הוּא הָיָה אוֹמֵר: כָּל שֶׁמַּעֲשָׂיו מְרֻבִּין מֵחָכְמָתוֹ, חָכְמָתוֹ מִתְקַיֶּמֶת. וְכָל
שֶׁחָכְמָתוֹ מְרֻבָּה מִמַּעֲשָׂיו, אֵין חָכְמָתוֹ מִתְקַיֶּמֶת:

ALL WHOSE fear of sin. Avot de-Rabbi Natan 22, provides a prooftext for
this saying: "The fear of God is the beginning of wisdom" (*PS 111:10*).
Then, it clarifies the meaning of the saying with this striking saying of
Rabban Yoḥanan ben Zakkai, the teacher of Ḥanina ben Dosa:

 ❖ If one is wise and fears sin, what is he like?
  Lo, that's a craftsman with the tools of his craft in his hand.
  If one is wise but does not fear sin, what is he like?
  Lo, that's a craftsman without the tools of his craft in his hand.
  If one fears sin, but is not wise, what is he like?
  He is no craftsman, but the tools of the craft are in his hand.

All whose deeds. The second saying completes the first by emphasiz-
ing the importance not only of avoiding sin, but also of doing good
deeds—fulfilling both the negative and positive commandments.

The meaning of both sayings is clarified by Yoḥanan ben Zakkai's
comparison of the wise person and the craftsman. In order for a person's wisdom to make a difference in the world, he or she needs to have
the right motivation and goals. First, when people don't fear sin and
don't desire to do right, they will lack the motivation and courage to
put their ideas into practice. Second, if they act to make a positive difference only sporadically, they will not gain an understanding of how
to make their ideas work in practice. In either case, their actions will
not bear fruit. But with the right motivation, goals, and experience, a
person will become "a craftsman with the tools of his craft in his hand."

That person will be able to act effectively and make a positive difference in the world.

Maimonides and other commentators have read *mitkayemet,* translated here as "live on," as meaning that wisdom, once gained, will live on in a person himself or herself. Maimonides argues that when people do good deeds while they are young, doing such deeds becomes a habit. Then, adult Torah study and the resulting wisdom gained confirm and strengthen the good habits, the virtues. But if people are self-indulgent and undisciplined while young, then doing the right thing—following the wisdom of the Torah—will seem a burden, and they will tend to abandon the wise path, the path of virtue. This interesting observation is illustrated by the following related saying of Rabbi Elazar ben Azariah. He uses the metaphor of "a tree planted by waters" (JER 17:5–8) to explore the relationship between wisdom and deeds:

&♥ One whose wisdom exceeds his deeds, what is he like? Like a tree whose branches are many, and roots are few. The wind comes and uproots and overturns it. And one whose deeds exceed his wisdom, what is he like? Like a tree whose branches are few, and roots are many. Even if all the winds of earth come and blow on it, it will not be moved from its place. *(Avot 3:22)*

Modern Life

Lee Kuan Yu, the brilliant founder of the nation of Singapore who led it to prosperity, said, "It is amazing how many brilliant people have no impact on the world." This is true enough, and raises the question: what "deeds" help a person with ideas or insight to make a difference in the world?

Are these deeds a matter of good and effective action? In other words, does a wise person need the same skills that a bad person might use to achieve his or her ends in order to have a positive impact? These might include social skills like being able to influence others to get them to go along with what you want, and using strategy to gain allies and defeat the opposition.

I suspect that those skills are indeed needed, and that people with good ideas will be frustrated without them. And with good ideas and good strategy, people with integrity have an advantage: they can more easily gain and sustain the trust and cooperation of others. Furthermore, those with the passion to do the right thing also often have greater staying power, and greater enjoyment in their efforts.

*Morning sleep, midday wine, childish talk,
and sitting in the gathering places of the ignorant
drive a person from the world. (3:14)*

רַבִּי דוֹסָא בֶּן הָרְכִּינַס אוֹמֵר: שֵׁנָה שֶׁל שַׁחֲרִית, וְיַיִן שֶׁל צָהֳרַיִם, וְשִׂיחַת הַיְלָדִים, וִישִׁיבַת בָּתֵּי כְנֵסִיּוֹת שֶׁל עַמֵּי הָאָרֶץ, מוֹצִיאִין אֶת הָאָדָם מִן הָעוֹלָם.

Rabbi Elazar HaKappar:

Envy, lust, and ambition drive a person from the world. (4:28)

רַבִּי אֶלְעָזָר הַקַּפָּר אוֹמֵר: הַקִּנְאָה, וְהַתַּאֲוָה, וְהַכָּבוֹד, מוֹצִיאִין אֶת הָאָדָם מִן הָעוֹלָם.

Morning sleep. Rabbi Dosa ben Harkinas' observation is that a self-indulgent way of life leads first to dissolution and then to irresponsibility. The people who are let down by the irresponsible person then shun him or her. Then, as the person's reputation for irresponsibility spreads, people will avoid working with or marrying him or her.

Envy, lust. The Hebrew *kin'ah* refers to both envy and jealousy. Envy can lead us to tear down other people, alienating them and making them hostile toward us. Jealousy leads us to treat even those close to us as enemies.

Lust can lead us to betray those we love, and can wreck relationships at work. *Ta'avah*, "lust," refers not only to sexual desire, but also to any powerful craving. People's craving for getting "high" through alcohol and other drugs has become a leading cause of their being "driven from the world." Compulsive pleasure-seeking leads youths to neglect their education, harm their future, and break their parents' hearts; it leads adults to neglect their children, destroy their marriages, and lose their jobs.

One of the contemporary theories on addictions says they are a substitute for satisfying relationships. In a vicious cycle, people crave pleasure as an escape from dealing with relationship problems, and that withdrawal makes the problems worse, driving the other person away.

Kavod, "ambition," literally means "honor," but in this context the term refers to a craving for honor or high status. In other words, envy, lust, and ego drive a person from the world. Mark Twain vividly described this weakness: "A man will do many things to be loved; he will do all things to get himself envied" (*Following the Equator*, ch. 21).

The Rabbinic suspicion of some emotions, such as envy and lust, is part of their view that human nature has *yetzer ha-ra*, "the bad inclination," as well as "the good inclination," *yetzer ha-tov*. Sometimes there was a tendency to view the *yetzer ha-ra* as a separate, negative force in life. A more complex view of the motivations for sin is alluded to in the midrash noted earlier (see 2:16): without the *yetzer ha-ra*, particularly the element of rivalry, people would not be motivated to build a house, marry, and excel in work. A story in the Talmud relates that a group of people once captured the *yetzer ha-ra*. A prophet warned them: "Realize that if you kill him, the world goes down. They imprisoned him for three days, then looked in the whole land of Israel for a fresh egg and could not find it" (YOM 69b). In other words, the very emotions that motivate us to do wrong and to harm ourselves or others can also be a positive force. Ben Azzai seems to advocate this view:

❧ If one's mind is serene because of his *yetzer*, it is a good sign for him; if his mind is distressed because of his *yetzer*, it is a bad sign. (ARN 25)

MODERN LIFE

THE DUAL power of emotions to help and harm, to motivate both sins and good deeds, raises the question: how can we channel our emotions so that they work *for* us rather than *against* us? Psychologists suggest that powerful emotions can impair our thinking when we face a decision. Instead of trying to understand others' goals and feelings, we label them as good or bad. We just attack or give our trust, even if neither of these reactions is merited. Thus, we fail to deliberate carefully before coming to a decision (*Avot* 1:1), or to judge others in favorable light (1:6), or to foresee consequences of the actions we might take (2:13).

To counteract the way extreme emotion can impair us, we need to take a step back from the issue we are facing, postpone a decision if possible until we are calmer, and discuss the issue with someone else. Then, we can take time to understand the problem more deeply, foresee consequences, and seek a course of action that serves both ourselves and others.

A popular view in conflict with that of the Sages says that we can't be rational about love—it makes deliberation and self-control impossible. There is no doubt that resisting immediate temptation is difficult, but in many situations, people can and do exert self-control in love. The theory that they can't is more of an excuse for lack of self-control and bad behavior than it is a reality.

RABBI ELAZAR OF MODIN:

Whoever profanes sacred things, desecrates the festivals,
humiliates his colleague in public, annuls the covenant of
Abraham our father, or perverts the meaning of the Torah,
even if he has Torah and good deeds,
he will not have a share in the world to come. (3:15)

רַבִּי אֶלְעָזָר הַמּוֹדָעִי אוֹמֵר: הַמְחַלֵּל אֶת הַקֳּדָשִׁים, וְהַמְבַזֶּה אֶת הַמּוֹעֲדוֹת,
וְהַמַּלְבִּין פְּנֵי חֲבֵרוֹ בָּרַבִּים, וְהַמֵּפֵר בְּרִיתוֹ שֶׁל אַבְרָהָם אָבִינוּ, וְהַמְגַלֶּה פָנִים
בַּתּוֹרָה שֶׁלֹּא כַהֲלָכָה, אַף עַל פִּי שֶׁיֵּשׁ בְּיָדוֹ תּוֹרָה וּמַעֲשִׂים טוֹבִים, אֵין לוֹ
חֵלֶק לָעוֹלָם הַבָּא.

RABBI YOHANAN BEN BEROKA:

All who profane the Name of Heaven in secret,
they will be punished in public. Unwittingly or wittingly—
it is all the same for profanation of the Name. (4:5)

רַבִּי יוֹחָנָן בֶּן בְּרוֹקָא אוֹמֵר: כָּל הַמְחַלֵּל שֵׁם שָׁמַיִם בַּסֵּתֶר, נִפְרָעִין מִמֶּנּוּ
בְּגָלוּי, אֶחָד שׁוֹגֵג וְאֶחָד מֵזִיד בְּחִלּוּל הַשֵּׁם.

THESE TWO rabbis lived during the turbulent period between 70 CE, when the Temple fell, and the Bar Kokhba rebellion in 135. At that time, the Sages were contending against many varieties of Gnosticism, several kinds of Christianity, and those who wanted to assimilate into Hellenistic (Greek) culture. All of these rejected Rabbinic Judaism.

Humiliates his colleague. Here, Rabbi Elazar of Modin warns us not to let strife and anger lead us to act viciously. The Rabbis came to view the sin of *halbanat panim*, literally "blanching the face" of another person by embarrassing him or her in public, as very grave: "He who publicly shames his neighbor is as though he shed blood" (BM 58b). Not only does this sin cause blood to drain from the victim's face, but it can lead to bloodshed. A striking example of insults leading to bloodshed, though other factors have also been involved, is the series of school shootings by previously ridiculed students.

Annuls the covenant. This phrase refers to those who wanted to assimilate so much that they would try to reverse the effects of circumcision. They could then participate in Greek athletic contests—which were done in the nude—without being noticed as different.

Perverts the meaning of Torah. This phrase, which literally translates to "reveals a face in the Torah not according to *halakhah*," is read by medieval commentators in the *Maḥzor Vitry* (a prayer book with commentaries) as meaning "to ascribe disgraceful or improper meanings to the contents of the Torah." It may have been originally directed against rival sects, such as the different varieties of Gnostics and Christians that existed in the days of the Sages, which had radically different readings of the Torah.

All who profane. Rabbi Menaḥem ben Shlomo Hameiri, a medieval commentator, explained that profanation is grave because it represents not simply yielding to temptation, but a willful decision to show contempt for the Torah and to deny the guiding hand of God. The *Maḥzor Vitry* explains that when someone profanes in secret, his or her character is corrupted. Since this corruption will be seen by others, God will punish him or her openly as a lesson. Maimonides says that, even though both are punished publicly, the punishment for unwitting profanation of the Name is lighter than if the profanation is deliberate.

During this era of bitter rivalry, Shmuel HaKatan composed the *Birkat Haminim*, the benediction against sectarians that Rabban Gamliel added to the *Tefillah* (see *Avot* 2:18). It is interesting that, even in the midst of this bitter strife, the Rabbis were aware of the danger of demonizing the opponent. Shmuel HaKatan is reported in *Avot* as fond of quoting this passage from Proverbs (24:17–18):

🍃 If your enemy falls do not exult; if he trips, do not rejoice, lest God see it and be displeased, and avert wrath from him [to you]. (*Avot* 4:24)

MODERN LIFE

INSULTING A person in front of others is a typical tactic of bullies at school, boys and girls alike. Public insults have also become routine between politicians opposing one another in elections. This is sometimes called "smash mouth" politics. In addition, the anonymity of the Internet has loosened restraints, and insults regularly fly as they would not in face-to-face interaction. All of this has fostered a culture where anger causes hurt and hurt causes anger in a vicious cycle. We can uplift our culture if we can break this cycle. Fortunately, in the U.S., there is now a concerted effort to counteract bullying among children and teens. But there is not yet a campaign to reduce such behavior among adults, as it exists in political debate, or on the Internet.

Joking and frivolity accustom a person to lewdness. (3:17A)

רַבִּי עֲקִיבָא אוֹמֵר: שְׂחוֹק וְקַלּוּת רֹאשׁ מַרְגִּילִין אֶת הָאָדָם לְעֶרְוָה.

RABBI AKIVA, Akiva ben Yosef, is at the historical center of Jewish tradition. In him, we can see different strands of tradition from the previous 2000 years coming together, and the next 2000 being influenced by these strands and by Rabbi Akiva's personal efforts.

Rabbi Akiva's comprehensive redaction of *halakhah* formed the basis for Yehudah haNasi's definitive Mishnah, itself the basis for the Talmud. The scholars who followed him were all his students in one way or another. He lived through the split with Christianity and he was well aware of Greek and Roman culture. He kept to the liberal and rationalist path of Hillel and Yehoshua ben Ḥanania, but was also deeply influenced by mysticism. The different strands in Jewish tradition that came together in Akiva later became separated and at times even opposed to each other. Their unity in Rabbi Akiva make his views a touchstone of Classical Judaism.

Akiva ben Yosef's life story is dramatic. He began life as a poor, illiterate shepherd boy. During those early days, he says that if he had ever come across a scholar, he would have broken his bones. He labored on the estate of Kalba Savua, one of the richest men in Judea. He fell in love with the Kalba Savua's daughter, Raḥel. She offered to marry Akiva on the condition that he study Torah. Raḥel's father cut her off and expelled both of them. Then, Akiva learned to read along with his son and eventually studied with Rabbis Yehoshua ben Ḥanania and Eliezer ben Hyrcanus, becoming a leading scholar. When he returned many years later to his father-in-law as a luminary of Torah wisdom with thousands of students, Kalba Savua gave Akiva half of his family's wealth.

Joking and frivolity. In our day, when both humor and lewdness rule entertainment, this reads as rather sour and puritanical. However, Rabbi Akiva was no puritan. He explained: "When husband and wife are worthy, the *Shekhinah* [holy Presence] abides with them; when they are not worthy, fire consumes them" (SOT 17a). Rabbi Akiva's lesson plays on the spelling of "woman" (אשה) and "man" (איש) in Hebrew. When you take away the Hebrew letters *yud* and *heh*, which spell one of the names of God in the Torah, you are left with only the words אש, אש, *esh, esh,* meaning "fire, fire." Thus, with God present, sexuality is holy within marriage. But when God is taken out of the relationship, then men's and women's sexuality becomes a burning fire that can destroy both of them.

Rabbi Akiva's concern here is with humor that can lead to sexual behavior forbidden by the Torah. The word *ervah*, translated here as "lewdness," literally means "nakedness" and is used in the Torah to label sexual sins. The commentary of the *Mahzor Vitry* says that this mishnah is a warning that humor between men and women leads to seduction and adultery.

Overall, Jewish sacred literature is remarkably humorless, given that there is, in fact, a rich tradition of humor within the Jewish community. Yet, as always, there is another side—one that is deeply appreciative of the positive power of humor. According to a talmudic legend, Rabbi Berokah Hoza'ah often attended a market where the prophet Elijah (who had not died, but ascended directly to heaven) would come down to visit him. The Rabbi asked him, "Who in the market will have a share in the world to come?" Elijah answered, "None." Then two passed by and he said, "These two." Rabbi Berokah asked them, "What is your occupation?" They replied, "We are jesters. When we see men depressed we cheer them up; furthermore, when we see two people quarreling we strive hard to make peace between them" (ta'an 22a).

Modern Life

Our view of this mishnah depends on how we view sexual impropriety and how we view humor. Since the 1960s, there has been a strong current of "sexual modernism," advocating acceptance of what was formerly regarded as improper. Adultery has been seen as a minor, private sin affecting only the people involved, and divorce as a benefit to both a discontented couple and their children.

In reaction against this "sexual modernist" view, the "marriage movement" has found that divorce among merely unhappy couples has a profoundly negative effect on children, and that one side of the couple is often hurt much more than the other, and for much longer. This view reinstates a sharp moral distinction between positive and destructive sexuality—between that which promotes and preserves the strength of the family, and that which can lead to its break-up, and hence to lasting harm for its members, most profoundly children. Thus, adultery is the private sin with the biggest social impact.

Tradition is a fence for the Torah;
Tithes are a fence for riches;
Vows are a fence for abstinence;
A fence for wisdom—silence. (3:17B)

מַסוֹרֶת–סְיָג לַתּוֹרָה, מַעְשְׂרוֹת–סְיָג לָעשֶׁר, נְדָרִים–סְיָג לַפְּרִישׁוּת, סְיָג
לַחָכְמָה–שְׁתִיקָה.

HERE, RABBI AKIVA takes up the idea of the *seyag*, the protective hedge or fencing that *Avot* 1:1 says we should make around the Torah.

Tradition. Masoret, or "tradition," here means the traditions concerning the accurate writing, voweling, and chanting of the Torah text. The accuracy of the text was particularly important to Akiva because he believed that every letter—and even the traditional decorative crowns on the letters—has significance. Historical discoveries have confirmed the high degree of accuracy in transmission of the Torah text over time.

Rabbi Akiva probably also had a more general meaning of tradition in mind: the Oral Torah, the tradition of the Sages, helps to preserve the spirit of the Written Torah and the observance of its commandments.

Tithes. Rabbi Akiva's saying is an outgrowth of the Sages' view that all belongs to God. In a later mishnah, he explains that we are all just borrowers:

🍂 Everything is given on pledge, and a net is spread out over all who live. The shop is open, and the shopkeeper gives credit. The ledger is open, the hand writes, and all who want to borrow, come and borrow. The collectors go around regularly every day and settle accounts, whether the person knows it or not. They have reliable information, and the judgment is true. And all is arranged for the banquet. (*Avot* 3:20)

In saying that tithes are a fence for wealth, Rabbi Akiva may be referring to divine rewards and punishments for individuals, but possibly also to human society. When we give to charity, we show an acceptance that all is God's. As stewards of God's possessions, we are to follow God's laws on how to deal with them. This humility will help ward off the enmity of others, whereas arrogance may lead to our downfall, either through foolish decisions or envy, or both.

Vows. Vows, *nedarim* in Hebrew, are promises to God to do or not to do something. Jewish tradition has had a changing view of such vows and of the abstinence or self-denial that often results from them. The Torah describes a class of self-deniers, the Nazarites, and a tractate of the Talmud is dedicated to vows. However, the Rabbis conclude that one should avoid formal vows. Any verbal agreement, though, has the force of a vow, so that keeping promises is a sacred obligation. Vows are still permissible if their intent is to break bad habits, and this may be the thrust of Rabbi Akiva's saying here.

There is a strand of asceticism—the idea that self-denial is holy—in Jewish tradition. But it is a minor strand, and is strictly limited. Rabbi Akiva ruled against hurting oneself (BK 15b), and there is a general rule that you should not deny yourself things that are not already denied by the Torah and Rabbinic law. A later Sage, Rav, said that on the day of judgment a person will have to answer for every good permissible thing that he or she could have enjoyed but did not (P KID 4:12, 66d).

A fence for wisdom. Knowing when to be silent and when to speak is a mark of wisdom, and protection for it, as well. This a stronger admonition than the popular saying, "If you can't say something nice about a person, don't say anything at all." When should we be silent, aside from avoiding *lashon ha-ra* (defamation)? Rabbi Naḥmias, a medieval commentator, in his commentary on this mishnah said, "The Holy One, blessed be He, created for you two ears and a mouth, so that you might listen twice as much as you speak."

MODERN LIFE

KOHELET WROTE there is "a time for silence and a time for speaking" (ECCL 3:7), but knowing our times, it is obviously not an art mastered by many. We see people with expertise in one area speaking where they have no expertise, showing an embarrassing lack of understanding. And we see highly intelligent people in public life making foolish gaffes.

We can learn from *Avot* 2:7, "The bashful do not learn," that one of the times for silence is not as a student in class. Fear of looking foolish is a barrier to learning, and asking questions promotes learning. Yet we also learn from *Avot* 1:11 that teachers need to be careful in their words, and from *Avot* 2:7 that you shouldn't say something privately that you think should never be heard publicly. In *Avot* 5:6 we read that a wise person is silent until someone more knowledgeable has finished speaking. So one part of "silence" is the humility to listen and to learn throughout all of one's life.

RABBI AKIVA:

Beloved is humanity, for it is created in the image of God;
  still more beloved, that it was made known to humanity
  that it is created in the image of God.
Beloved is Israel, for they were called children of God;
  still more beloved, that it was made known to them
  that they were called children of God.
Beloved is Israel, for they were given a precious implement;
  still more beloved, that it was made known to them
  that they were given a precious implement
  through which the world was created. (3:18)

הוּא הָיָה אוֹמֵר: חָבִיב אָדָם שֶׁנִּבְרָא בְצֶלֶם. חִבָּה יְתֵרָה נוֹדַעַת לוֹ שֶׁנִּבְרָא
בְצֶלֶם, שֶׁנֶּאֱמַר: "כִּי בְּצֶלֶם אֱלֹהִים עָשָׂה אֶת־הָאָדָם." חֲבִיבִין יִשְׂרָאֵל
שֶׁנִּקְרְאוּ בָנִים לַמָּקוֹם. חִבָּה יְתֵרָה נוֹדַעַת לָהֶם שֶׁנִּקְרְאוּ בָנִים לַמָּקוֹם,
שֶׁנֶּאֱמַר: "בָּנִים אַתֶּם לַיָי אֱלֹהֵיכֶם." חֲבִיבִין יִשְׂרָאֵל שֶׁנִּתַּן לָהֶם כְּלִי חֶמְדָּה.
חִבָּה יְתֵרָה נוֹדַעַת לָהֶם, שֶׁנִּתַּן לָהֶם כְּלִי חֶמְדָּה, שֶׁבּוֹ נִבְרָא הָעוֹלָם. שֶׁנֶּאֱמַר:
"כִּי לֶקַח טוֹב נָתַתִּי לָכֶם, תּוֹרָתִי אַל־תַּעֲזֹבוּ."

THE HEBREW contains a prooftext for each of the three sentences above:
- In the image of God was man created. (GEN 9:6)
- Children are you to your God. (DEUT 14:1)
- I have given you a good teaching; do not forsake my Torah. (PROV 4:2)

Here "man" translates *adam,* the first man, but also means all humanity.

Rabbi Akiva here emphasizes the greatness of God's love for humanity, and for the Jewish people. He emphasizes that it is a special gift that Jews are aware of this love. That awareness comes from the Torah.

Rabbi Akiva said that another principle of the Torah is, however, still greater than our awareness of being made in the image of God: "You shall love your neighbor as yourself" (LEV 19:18). His colleague Ben Azzai (see *Avot* 4:2) argued that the principle of being "made in the image" of God is more fundamental, because otherwise we might cause shame to someone who shames us. Thus, respect, which comes from seeing another person as made in the image of God, is more fundamental than love (GEN RAB 24:7 and *Sifra, Kedoshim* 4:12).

When Rabbi Akiva was very old, a new rebellion against Rome, led by Bar Kochba, arose. Rabbi Akiva, unlike Yoḥanan ben Zakkai 60 years earlier, supported the rebellion, and also regarded Bar Kokhba as a messiah—one who would reestablish the Jewish state. Rome was beaten initially, and a rebel state existed briefly. But in the end, Rome reasserted its power. Rome forbade the study of Torah, but Akiva continued to study and to teach. When Akiva was warned to be afraid of the government, he replied with a parable. A fox asked some fish what they were fleeing from. They said: the nets of men. The fox told the fish that they should come up on land where there are no nets to trap fish. The fish replied that they would surely die out of water. So, too, Rabbi Akiva said, is study of the Torah for Jews; without the Torah they cannot live (BER 61b).

Akiva was thrown into prison by the Romans for teaching Torah against their edict. He continued teaching until his last breath:

> When R. Akiva was taken out for execution, it was the hour for the recital of the Shema, and while they combed his flesh with iron combs, he was accepting upon himself the kingship of Heaven [saying the Shema]. His disciples said to him: Our teacher, even to this point? He said to them: All my days I have been troubled by this verse, "with all thy soul," [which I now interpret,] "even if He takes thy soul." I said: When shall I have the opportunity of fulfilling this? Now that I have the opportunity shall I not fulfill it? He prolonged the word *ehad* until he expired saying it. (BER 61b)

It is still customary for the *Shema* to be the last words of the faithful.

Hadrian's persecutions, which followed the collapse of the Bar Kochba rebellion in the year 135, amounted to the worst mass murder of Jews up until the Holocaust, with hundreds of thousands killed, and the streets of Jerusalem running with blood. Jews were exiled from Judea, and Hebrew gradually ceased to exist as a living language. However, the students of Rabbi Akiva set up a new academy at Usha in the Galilee, keeping alive the traditions of the Sages, and enabling Judaism to survive and develop to this day.

MODERN LIFE

WHETHER OR not respect is more fundamental than love, it is certainly less fickle. Love, at least as it is most commonly understood, is a feeling that can come and go. Respect is a principle that one can always act on, and it is usually pretty clear how to act on it if one wants to. The realism of Rabbinic ethics tells us: commit yourself to respecting other people; love them if you can.

RABBI AKIVA:

All is foreseen, and freedom of choice is granted.
With goodness the world is judged, and
All is according to the preponderance of deeds. (3:19)

הַכֹּל צָפוּי, וְהָרְשׁוּת נְתוּנָה, וּבְטוֹב הָעוֹלָם נִדּוֹן, וְהַכֹּל לְפִי רוֹב הַמַּעֲשֶׂה:

As WITH Hillel's three questions (1:14), Rabbi Akiva here summarizes a whole religious philosophy in a few choice phrases.

All is foreseen. Reshut, translated here as "freedom of choice," is literally "permission" or "authority." Here, this refers to God's granting of authority to humankind to make our own individual choices. A similar idea is presented in the saying, "All is in the hand of Heaven except the fear of Heaven" (BER 33B).

Rabbi Akiva asserts here both that God's power to foresee events is unbounded, and that, nonetheless, God's foresight does not determine our choices; we are empowered to make our own decisions. Rabbi Akiva thus preserves both God's unlimited power and human moral agency and responsibility. Taking this position, he was demarcating between the theology of the Sages and those of two rival Jewish sects. According to the historian Josephus, the Sadducees had denied that God's hand guides the world, or in other words, they denied "providence" (though they must have accepted the doctrine of God's reward and punishment as this is clearly stated in the Torah). The Essenes, the monastic sect, instead rejected free will and said that all is pre-determined.

Reconciling providence and free will has been a troubling problem for Judaism, ever since its contact with the Greeks, and the Stoic idea of the "cosmos," a world that runs under orderly laws. Christianity and Islam have been even more troubled by the problem. Rabbi Akiva's aphorism gives an idea of the needed solution, but does not explain it.

The philosopher and psychologist Émile Meyerson pointed out that our minds tend to be satisfied with deterministic explanations. This makes free will a baffling concept to understand, while it seems to be an obvious fact when it comes to our personal decision making. Philosopher Immanuel Kant said that this conflict represents an inherent limitation of human reason, and a conflict that cannot be fully resolved. Whatever the case, Rabbi Akiva was not concerned with giving a justification of providence and free will, but with asserting the importance of both, leaving it to the ages to study.

With goodness. There are two aspects of God's goodness or mercy in judging. The first is the possibility of repentance, *teshuvah.* According to the Sages, even if people are wicked all their lives, they will generally be forgiven by God if they sincerely repent. Some Sages argued that there are exceptions, such as for a person who sins with the intention of repenting later so that they will be forgiven, or for "profanation of the name." The other aspect of God's goodness in judging us is that when our deeds are nearly balanced, God will still judge us as meritorious.

All is according. The idea that all is according to the preponderance of deeds—the weight of good versus bad deeds—has two important implications. First, it is our deeds and not our beliefs by which God judges us. There is a legend in the Talmud in which God laments, "If only they forgot Me and obeyed My commandments." This characteristic view of Classical Judaism contrasts particularly with the Protestant Christian view of "justification by faith," that belief is essential. The second consequence is, as Rabbi Yehoshua ben Ḥanania put it, "The righteous of all nations will have a portion in the world to come" (*Tosefta,* SAN 13:2). Differences of belief do not ultimately matter; individual deeds are all-important.

Akiva's emphasis on the preeminence of deeds did not decrease the importance of Torah knowledge:

> The question was raised: Is study greater, or deeds? R. Tarfon answered: Deeds are greater. R. Akiva answered: Study is greater. Then they all answered and said: Study is greater, for it leads to deeds. (KID 40b)

Notice that the agreed upon answer keeps Rabbi Akiva's saying here intact: we will be judged by our deeds, but only study will give us the knowledge to keep on the right path.

MODERN LIFE

RABBI AKIVA'S combined belief in free choice and providence enabled him to be a decisive leader in tempestuous times, yet to have a wonderful inner peace. Whatever happened, he would always say, "Whatever the Compassionate One does, He does for the good" (BER 60b). One of the great beauties of the "old-time religion" of Rabbi Akiva and the Sages is that their belief system supported initiative, action, and inner peace all at the same time.

The prime challenge to any modern modification of Akiva's religion is to duplicate that power to help and inspire the faithful.

> *Without Torah, there is no proper worldly conduct;*
>   *without proper worldly conduct, there is no Torah.*
> *Without wisdom, there is no awe of God;*
>   *without awe of God, there is no wisdom.*
> *Without understanding, there is no knowledge;*
>   *without knowledge, there is no understanding.*
> *Without flour, there is no Torah;*
>   *without Torah, there is no flour. (3:21)*

רַבִּי אֶלְעָזָר בֶּן עֲזַרְיָה אוֹמֵר: אִם אֵין תּוֹרָה, אֵין דֶּרֶךְ אֶרֶץ; אִם אֵין דֶּרֶךְ,
אֶרֶץ אֵין תּוֹרָה. אִם אֵין חָכְמָה, אֵין יִרְאָה; אִם אֵין יִרְאָה, אֵין חָכְמָה. אִם
אֵין דַּעַת, אֵין בִּינָה; אִם אֵין בִּינָה, אֵין דַּעַת. אִם אֵין קֶמַח, אֵין תּוֹרָה; אִם
אֵין תּוֹרָה, אֵין קֶמַח.

WITHOUT TORAH. The Hebrew *derekh eretz*, "proper worldly conduct," doesn't have an exact English equivalent. Translated literally as "the way of the land," this phrase refers to a combination of courtesy, respect, and skill in dealing with people. Good and skillful manners support another person's dignity and avoid embarrassment and hurt feelings. Morals are concerned with the substantive effect on the other person's welfare. Underlying both is an attitude of respect and kindness for the other person. Thus, the deep moral commitment engendered by Torah strongly supports good social skills and considerate, courteous conduct.

A person may have polished manners but lack underlying respect for others. However, their good manners are likely to be dropped at any moment, and the person can turn vicious. Similarly, a person may be brusque and abrasive in his or her speech, but have a kind heart. A hurtful tongue shows at least a temporary lack of empathy, though, and the person with that tongue can easily slide into committing callous actions.

Finally, another interpretation of the first saying concerns the learning of Torah: when a student and teacher are inconsiderate of each other or of the class, learning is compromised.

Without wisdom. Here, wisdom is linked to *yirah*, fear or awe of God, or, in other words, reverence. As it is written: "The fear of God is the beginning of wisdom" (PROV 9:10). Without humility before God, we will not approach learning with the proper spirit, and our learning will be shallow and lacking wisdom. And similarly, without some deeper understanding—wisdom—we may dismiss faith as shallow and foolish.

Without understanding. Here the knowledge referred to is probably, as the *Maḥzor Vitry* notes, what a person learns formally in school. Without understanding, this knowledge is just a useless bundle of facts that a person carries around—a "camel carrying silk." Yet one cannot build a conceptual grasp of a subject from thin air. Some knowledge of facts is needed. The challenge, both for teacher and student, is to build knowledge of facts and understanding of them in tandem. With knowledge and understanding joined, our learning becomes applicable to life, a powerful guide and tool.

Without flour. A blunt, arresting truth. We should first earn a livelihood, and then harmonize our work with serious study—not an easy task. This saying can also be viewed as a comment on leadership. Without the moral leadership that provides stability and peace, economies fall apart and societies fall into war and corruption. Modern famines are caused by war, social strife, and bad government. As Nobel Prize laureate economist Amartya Sen points out, there has never been a modern famine in a country with a free press. Ethical leadership is the key.

MODERN LIFE

ANTHROPOLOGISTS HAVE pointed out a trade-off between clarity and politeness. Good manners require that we use artful ambiguity and discrete silence to protect other people from embarrassment. The effort to discover the truth, though, requires clarity, whether egos are bruised or not. The Talmud records this debate over truth verses good manners:

> What is sung as one dances before the bride? The School of Shammai says: the bride as she is. The School of Hillel says: one sings "Oh beautiful and graceful bride." (KET 16b)

The decision was for the school of Hillel (see *Avot* 1:18). Because of the need for clarity, academic debates tend to be rather brutal, and the style of debate in the talmudic academies has been similar. Unfortunately, this sometimes goes over the line into rudeness. The Talmud records that, in the Land of Israel, debates were courteous, but in Babylonia, they became less so. Jews have adapted well to modern academic life, but in social life we have sometimes been tarnished by a reputation of unjustified bluntness, to the point of rudeness.

RABBI ELAZAR ḤISMA:

The reckoning of bird sacrifices and the onset of a woman's
unclean period—these, these are the body of Torah law;
The calculations of heavenly cycles and geometry
are side dishes for wisdom. (3:23)

רַבִּי אֶלְעָזָר (בֶּן) חִסְמָא אוֹמֵר: קִנִּין וּפִתְחֵי נִדָּה הֵן הֵן גּוּפֵי הֲלָכוֹת; תְּקוּפוֹת
וְגִימַטְרִיָאוֹת–פַּרְפְּרָאוֹת לַחָכְמָה.

THE TALMUD says of Rabbi Elazar that he "could calculate the number of drops in the ocean" (HOR 10a) and was recruited to the rabbinate for his brilliance. Rabbi Elazar here makes an obscure but brilliant comparison between Jewish and Greek learning. To understand it we need some background information about Greek learning and talmudic law.

Heavenly cycles and geometry. The mathematics of the most advanced Greek geometer, Archimedes, was required to calculate volumes, "the number of drops in the ocean." The other peak achievement of Greek mathematics and science concerned the calculation of the paths of the planets. Elazar was a contemporary of Ptolomy, the Alexandrian astronomer who did the most advanced work on planetary cycles. Thus, Elazar refers to these twin peaks, the greatest achievements of Greek science.

Bird sacrifices. Elazar compares obscure corners of Jewish law to the magnificence of Greek science. How can these be more important?

Ritual purity is the issue in the question of the onset of menstruation. The laws of family purity forbid sexual intercourse between man and wife during the wife's menstrual period and for a number of days afterward. If the time of the onset of menses is figured incorrectly, the wife could possibly begin to bleed during intercourse, violating the laws of family purity. The onset of menses was especially difficult to reckon because of the then primitive state of knowledge about the physiology of reproduction.

Kinin, literally "nests," is an obscure tractate of the Mishnah that is concerned with bird sacrifices. When the Temple—destroyed by Elazar's time—stood, doves and other birds were sacrificed to restore ritual purity to people, including men who became ritually impure because of accidentally violating the laws of family purity. The passages in the Torah and Mishnah on the number and types of birds needed and their proper sacrifice are difficult, and there is no commentary clarifying them.

The theoretical importance of these issues is that with repeated violations of family purity, and with no proper cleansing of sin through bird sacrifices, a man could, in principle, be forbidden to his wife and thus pushed to divorce. Reckoning of the onset of menstruation, and restoring ritual purity through bird sacrifices if there were violations, was thus logically linked to the to maintenance of Jewish marriage and to the creation of the next generation. Even these obscure corners of Jewish law turn out to be about love, sex, marriage, and reproduction.

Rabbi Elazar is, then, comparing two types of calculation—one Greek and one Hebrew. The Hebrew calculations, even those on obscure issues, do concern sex between man and wife, the maintenance of a marriage, and the birth of the next generation—the stuff of life. The Greek calculations are concerned with the paths of the planets and the exact calculation of volumes—fascinating subjects, but not then important to humanity.

MODERN LIFE

RABBI ELAZER ḤISMA put his finger on the exact peak of Greek learning, and for a very long time he was right about its lack of importance to human welfare. Even a thousand years later, the poet and philosopher Yehudah Halevi could rightly say that Greek wisdom is like flowers that bear no fruit, but that Jewish wisdom is like bread, which sustains life. Then, however, a change came. Archimedes and Ptolomy were translated into Latin, and three generations of brilliant scholars—led by Copernicus, Galileo, and Newton—took up the development of Greek science from where it had ceased (in the time of Elazar) and created modern science. Modern science discovered laws of nature and provided dazzling new insights, including into the biology and chemistry of reproduction. From these scientific discoveries came breakthroughs in technology and medicine that have transformed the modern world. Not least of these breakthroughs is effective contraception, which affects exactly the issues Rabbi Elazar commented on.

Now it is modern science that has turned the tables, and by its powerful relevance to life it challenges Judaism, and all religions, to show their relevance and importance to humanity today. Many defenders of religion argue that science can ascertain observable facts, but never deal with the values, purpose, and meaning in life. (For more on religion and science, see the commentary to *Avot* 2:19.)

Chapter Four

BEN ZOMA:

Who is wise? One who learns from every person. *(4:1A)*

בֶּן זוֹמָא אוֹמֵר: אֵיזֶהוּ חָכָם? הַלּוֹמֵד מִכָּל אָדָם, שֶׁנֶּאֱמַר: "מִכָּל-מְלַמְּדַי
הִשְׂכַּלְתִּי."

WHO IS WISE? The prooftext in the Hebrew is: "From all my teachers have I gained wisdom" (*PS 119:99*). Hillel exemplified a devotion to learning from every source, even from nature and popular lore:

> It was said of Hillel that he had not neglected any of the words of the Wise, but had learned them all; he had studied all languages, even that of the mountains, hills, and valleys, of the trees and herbs, of beasts, wild and tame; tales of demons, popular stories, and parables, everything he learned. (SOF 16:9)

Most of us are willing to learn from teachers and those in power over us. It is more unusual to be willing to learn from those who have less schooling, are younger, or are in positions subordinate to us—and that is probably the point of this saying. An example of the right attitude is that of Yehuda haNasi:

> Much Torah I learned from my teachers, from my companions still more, and from my students most of all. (MAK 10a)

This eagerness to learn requires humility, and lack of such humility is a common failing of those with unusual brilliance. The story of the rivalry between the school of Hillel and the school of Shammai is instructive here. It is said that the views of the school of Hillel won out because Hillel's followers were "kindly and humble, and studied both their own commentaries and those of the school of Shammai, and mentioned the views of the school of Shammai before their own" (ER 13b).

MODERN LIFE

THE WILLINGNESS to learn from others of whatever station in life is a great source of strength. English philosopher Edmund Burke observed:

> I have known and, according to my measure, cooperated with great men; and I have never yet seen any plan which has not been mended by the observations of those who were much inferior in understanding to the person who took the lead in the business. (*Reflections on the French Revolution,* ¶280)

Following the same idea, contemporary management experts have emphasized the importance of consultation with others, even when the ultimate decision lies with one person. This process can catch and avoid disastrous mistakes, and almost always strengthens the final plan.

A step beyond consultation is actually seeking out criticism of the solution or decision you favor. This is emotionally difficult to do, but, as philosopher Karl Popper explained, it can help you find new solutions and discover new ideas.

An impressive story of the power of self-criticism is told by J.C. Eccles. Eccles was a scientist who studied how nerve cells transmit information to one another. He had supported the view that the main method of transmission is electrical, rather than chemical, but he thought the evidence was going against his view "and was in a state of extreme depression about it."

Then Eccles learned from Popper that it is "not disgraceful to have one's favorite hypothesis falsified," but on the contrary, the learning that comes from a clear falsification is important in itself. Inspired by this idea, Eccles sharpened his theory to make it more testable, and then cooperated in experimental refutation of his theory of electrical transmission, "the brain-child which I had nurtured for nearly two decades ... I was able at once to contribute to the theory of chemical transmission that was the brain-child of [others]" (*The Philosophy of Karl Popper* I, 350). He modestly does not mention that he received the Nobel Prize for this work.

Ben Zoma's advice to learn from every person is, like most advice, much easier to give than to take. There are many reasons why we are reluctant to seek counsel, including defensiveness and pride. Because of pride, teens are often reluctant to seek a parent's counsel, and adults hesitate to seek advice from someone they fear they are vulnerable to.

This reluctance to seek counsel does have some rational grounds. If you want to seek counsel, you need to confide in another person. If that other person is unscrupulous he or she can take advantage of you or humiliate you. Here, the solution is to seek counsel from people whom you know and trust, as well as those with special expertise on the issue you are facing.

Another prime reason for avoiding counsel is that we are afraid we might be told bad news: that there is a serious difficulty we must face, or that we cannot realize our dreams. The drawbacks to acting on the basis of fear, however, are often severe. If we decide impulsively, we are much more likely to make a serious blunder. If we are indecisive and drift, then the price is the emotional strain of continual anxiety, anger, or depression. The courage to consult others is almost always well-rewarded.

BEN ZOMA:

Who is valiant? One who conquers his impulses. (4:1B)

אֵיזֶהוּ גִבּוֹר? הַכּוֹבֵשׁ אֶת יִצְרוֹ, שֶׁנֶּאֱמַר: "טוֹב אֶרֶךְ אַפַּיִם מִגִּבּוֹר, וּמֹשֵׁל
בְּרוּחוֹ מִלֹּכֵד עִיר."

THE PROOFTEXT in the Hebrew is: "He who is slow to anger is better than the mighty, and he who rules over his spirit than he who captures a city" (*PROV 16:32*). *Yetzer*, translated here as "impulses," alludes to *yetzer ha-ra*, the bad inclination. As we see also in the discussions of *Avot* 2:16 and of *Avot* 4:28 (p. 116), the Rabbis recognized that passions such as envy and lust, which easily become destructive, also play an important positive role in life and in society. The best interpretation of this mishnah, then, is that it urges us to channel our passions in the most constructive direction, curbing or suppressing them where they may do harm and focusing them where they can help.

Self-control is an important value in all rationalist traditions, including those of the Jewish Sages and Aristotle. Maimonides synthesized the two, and in his philosophy self-control is central to the good life. Following Aristotle, he holds that our goal in living should be to fulfill our highest potential as human beings. And this highest potential is, according to Maimonides, our real though limited ability to know God.

All of our actions, according to Maimonides, should ultimately be "for the sake of Heaven" (*Avot* 2:17a), and directed to the goal of knowing God. For example, our health is important to our ability to carry out the mitzvot and to know God. Thus, when a pleasurable act such as eating serves our health, we should do it, but when it does not—as when it turns into overeating—then we should refrain. Maimonides explains:

&❧ This represents thoughtful conduct. Through such acts a human being distinguishes himself from other living creatures. Similarly, if a person engages in sexual relations whenever he desires without considering the benefit and the possible damage, he is conducting himself like an animal and not like a human being . . . 'Valiant' [above] refers to . . . the ability to direct one's potential in accord with one's thought. (Maimonides, *Eight Chapters*, ch. 5, 7, trans. E. Touger)

MODERN LIFE

IN THE Romantic reaction against the Age of Reason, self-control came under attack. Jean-Jacques Rousseau's Romantic vision of a purely good, natural self has been extremely influential, especially in the United States.

In the 19th century, Ralph Waldo Emerson spoke of "self-reliance" as a primary virtue, and poet Walt Whitman sang of "Spontaneous Me." In the 20th century, the "self-actualization" movement combined Aristotle's idea that we should fully realize our human potential and Rousseau's notion that our natural self is wise and healthy. According to that movement, we should be true to our natural self and realize the potential of the self. Hence, not self-control, but "authenticity" and "growth" are important. In recent times, self-control has become a most unpopular virtue—even a vice.

The ideal of realizing our full potential is not in conflict with the Sages' values, though it is foreign to their thinking. What God asks of us is justice, kindness, and humility. There is no ambition, as with Maimonides, to know God intimately, or to achieve some peak of human perfection. It is demanding enough simply to be decent to one another and to achieve the ordinary pleasures of love and family, and of peace and prosperity.

Rousseau's idea that people are naturally good, and that we should simply follow our natural inclinations flatly contradicts the Sages' views. First of all, what our impulses tell us to do in the moment may be detrimental to us in the long run (cf. *Avot* 2:13). Even if our goal is simply to maximize pleasure, self-control is necessary. Secondly, the Sages believed that natural emotions such as anger, envy, lust, and hatred (2:15, 5:14, 2:16) can become very destructive, to both ourselves and others, if we don't keep them under control.

Looking at these issues from the point of view of modern psychology, strong negative emotions lead us to think primitively. We have a "fight or flight" reaction in which we divide the world into "for me" and "against me," and fight or run. We fail to ask: What are my interests and goals? What are the goals of the other person? What are the consequences of different courses of action?

Psychologist Steven Stosney has pointed out that compassion and anger tend to dissolve each other; they are incompatible. Achieving self-control requires, then, both an inclusion of positive emotion, to balance and guide negative emotions, and an effort to include both the interests of other people and the consequences of our actions in our thinking.

Who is rich? One who rejoices in his portion.
Who is honored? One who honors others. (4:1C)

אֵיזֶהוּ עָשִׁיר? הַשָּׂמֵחַ בְּחֶלְקוֹ, שֶׁנֶּאֱמַר: "יְגִיעַ כַּפֶּיךָ כִּי תֹאכֵל אַשְׁרֶיךָ וְטוֹב
לָךְ." אַשְׁרֶיךָ–בָּעוֹלָם הַזֶּה, וְטוֹב לָךְ–לָעוֹלָם הַבָּא: אֵיזֶהוּ מְכֻבָּד? הַמְכַבֵּד
אֶת הַבְּרִיּוֹת, שֶׁנֶּאֱמַר: "כִּי־מְכַבְּדַי אֲכַבֵּד וּבֹזַי יֵקַלּוּ."

WHO IS RICH? This saying is followed by a prooftext: "When you eat
the labor of your hands, you are happy, and it will be well with you (*PS
128:2*). 'Happy are you'—in this world. 'And it will be well with you'—
in the world to come."

This classic statement of a key to happiness is reminiscent of the view
of the Greek and Roman Stoic philosophers, who may have influenced
ben Zoma's outlook. Here is the Stoic teacher Epictetus, in his *Manual:*

> Remember that you ought to behave in life as you would at a banquet.
> As something is being passed around it comes to you; stretch out your
> hand, take a portion of it politely. It passes on; do not detain it. Or it
> has not come to you yet; do not project your desire to meet it, but wait
> until it comes in front of you. So act toward children, so toward a wife,
> so toward office, so toward wealth. (*Enchiridion*, trans. E. Carter, §15)

The larger context of the Stoic philosophy is, however, quite different from that of Judaism. For the Stoics, happiness and virtue are identical, and pursuit of pleasure is an evil. The goal of life is to be free of
distress, to achieve "*apathia.*"

The Stoics tried to combine the goal of emotional invulnerability and
action within the world. Their concept was that we should be indifferent to pleasure and pain, and pursue only virtue, which is identical to
happiness. Virtue means doing the best within your power to carry out
your duties according to your role in society. Ben Zoma's Jewish ideal
of "rejoicing in your portion," by contrast, does not imply indifference
to pleasure and pain, but rather enjoyment of life and freedom from
envy, based on gratitude to God.

MODERN LIFE

WHO IS RICH? In the contemporary Western world, the most popular
philosophy for peace of mind is Buddhism. The "Four Noble Truths"
of Buddhism are: 1. Life is suffering. 2. Suffering is caused by "craving"
(desiring things for oneself). 3. Suffering ceases when we cease craving.
4. The way to extinguish craving is through the Eightfold Path: right

views, right aspiration, right speech, right conduct, right livelihood, right effort, right mindfulness, and right contemplation. Buddhist ethics bears a resemblance to Rabbinic ethics in its great—in fact even greater—emphasis on compassion. However, its ultimate goal is quite different.

Detachment from suffering is the goal in Buddhism, a goal epitomized by the celibate Buddhist monk spending his days in meditation and prayer in a mountain retreat. In Judaism, the goal is not detachment, but commitment to marriage and family, to productive work, and to bettering society. We pay an unavoidable price in terms of worry and sorrow for such whole-hearted engagement in life. Anxiety, as historian of ancient Greece Edwyn Bevan noted, is the price we pay for love. If we make serenity our top priority, then we have to give up on marriage and family, and on the effort to struggle for a more just society. The goal of detachment, which Stoic philosophy, like Buddhism, adopted was not an advance of the ancient Greek world, argued Bevan, but rather a failure of nerve, a shrinking from challenge—the twilight of ancient Greece's glory.

This mishnah presents a way to achieve a degree of peace of mind even in the midst of the struggles an engaged life entails. Philosopher Bertrand Russell wrote, "There is nothing so destructive of happiness as the habit of comparing one's self to others." And the notion of rejoicing in one's lot is the antidote to this habit. The mood of the Psalms and the siddur, the traditional Jewish book of prayer, is of overflowing gratitude and joy for our gifts from God, whether they be small or large.

It is human nature to strive for more and for better. This has the positive effect of bettering our own individual lot, and that of humanity. But this striving for excellence requires a focus on what is lacking, what is wrong, and that can create discontent and dissatisfaction. The challenge to us is to strive for excellence, but to be content with what we have. The principle of "making peace with the future," mentioned in connection with *Avot* 3:13, can help, but it remains a serious challenge.

Who is honored? This saying is also followed by a prooftext: "For I honor those who honor me, but those who spurn me shall be dishonored" (1 SAM 2:30). Among those we have personal contact with, respect for others no doubt fosters respect. However, I think it has to be acknowledged that a lot of people obtain positions of honor who don't deserve them. For public honor, this mishnah alas applies imperfectly.

BEN AZZAI:

> *Run to do a small mitzvah, and flee from sin.*
> *For mitzvah leads to mitzvah, and sin leads to sin.*
> *For the reward of a mitzvah is a mitzvah,*
>   *and the punishment of a sin is a sin. (4:2)*

בֶּן עַזַּאי אוֹמֵר: הֱוֵי רָץ לְמִצְוָה קַלָּה, וּבוֹרֵחַ מִן הָעֲבֵרָה. שֶׁמִּצְוָה גוֹרֶרֶת מִצְוָה,
וַעֲבֵרָה גוֹרֶרֶת עֲבֵרָה, שֶׁשְּׂכַר מִצְוָה מִצְוָה, וּשְׂכַר עֲבֵרָה עֲבֵרָה.

RABBI ELIEZER BEN YA'AKOV:

> *If you do one mitzvah*
>   *you acquire for yourself one advocate,*
>   *and if you commit one sin*
>   *you acquire for yourself one prosecutor.*
> *Repentance and good deeds*
>   *are as a shield against calamity. (4:13)*

רַבִּי אֱלִיעֶזֶר בֶּן יַעֲקֹב אוֹמֵר: הָעוֹשֶׂה מִצְוָה אַחַת, קוֹנֶה לוֹ פְּרַקְלִיט אֶחָד,
וְהָעוֹבֵר עֲבֵרָה אַחַת, קוֹנֶה לוֹ קַטֵּגוֹר אֶחָד, תְּשׁוּבָה וּמַעֲשִׂים טוֹבִים כִּתְרִיס
בִּפְנֵי הַפּוּרְעָנוּת.

SIN LEADS to sin. Other passages of the Talmud vividly describe how one sin leads to another.

🙰 Sins repeated seem permitted. (YOM 86b)

🙰 At first the impulse to evil is as thin as a spider's thread, but in the end it is as thick as a cart rope. (SUK 52a)

🙰 The impulse to evil is first called "passer-by," then "guest," and finally "master." (SUK 52b)

The first passage says that we become desensitized to the wrong we do, and to the harm we cause, and thus tend to repeat sins. The second two describe how our character can become warped, a fact especially exemplified by addictions, and by any habit destructive to oneself or others (see also *Avot* 3:14).

A third way one sin leads to another is described in Scottish poet Robert Burns' famous couplet: "Oh what a tangled web we weave/When first we practice to deceive." Here, the idea is that in order to cover up one deception—and almost all wrongdoing involves deception—we have to practice further deception, so we become trapped in a web of lies and sins. This idea is implied by the Hebrew, as *goreret*, here translated as "leads to," literally means "drags." Rabbi Joseph Hertz translates ben Azzai's mishnah as: "One good deed draws another good deed in its train, and one sin, another sin."

Mitzvah leads to mitzvah. How does one good deed lead to another? A dramatic example of this linkage is the deeds of the "righteous gentiles" who hid Jews during the Holocaust. Very often they would first agree to hide their neighbors briefly because they couldn't conceive of giving them up to be murdered. But once having helped them, they grew more courageous and hid neighbors for a long period of time, at the risk of their own lives. In a decent society, doing acts of kindness and being fair to others engenders trust, and encourages people to ask for your cooperation in efforts that enable you to help people further. In other words, your mitzvah will lead to doing other mitzvot, including those that benefit you. So your mitzvah leads not only to doing more mitzvot, but also to influencing others to do mitzvot.

The reward of a mitzvah. This may refer not only to the opportunity to do more good, but also to the emotional and spiritual reward of doing the right thing, of "serving out of love." This idea resembles the Stoic idea that virtue and happiness are identical, or as it is usually put, "Virtue is its own reward." The sins that follow sin may be not only those of the original sinner, but also those of the person who is induced to sin against the sinner in revenge.

Do one mitzvah. This describes how good and bad deeds affect us in this world and the next. *Puranut*, "calamity," also means divine retribution. Good and bad deeds are the basis of God's final judgment.

MODERN LIFE
WHEN WE look back over our lives, or the lives of others, we can often see in retrospect that one decision was a turning point, for good or ill, and that many other decisions flowed out of it. Our experience validates this mishnah, and a related point of Maimonides: doing good deeds while young develops good character, and sinning leads to weak character (see *Avot* 1:14). The evidence of addictions confirms this: a person who doesn't develop an addiction in youth is far less likely to become an addict later in life. The "corruption of youth" is sometimes laughed at today, but evidence shows it is very real, as is the uplift and inspiration of youth through setting a good example and doing good deeds.

BEN AZZAI:

Despise no man and dismiss no thing;
for there is no man who does not have his hour,
and no thing that does not have its place. (4:3)

הוּא הָיָה אוֹמֵר: אַל תְּהִי בָז לְכָל אָדָם, וְאַל תְּהִי מַפְלִיג לְכָל דָּבָר, שֶׁאֵין
לְךָ אָדָם שֶׁאֵין לוֹ שָׁעָה, וְאֵין לְךָ דָבָר שֶׁאֵין לוֹ מָקוֹם.

RABBI LEVITAS OF YAVNEH:

Be very, very humble, for the hope of Man is the worm. (4:4)

רַבִּי לְוִיטַס אִישׁ יַבְנֶה אוֹמֵר: מְאֹד מְאֹד הֱוֵי שְׁפַל רוּחַ, שֶׁתִּקְוַת אֱנוֹשׁ רִמָּה.

YEHUDAH BEN TEIMA:

Be as bold as a leopard, as light as an eagle, as swift as a
gazelle, and as brave as a lion
to do the will of your Father in heaven.
Bold-faced to hell, shame-faced to heaven. (5:23)

יְהוּדָה בֶּן תֵּימָא אוֹמֵר: הֱוֵי עַז כַּנָּמֵר, וְקַל כַּנֶּשֶׁר, רָץ כַּצְּבִי, וְגִבּוֹר כָּאֲרִי
לַעֲשׂוֹת רְצוֹן אָבִיךָ שֶׁבַּשָּׁמַיִם. הוּא הָיָה אוֹמֵר: עַז פָּנִים לְגֵיהִנֹּם, וּבוֹשֶׁת
פָּנִים לְגַן עֵדֶן.

DESPISE NO man. Ben Azzai here identifies a key danger of lacking humility: arrogance, giving oneself permission to abuse and oppress others. The attitude of respect for each person in his or her role in life is explained in this "favorite saying of the sages of Yavneh":

&☙ I am a creature of God and you are a creature of God. My work is in the city, yours in the field. As you rise early to your work, I rise early to my work. Just as you do not intrude in my work, so I do not intrude in yours. Lest we say, "I do much and you do little," we have learnt: More or less, it does not matter, provided the heart is directed toward Heaven. (BER 17a)

Be very, very humble. Humility is a core virtue in the eyes of the Sages, as well as in the Bible. In the Sages' view, human beings have both good and bad impulses (*yetzer ha-tov* and *yetzer ha-ra*). Arrogance unleashes many of the bad impulses, whereas humility keeps them in check and enables our good side to flourish. The Sages did limit humility, banning people from hurting themselves. Rabbi Shimon ben Tzemaḥ (c. 1400) notes that Rabbi Levitas "commanded [us] . . . not to speak to others with arrogance and contempt, but he most certainly did not command a man to humiliate himself in front of others." Still, because the tendency toward pride is so strong, Maimonides argues in his commentary on this mishnah that even though self-abasement is improper, people should push in the direction of humility as far as they can.

Be as bold as a leopard. If arrogance is clearly an evil, can one overdo humility? Even though he is blunt about condemning the arrogant and haughty, Yehudah ben Teima advocates being extremely bold and assertive in pursuit of the right goals, those that are "for the sake of Heaven." So humility is not the same as timidity.

Can't one, however, legitimately value his or her own personal qualities? The medieval moralist Baḥya ibn Paquda, in his book *Duties of the Heart,* identifies a bad kind of humility. If we wrongly say we aren't good enough to do something, and hence shrink from taking on responsibilities and doing mitzvot we could do, this is a bad kind of humility. This critique also implies that there is a good kind of pride. If we know our special strengths, and see them as gifts to develop and use to serve others, this is a good kind of pride. Real humility, then, is not underestimating our strengths or overestimating our weaknesses, but rather honestly assessing ourselves, and using our strengths in a way that benefits others, and not only ourselves.

Modern Life

Humility has become so unpopular in our time that it is often viewed as a vice. This rejection of humility is an offspring of Rousseau's view that our natural self is purely good, and only becomes corrupted by society. An influential heir to Rousseau's view is Erich Fromm's idea that self-love is the basis for love of others. In its current version, "self-esteem" is seen as the core virtue, and lack of it as the source of all evil. This idea is now virtually a religion in America.

While the Rabbinic view of humility is vulnerable to criticism that it goes too far, ibn Paquda provides an important clarification. The self-esteem movement, by contrast, has little or no recognition that some kinds of positive self-regard can be harmful. It has no place for humility. This is a disastrous oversight, because humility is a foundational value. The prophet Micah said that all God asks of us is to "Do justice, love kindness, and walk humbly with your God" (6:8). Humility is a prerequisite to both reverence and compassion. If we are full of ourselves, we cannot experience awe of God, and if we don't view the other person as worthy, our hearts will not be open to compassion.

RABBI YISHMAEL:

All who learn in order to teach:
  they will be granted enough to learn and to teach;
All who learn in order to do:
  they will be granted enough to learn and to teach,
  to keep the commandments and to do them. (4:6)

רַבִּי יִשְׁמָעֵאל בַּר רַבִּי יוֹסֵי אוֹמֵר: הַלּוֹמֵד עַל מְנָת לְלַמֵּד, מַסְפִּיקִין בְּיָדוֹ
לְלְמוֹד וּלְלַמֵּד, וְהַלּוֹמֵד עַל מְנָת לַעֲשׂוֹת, מַסְפִּיקִין בְּיָדוֹ לִלְמוֹד, וּלְלַמֵּד,
לִשְׁמוֹר, וְלַעֲשׂוֹת.

RABBI TZADOK:

Do not make of it a crown to glorify yourself,
  nor a spade to dig with.
Anyone who uses the words of Torah for material gain
  removes his life from the world. (4:7)

רַבִּי צָדוֹק אוֹמֵר: אַל תִּפְרוֹשׁ מִן הַצִּבּוּר, וְאַל תַּעֲשׂ עַצְמְךָ כְּעוֹרְכֵי הַדַּיָּנִין,
וְאַל תַּעֲשֶׂהָ עֲטָרָה לְהִתְגַּדֵּל בָּהּ, וְלֹא קַרְדּוֹם לַחְפָּר בָּהּ, וְכָךְ הָיָה הִלֵּל
אוֹמֵר: וּדְאִשְׁתַּמֵּשׁ בְּתָגָא חֲלָף. הָא לָמַדְתָּ, כָּל הַנֶּהֱנֶה מִדִּבְרֵי תוֹרָה נוֹטֵל
חַיָּיו מִן הָעוֹלָם.

ALL WHO learn. These sayings raise key issues on leadership in the Jewish community. In a variant text of this mishnah in *Avot de-Rabbi Natan*, the first sentence reads "... they will *not* have enough to learn and to teach." In this variant, the mishnah says that learning in order to do mitzvot is necessary for achievement of any reward. According to both versions of this mishnah, devotion to Torah is supposed to be rewarded in this life: the person will earn at least enough of a livelihood to continue studying, teaching, and doing.

The following two sayings, from Rabbi Yose and Rabbi Yonatan, respectively, reinforce the idea of rewards for studying Torah:

🍃 All who honor the Torah will be honored by their fellow men, and all who dishonor the Torah will be dishonored by their fellow men. (*Avot* 4:8)

🍃 All who fulfill the Torah in poverty will in the end fulfill it in wealth, and all who neglect the Torah in wealth will in the end neglect it in poverty. (*Avot* 4:11)

Since we are talking about this world, it is clear that the rewards will depend on the behavior of the community. This claim is remarkable, as it promises rewards in this life—something the Sages usually avoid.

Do not make of it a crown. "It" here is Torah. This arresting image is a classic statement against professional religious leadership, and in favor of a totally lay leadership. This saying of Rabbi Tzadok begins here in some manuscripts with quotations from earlier *mishnayot*: "Do not separate yourself from the community" (2:5) and "[while a judge] do not act as an advocate" (1:9). And to support his own saying, he cites Hillel (1:13): ". . . exploit the crown—you perish."

In his commentary on this mishnah, Maimonides argues that the only remuneration a scholar should accept is relief from communal taxes and pay in lieu of lost income when he acts as a judge. By the late Middle Ages, rabbis were, however, paid by the community. And Judaism now in fact has a primarily professional leadership.

Modern Life

PAID AND unpaid leadership each have their own problems. Paying leaders can lead to "professional distortions," in which people bend to the pressures of their profession, in a negative way. Pressures are placed on current American rabbis to focus on the ceremonies that they lead more than on ethical issues, and to bend to please members of their congregations. The pressure on academic teachers of Judaism is to do "objective" studies rather than to make the Judaism relevant for life. The pressure on professional educators is just to get children through their bar and bat mitzvah ceremonies. Unpaid leaders have time pressures that can cause them to neglect the studying needed to be a religious leader, while they're expected to give their financial support.

Each group, however, also has its strengths. Rabbis have deep knowledge of Jewish religious tradition, and the skills needed to lead others in celebration of its rituals and festivals, and to give counsel and comfort to those in need. Academics have unparalleled knowledge of Jewish history in all its facets, particularly as it relates to how Jewish beliefs have interacted with Jewish culture and society over time. And the laity have expertise in other fields, as well as the essential funds and volunteer energy necessary to make communal institutions succeed.

Religious denominations that are predominantly professional, such as Catholicism, or purely lay, such as Mormonism, each have their drawbacks. Judaism relies on both professional and lay people to rise above the pressures and work for the community "for the sake of Heaven."

RABBI ISHMAEL:

He who refrains from judging saves himself
from animosity, plunder, and false oaths;
He who brashly issues judgments
is foolish, wicked, and arrogant. (4:9)

רַבִּי יִשְׁמָעֵאל בְּנוֹ אוֹמֵר: הַחֹשֵׂךְ עַצְמוֹ מִן הַדִּין, פּוֹרֵק מִמֶּנּוּ אֵיבָה, וְגָזֵל,
וּשְׁבוּעַת שָׁוְא, וְהַגַּס לִבּוֹ בְּהוֹרָאָה, שׁוֹטֶה, רָשָׁע, וְגַס רוּחַ.

Do not judge alone,
for none can judge alone except One.
And do not say, "Accept my opinion!"
for they are entitled, not you. (4:10)

הוּא הָיָה אוֹמֵר: אַל תְּהִי דָן יְחִידִי, שֶׁאֵין דָן יְחִידִי אֶלָא אֶחָד. וְאַל תֹּאמַר:
קַבְּלוּ דַעְתִּי שֶׁהֵן רַשָׁאִין וְלֹא אָתָּה.

RABBI ISHMAEL here is the son of Rabbi Yose, author of *Avot* 4:8, the previous mishnah. (The translation reflects an all-male judiciary.)

He who refrains. The conduct of judges is vitally important in Jewish law, in which cases are judged by a panel of judges, not by a jury. Traditional commentators read this mishnah as a warning against being eager to act as a judge and being arrogant as a judge. However, *din*, here translated as "judgment," is also the word for "lawsuit," and the *Mahzor Vitry* interprets this mishnah as referring to the would-be litigant, meaning: "He who refrains from lawsuits saves himself from animosity, plunder, and false oaths." The second sentence could also refer to a litigant and mean that the person who uses the courts for self-aggrandizement is foolish, wicked, and arrogant. Whichever way we take this mishnah, Rabbi Ishmael had a lively appreciation of the mischief that can be caused by abuse of the legal system.

Do not judge alone. Here, Rabbi Ishmael considers the conduct of judges toward one other, and again warns against arrogance. These sayings harshly condemn misuse of the courts, but they should not be misconstrued as arguments against the value of a legal system. As noted earlier (2:7), in the "Noahide laws," the Sages included courts of law as essential to a civilized society. More than that, they viewed the laws in the Torah as a gift from God at Mount Sinai.

MODERN LIFE

THESE SAYINGS may also be read as warnings against being too judgmental of other people. The injunctions to judge others in a favorable light (1:6) and to avoid saying bad things about others (1:17) support this idea of avoiding negative judgments. But the Sages did recognize that we do need to make judgments of other people (1:1a). The commandments to rebuke and not to share in our neighbor's sin (LEV 19:17), and not to stand by in the face of evil (LEV 19:16) require us to judge others. To keep away from a bad neighbor and to not associate with the wicked also require that we judge other people's characters. There is no simple rule to resolve this conflict, but we can conclude that we should be reluctant to judge, unless there is a compelling reason to do so.

A step beyond judging is expressing negative judgments, or rebuking. In our time, those people with the most "black and white" views of what is ethical and with the most authoritarian outlook are often quite willing to rebuke. In contrast, those who take a more humane and nuanced view, and see many ethical issues in shades of gray—with "right verses right" and "lesser of evils" choices—are often reluctant to speak out. And some are relativists (see *Avot* 1:1b), who are in principle opposed to rebuking others.

The Sages advocate a very humane system of ethics, but nonetheless see an important role for rebuke. The need to rebuke is based on the commandment to "surely rebuke your neighbor, and incur no guilt because of him" (*LEV 19:17*). The second clause is interpreted two ways. First, in order not to share in the guilt of the sinner, we have to rebuke in an effort to stop him or her from sinning. The other interpretation is that we should not sin by embarrassing the sinner; rebuke generally should be done in private.

A further important qualification comes from the proverb, "Do not rebuke a scoffer, for he will hate you; reprove a wise man and he will love you" (PROV 9:8). The conclusion is that if we are reasonably sure that a rebuke won't help, we should not rebuke (YEV 65b). This greatly restricts when rebuke is appropriate, but Sages nevertheless say "All love that has no reproof with it is not true love," and "Reproof leads to peace" (GEN R 54:3). Finally, the Sages recognize that reproofing in a way that leads to a good result is very difficult. Rabbi Akiva said: "I wonder whether there is anyone in this generation who knows how to give reproof" (AR 16b).

RABBI MEIR:

Do less business, and busy yourself with Torah.
And be humble before every person.
Neglect Torah, and many causes for neglect
will confront you.
Toil in the Torah and a great reward will be given you. (4:12)

רַבִּי מֵאִיר אוֹמֵר: הֱוֵי מְמַעֵט בְּעֵסֶק, וַעֲסוֹק בַּתּוֹרָה, וֶהֱוֵי שְׁפַל רוּחַ בִּפְנֵי
כָל אָדָם, וְאִם בָּטַלְתָּ מִן הַתּוֹרָה, יֵשׁ לָךְ בְּטֵלִים הַרְבֵּה כְּנֶגְדָּךְ, וְאִם עָמַלְתָּ
בַּתּוֹרָה, יֵשׁ לוֹ שָׂכָר הַרְבֵּה לִתֵּן לָךְ.

RABBI NEHORAI:

Emigrate to a place of Torah,
and don't say that it will come to you;
For your fellow students will establish it as your possession.
And do not rely on your own understanding. (4:18)

רַבִּי נְהוֹרַאי אוֹמֵר: הֱוֵי גּוֹלֶה לִמְקוֹם תּוֹרָה, וְאַל תֹּאמַר שֶׁהִיא תָבוֹא תָבוֹא אַחֲרֶיךָ
שֶׁחֲבֵרֶיךָ יְקַיְּמוּהָ בְּיָדֶךָ, וְאֶל בִּינָתְךָ אַל תִּשָּׁעֵן.

RABBI MEIR, whose acquired name means "enlightener," was the most
influential student of Akiva. To escape the persecutions of the Roman
emperor Hadrian, he and other scholars gathered at Usha, in the Galilee,
to reestablish the Sanhedrin and the leadership of the Sages. Meir preserved and further developed Akiva's Mishnah, and his version became
the basis for the authoritative version we have from Yehudah haNasi,
which includes *Avot*.

Do less business. In a period of retrenchment, Rabbi Meir emphasized
both good relations with non-Jews and strict commitment to a Jewish
life. Here, he clearly places the priority on devotion to Torah: you need
to make less money, if that is what it takes to be steeped in Torah learning and the practice of mitzvot. And, as in earlier *mishnayot*, learning is
joined with the need for humility. In this context, "before every person"
emphasizes humility before those of lesser learning or wealth.

Emigrate. This saying can be read as a justification of the establishment of the schools in exile. (*Hevei goleh*, "emigrate," is literally "be exiled.") However, there is a broader meaning: advanced education is key
to the future of Judaism, and fellow students are a key factor in higher
education. By the time of the fall of the Temple in 70 CE, universal

education for boys was seen as a vital part of Judaism. Outside Judea, and later in the exile, schools of higher education for elite scholars also were seen as vital.

Do not rely. This saying is a quotation of Proverbs 3:5. In this context, the point is clearly that students should not think that they can rely on their own idiosyncratic interpretation of the religious and legal tradition, and ignore the views of their teachers and other students. Sound views come from the process of discussion with teachers and arguments with other students.

Modern Life

A MODERN philosophy that challenges the need for consultation with others is extreme individualism. An important movement for individualism evolved from the Protestant Reformation in Europe. The ultimate authority in moral and religious matters was no longer seen as being the Church, but rather the conscience of the individual. The peak of this individualist theory was philosopher Immanuel Kant's principle of the "autonomy of the will." According to Kant, every person has the individual capacity to judge right and wrong and should not be influenced by the judgment of others. It would be an abdication of responsibility, and hence immoral, to rely on others' judgment.

The Sages clearly believed that the individual has the ability and responsibility to choose between right and wrong (see 3:19). And the Torah warns: "You shall not follow a multitude to do evil" (EX 23:2). Yet the Sages are equally clear that study and consultation with others is vital for us to achieve our full capacities for sound moral judgments.

How are we to reconcile these positions? In most situations, identifying what is morally wrong is usually much easier than seeing what is the best course of action, including what is morally best. This is because what is wrong is a matter of immediate harm or of violation of the dignity of another person. But to see what is the best thing to do, we need to take into account the impact of our actions on many people over the long term, which is much more difficult to ascertain. Thus, when it comes to the negative commandments, such as those not to steal, to murder, or to commit adultery, the main danger is corrupt influence from others, or one's own lack of self-control. But when it comes to positive commandments, such as the pursuit of justice or loving one's neighbor, study and consultation with others are invaluable.

Beyond our grasp are the well-being of the wicked
and the sufferings of the righteous. (4:19)

רַבִּי יַנַּאי אוֹמֵר: אֵין בְּיָדֵינוּ לֹא מִשַּׁלְוַת הָרְשָׁעִים וְאַף לֹא מִיִּסּוּרֵי הַצַּדִּיקִים.

Calamities in the World:

Seven kinds of calamity come into the world
because of seven classes of sin:

If some tithe and some do not, a famine comes from drought;
some go hungry and some are full.

If all do not tithe, a famine comes from riots and drought.

If they also do not separate the ḥallah,
an annihilating famine comes.

Plagues come into the world because of capital crimes
mentioned in the Torah that are not handed over to a court,
and because of forbidden use of produce in a sabbatical year.

The sword comes into the world because of
delay of justice and perversion of justice,
and because of teaching the Torah improperly.

Wild beasts come upon the world because of false oaths
and profanation of the Name.

Exile comes to the world because of worshipping the stars,
forbidden sexual relations, the shedding of blood,
and not leaving the earth fallow in the sabbatical year. (5:11)

שִׁבְעָה מִינֵי פוּרְעָנִיּוֹת בָּאִים לָעוֹלָם עַל שִׁבְעָה גוּפֵי עֲבֵרָה. מִקְצָתָן מְעַשְּׂרִין
וּמִקְצָתָן אֵינָן מְעַשְּׂרִין, רָעָב שֶׁל בַּצּוֹרֶת בָּא, מִקְצָתָן רְעֵבִים וּמִקְצָתָן שְׂבֵעִים.
גָּמְרוּ שֶׁלֹּא לְעַשֵּׂר, רָעָב שֶׁל מְהוּמָה וְשֶׁל בַּצּוֹרֶת בָּא, וְשֶׁלֹּא לִטּוֹל אֶת הַחַלָּה,
רָעָב שֶׁל כְּלָיָה בָּא. דֶּבֶר בָּא לָעוֹלָם–עַל מִיתוֹת הָאֲמוּרוֹת בַּתּוֹרָה שֶׁלֹּא
נִמְסְרוּ לְבֵית דִּין, וְעַל פֵּרוֹת שְׁבִיעִית. חֶרֶב בָּאָה לָעוֹלָם–עַל עִנּוּי הַדִּין, וְעַל
עִוּוּת הַדִּין, וְעַל הַמּוֹרִים בַּתּוֹרָה שֶׁלֹּא כַהֲלָכָה. חַיָּה רָעָה בָּאָה לָעוֹלָם, עַל
שְׁבוּעַת שָׁוְא וְעַל חִלּוּל הַשֵּׁם. גָּלוּת בָּאָה לָעוֹלָם–עַל עֲבוֹדַת כּוֹכָבִים, וְעַל
גִּלּוּי עֲרָיוֹת, וְעַל שְׁפִיכוּת דָּמִים, וְעַל שְׁמִטַּת הָאָרֶץ.

These two mishnayot display conflicting attitudes among the Sages regarding the problem of evil—the problem of how God can allow that "bad things happen to good people," as Rabbi Harold Kushner has put it. These reflect an ongoing search for understanding within Judaism.

The second, anonymous mishnah speculates on specific causes of suffering. Such speculation, no doubt engendered by the faith that all is in God's hands, is today often seen as presumptuous. For example, a leading *haredi* rabbi in Israel recently speculated that the Holocaust was delivered on the Jews because of impiety. Israelis reacted with outrage and derision—not least of all because the more observant Eastern European Jews suffered greater losses in the Holocaust than less observant Western European Jews.

As opposed to seeking and in fact specifying reasons for calamities, the first mishnah humbly confesses that the seemingly random injustice of the world is beyond human understanding.

MODERN LIFE

THE IRON consistency of natural law, as revealed by modern science, has compounded questions about "the problem of evil," leaving people to doubt the existence of a God who intervenes in humanity's problems, a God who rewards and punishes. Many now believe in a God who influences us primarily through the hearts of individuals. And it is a remarkable fact that, through a feeling of connection to God, many people find the strength to do things (such as overcome addictions to drugs and alcohol) that they could not otherwise do.

God hides from the mind, but speaks to the heart. Some Jewish theologians have attempted to go beyond this limited idea using ideas from Kabbalah. One of the core ideas from the *Zohar* (13th c.) is that there is a correlation between heaven and earth, so that worldly actions also affect heaven. Abraham Joshua Heschel argued similarly that God needs humanity to carry out God's will. According to both the *Zohar* and Heschel, God looks to humanity as a partner in completing Creation, which is done by humanity observing the mitzvot, the commandments.

Heschel said that the idea of an all-knowing and all-powerful God was an alien concept brought into Judaism by Maimonides, under the influence of Islam. But the notion of God's concern for human partners is more reflective of Jewish theology. The problem is that this theology still does not explain the mystery of why the good suffer, or provide a convincing doctrine of God's reward and punishment. So Rabbi Yannai's mishnah, admitting bafflement, still rings true today.

RABBI YA'AKOV:

This world is like an anteroom before the world to come.
Prepare yourself in the anteroom
  so that you may enter the banquet hall. (4:21)

רַבִּי יַעֲקֹב אוֹמֵר: הָעוֹלָם הַזֶּה דּוֹמֶה לִפְרוֹזְדוֹר בִּפְנֵי הָעוֹלָם הַבָּא. הַתְקֵן
עַצְמְךָ בִּפְרוֹזְדוֹר, כְּדֵי שֶׁתִּכָּנֵס לִטְרַקְלִין.

Better is one hour of repentance and good deeds in this life
  than all the life of the world to come.
And better is one hour of blissful spirit in the world
  to come than all the life of this world. (4:22)

הוּא הָיָה אוֹמֵר: יָפָה שָׁעָה אַחַת בִּתְשׁוּבָה וּמַעֲשִׂים טוֹבִים בָּעוֹלָם הַזֶּה
מִכָּל חַיֵּי הָעוֹלָם הַבָּא, וְיָפָה שָׁעָה אַחַת שֶׁל קוֹרַת רוּחַ בָּעוֹלָם הַבָּא מִכָּל
חַיֵּי הָעוֹלָם הַזֶּה.

THE HEBREW words for both "anteroom," *prozdor*, and "banquet hall,"
traklin, are derived from the ancient Greek names for these rooms in a
villa. The sentiment is, however, typically Rabbinic. Belief in the afterlife was of vital importance for the Sages, and this mishnah is one of
the more striking expressions of its importance. Even here, though, a
claim for the importance of the afterlife is followed by a claim that action in this life is most important.

Better is one hour. What is the meaning of this paradox? The life of
the world to come will not be worth much to you unless you repent and
do good deeds. For without these you will not earn a place in the world
to come, or at least not a high place in it. If you do gain that high place,
one where you have a blissful spirit, then just one hour of that bliss will
be better than all that you have experienced in this world.

That Rabbi Ya'akov resorted to a riddle here is indicative of the
fact that the nature of the afterlife has never been clear in Judaism.
Maimonides, writing in the Middle Ages, explains with his usual clarity: "Know that the Torah Sages have differences of opinion about the
happiness that a person will attain through fulfillment of the mitzvot"
(*Commentary on the Mishnah*, SAN 10). He describes the different views:

1. The ultimate happiness is in *Gan Eden*, the Garden of Eden, which is a
   better, completely happy version of our world, and retribution is exacted
   in Gehinnom, a place of horrible burning and torture.

2. Ultimate happiness is living in the era of the Messiah, during which all will live in happiness on earth.
3. Ultimate happiness is being resurrected to a happy life on earth forever, and retribution is not being resurrected.
4. Ultimate happiness is prosperity and the defeat of enemies on this earth, and retribution is the reverse. [This is the plain meaning of the Torah texts, applied usually to the whole people of Israel.]
5. A combination of all of the above. As Maimonides says, "The Messiah will come, he will resurrect the dead, and then we will enter the Garden of Eden, where we will eat and drink in health forever."

Finally, the concept of reincarnation, *gilgul* in Hebrew, which was traditionally rejected, began to be accepted late in Maimonides' life by Jewish mystics and later by Ḥasidim. Maimonides himself, writing later in *Guide to the Perplexed*, expressed views different from those of the Sages, which led others to accuse him of denying resurrection—a charge he rejected.

Modern Life

Why has this diversity of beliefs about the afterlife been tolerated in Judaism? The answer lies in the religion's foundations, in the teachings (*torah*) of Moses. Moses never mentions the afterlife, and his primary focus is on the rules of behavior. (As the late Berl Gross suggested in his book *Before Democracy*, Moses may have been reacting against the Egyptian society he had left, a society obsessed with the afterlife.) The function of the concept of God's reward and punishment within Judaism is to motivate good behavior—the performance of the mitzvot. Even after Jews accepted the idea of reward and punishment in a "world to come," the function of the afterlife was primarily to support the mitzvot. The Talmud generally does not try to settle issues of theology, but makes rulings only on actions.

The diversity of views about the afterlife within Judaism reveals the struggles that Jews have had over reconciling belief in one just God with the sufferings of the world. Today, many Jews refrain from speculation on the afterlife, as Moses also refrained long ago. They rely on the idea of "serving out of love" and reject the idea of serving for the sake of a reward or for fear of punishment (see *Avot* 1:3). Is this approach, which doesn't rely on divine judgment, weaker because it promises less? Or is it stronger because it does not hold God responsible for the tragedies of life and is therefore not shaken by such tragedies?

Do not placate your friend in the hour of his anger,
And do not console him in the hour when his dead
  lies before him,
And do not question him in the hour of his vow,
And do not try to see him in his hour of disgrace. (4:23)

רַבִּי שִׁמְעוֹן בֶּן אֶלְעָזָר אוֹמֵר: אַל תְּרַצֶּה אֶת חֲבֵרְךָ בִּשְׁעַת כַּעֲסוֹ, וְאַל
תְּנַחֲמֵהוּ בְּשָׁעָה שֶׁמֵּתוֹ מֻטָּל לְפָנָיו, וְאַל תִּשְׁאַל לוֹ בִּשְׁעַת נִדְרוֹ, וְאַל תִּשְׁתַּדֵּל
לִרְאוֹתוֹ בִּשְׁעַת קַלְקָלָתוֹ.

THE TRANSLATION here follows the original gendered Hebrew to emu-
late its concision and force. The counsel of this mishnah is, of course,
equally valid for men and women.

Rabbi Shimon ben Elazar had a keen appreciation that strong feelings can make us act irrationally, against our better interests and those
of others. In another place, he said, "Impulses *(yetzer)* should be pushed
away with the left hand, and drawn near with the right" (SOT 47a). The
idea is that the right hand is stronger, so that our emotions should indeed guide us, but we consciously need to keep them in balance so they
are channeled in a productive rather than destructive direction.

Just as managing our own emotions is a difficult challenge, so is handling others when their emotions are high. Here, Rabbi Shimon ben
Elazar points out that intervening when the negative emotions of the
other person—anger, grief, guilt, shame—are at their height is likely
not only to fail, but to make the situation worse. In response to all four
of these emotions, good or bad manners have serious consequences. In
such delicate situations, it is easy to make the wrong move, and if we
do, we may well do long-term damage to an important personal relationship. In all these situations, then, Rabbi Shimon ben Elazar advises us to wait until a person is not overwrought with emotion to interact
with him or her.

The Sages noted that we need to consider not only the feelings, but
also the character of the person before we act. As noted in connection
with *Avot* 4:11, the different character of the other person can completely reverse what is appropriate action: "As one is commanded to say that
which will be listened to, so is one commanded not to say that which
will not be listened to" (YEV 65b).

These striking warnings are all advice on *derekh eretz,* the Sages' term for proper worldly conduct, which includes ethics, good manners, and social skills. And in the view of the Sages, *derekh eretz* is essential to fulfilling a religious way of life, as is said in *Avot* 3:21: "Without proper worldly conduct, there is no Torah."

Modern Life

THE WISDOM of these warnings is rooted in a principle that modern psychology has confirmed, known as the Yerkes-Dodson Law. This law relates how much a person is emotionally aroused to how well they are able to function. If a person is not emotionally aroused at all, he or she will not be motivated to do anything. As emotional arousal increases, so does motivation, making the person perform better. But at a certain point, excessive arousal will cause the person to become less functional, and when extreme, it will render him or her dysfunctional and ineffectual. All the cases in this mishnah are examples of when emotions are at these dysfunctional extremes.

This mishnah advocates not talking with a person in these extreme situations, but postponing until the person is calmer, and able to deal with whatever we have to offer. Only then will what we have to offer be helpful. If we are able to help someone to respond effectively to the situation or person that caused him or her to be angry, he or she might be able to move on from the anger, and not fall into the trap of acting out against his or her own interests.

Postponing discussion is a case of a more general principle. In order for a conversation to be emotionally rewarding, or a discussion productive, as a rule both sides need a cooperative attitude. Cooperation is sometimes natural and effortless, but one or both people often have anxieties and suspicions that are barriers to cooperation. Overcoming these barriers and successfully winning cooperation becomes an essential first step to having any constructive conversation.

Psychologist John Gottman has found that, for married couples, a key to positive discussions is a "soft start." The person raising an issue does not attack, but waits for the right time to talk, formulating the issue in a way that demonstrates compassion and emphasizes shared goals. Whatever technique is used, how best to win cooperation is a question well worth conscious forethought and careful planning.

Learning as a child, what is it like?
Like ink written on new paper.
Learning as an old person, what is it like?
Like ink written on erased paper. (4:25)

אֱלִישָׁע בֶּן אֲבוּיָ אוֹמֵר: הַלּוֹמֵד יֶלֶד לְמָה הוּא דוֹמֶה? לִדְיוֹ כְתוּבָה עַל נְיָר חָדָשׁ, וְהַלּוֹמֵד זָקֵן לְמָה הוּא דוֹמֶה? לִדְיוֹ כְתוּבָה עַל נְיָר מָחוּק.

Rabbi Yose bar Yehudah:

Learning from the young, what is it like?
Like eating unripe grapes
and drinking wine from the vat.
Learning from the old, what is it like?
Like eating ripe grapes and drinking aged wine. (4:26)

רַבִּי יוֹסֵי בַּר יְהוּדָה אִישׁ כְּפַר הַבַּבְלִי אוֹמֵר: הַלּוֹמֵד מִן הַקְּטַנִּים לְמָה הוּא דוֹמֶה? לְאוֹכֵל עֲנָבִים קֵהוֹת, וְשׁוֹתֶה יַיִן מִגִּתּוֹ, וְהַלּוֹמֵד מִן הַזְּקֵנִים לְמָה הוּא דוֹמֶה? לְאוֹכֵל עֲנָבִים בְּשׁוּלוֹת, וְשׁוֹתֶה יַיִן יָשָׁן.

Rabbi Meir:

Do not look at the bottle, but at what is in it.
There are new bottles filled with aged wine,
and old bottles that don't even have new wine. (4:27)

רַבִּי מֵאִיר אוֹמֵר: אַל תִּסְתַּכֵּל בְּקַנְקַן אֶלָּא בְּמַה שֶׁיֵּשׁ בּוֹ, יֵשׁ קַנְקַן חָדָשׁ מָלֵא יָשָׁן, וְיֵשׁ יָשָׁן שֶׁאֲפִלּוּ חָדָשׁ אֵין בּוֹ.

These three sayings all concern the proper roles of youth and age and the relationships between them. It is interesting that the first mishnah is included at all, particularly under the name of its author. Elisha ben Avuya is the great Rabbinic scholar who abandoned his faith. Because he had such a deep understanding of Jewish law, the Talmud cites his pre-apostasy views, but under the name *aḥer,* "another." Here, a contemporary, perhaps his student Rabbi Meir, wanted to honor him for his contributions, and so his name is credited.

Learning as a child. This saying is part of a series of Elisha ben Avuya's sayings recorded in *Avot de-Rabbi Natan.* The validity of the other sayings, unlike the one quoted here, might be questioned because of Elisha ben Avuya's history. One of the most interesting is: "When one studies Torah as a child, the words of Torah are absorbed by his blood and come out of his mouth distinctly. But if one studies Torah in his old age, the words of the Torah are not absorbed by his blood and do not come out of his mouth distinctly" (ARN 24).

Here, the idea is not just that the young have better memories than the old, but also that there is a qualitative difference between the learning of the young and the old. What we learn as a child not only sticks, but is laid down as a framework, a set of lenses that we look through to interpret everything else. We understand that framework more deeply than anything else, and it forms a foundation for our other learning.

Learning from the young. Here is the flip side of the generational compact of passing on the wisdom of the past. Those who have learned and added to the tradition are best situated to pass it on in a way that helps the next generation. Traditions are amazingly powerful, but also fragile, and can easily turn destructive. Here, the warning is not to attempt to learn from those who are not seasoned, and who do not know the misunderstandings and distortions that a tradition is subject to.

Do not look at the bottle. A cautionary note about age. Despite the positive words above, there are many old fools, and young men and women of wisdom.

MODERN LIFE

TRADITIONALLY, THERE was broad agreement among the older generation on what should be taught to the younger. Partly under the influence of Rousseau, modern education has become more "child-centered." In a modest form, this approach emphasizes that one should connect to a child's existing knowledge and interests. In this form, Yehudah ha-Nasi agrees: "One can only learn well that part of the Torah which is his heart's desire" (AZ 19a). In its extreme form, the approach holds that the individual child is naturally good and wise and should determine the curriculum. This goes against the Sages' belief that we have good and bad tendencies, and that Torah study will improve us. They believe wholeheartedly that a curriculum set by adults is good for children.

A critical challenge for our community is developing a corps of teachers whose knowledge is "old wine." Only such teachers have the experience to help students develop a deep understanding of past wisdom.

Those who are born, die; those who are dead, live again;
*   and those who live again are judged.*
So know, make known, and have knowledge that He is God,
*   He is maker, He is creator, He is knower,*
*   He is judge, He is witness, He is plaintiff,*
*   and He will in future make judgment.*
Blessed be He, in whose court there is no wrongdoing,
*   no forgetting, no favoritism,*
*   and no bribe-taking—for all is His.*
*   And know that all depends on the accounting.*
And do not heed your evil inclination promising you
*   that sheol will be a place of refuge for you.*
For not by your choice were you created, and
*   not by your choice were you born, do you live, will you die,*
*   and will you be called to account before the Supreme*
*   King of kings, the Holy One, blessed be He. (4:29)*

הוּא הָיָה אוֹמֵר: הַיִּלוֹדִים לָמוּת, וְהַמֵּתִים לִחְיוֹת, וְהַחַיִּים לִדּוֹן. לֵידַע
וּלְהוֹדִיעַ וּלְהִוָּדַע, שֶׁהוּא אֵל, הוּא הַיּוֹצֵר, הוּא הַבּוֹרֵא, הוּא הַמֵּבִין, הוּא
הַדַּיָּן, הוּא הָעֵד, הוּא בַּעַל דִּין, הוּא עָתִיד לָדוּן. בָּרוּךְ הוּא, שֶׁאֵין לְפָנָיו
לֹא עַוְלָה, וְלֹא שִׁכְחָה, וְלֹא מַשּׂוֹא פָנִים, וְלֹא מִקַּח שֹׁחַד, וְדַע שֶׁהַכֹּל לְפִי
הַחֶשְׁבּוֹן, וְאַל יַבְטִיחֲךָ יִצְרְךָ שֶׁהַשְּׁאוֹל בֵּית מָנוֹס לָךְ, שֶׁעַל כָּרְחֲךָ אַתָּה נוֹצָר,
וְעַל כָּרְחֲךָ אַתָּה נוֹלָד, וְעַל כָּרְחֲךָ אַתָּה חַי, וְעַל כָּרְחֲךָ אַתָּה מֵת, וְעַל כָּרְחֲךָ
אַתָּה עָתִיד לִתֵּן דִּין וְחֶשְׁבּוֹן לִפְנֵי מֶלֶךְ מַלְכֵי הַמְּלָכִים הַקָּדוֹשׁ בָּרוּךְ הוּא.

RABBI ELAZAR HAKAPPAR urges us to abandon any doubt we may have about the reality of divine punishment—an admonition so powerful that it is as startling as a slap in the face.

Those who are born. Here, Elazar restates the basic Rabbinic belief in resurrection and judgment in the afterlife. Characteristically, he is most concerned about the reality of judgment, and is silent about the nature of the reward or punishment. This doctrine of reward and punishment in an afterlife is the feature of the Rabbinic synthesis that has been most rejected in modern times. There has been a tendency among those with Western higher education to be most skeptical of it.

Not by your choice. Elazar's ringing reminder of our powerlessness and the mystery of why we live and die cuts short the arrogance of Positivists, who have viewed modern science as a surrogate religion. The questions about life's purpose raised here have not been resolved by science and, as argued earlier (2:19), are not likely to be. In the past 50 years, there has been a decline in Positivism and a revival of all sorts of religiosity. One of the most popular versions of "spirituality" has been of the so called "New Age" variety. New Age spirituality is different from Judaism (or Christianity) in that it typically makes no ethical demands.

The wedding of holiness and the fulfillment of ethical demands is a bedrock feature of Judaism. As philosopher E. A. Burtt pointed out, earlier religions focused more on controlling nature. Beginning with Judaism, religion turned more toward creating the ethical basis for a good society. Later, similar ethical concerns arose outside of the Near East. In East Asia, Confucius, while accepting the traditional animist religion, tried to infuse society with an ethical consciousness. In South Asia, Buddha created his own new synthesis of ethics and spirituality. And in ancient Greece, Socrates tried to establish an ethical basis for society separate from any religious feeling.

Elazar here touches on the sense of awe at the mystery of life that is at the heart of religion, and at the same time sends Judaism's typical urgent call to heed ethical demands, demands that come from God.

Supreme King of kings. This metaphor of God as a powerful king is common throughout the Rabbinic literature, and is particularly used in connection with discussions of judgment after death. In the Seleucid empire, which the Maccabees successfully revolted against, the emperor was called (with the royal plural) "The Kings of Kings." The Rabbinic phrase, literally "King of the Kings of Kings," emphasizes that God is above any human ruler. Current translations in non-Orthodox Jewish liturgy avoid this expression, and avoid any reference to God as "He" in favor of gender-neutral expressions. Here, "King" is essential to the flavor of the original.

Modern Life

JEWISH PHILOSOPHER Martin Buber said that a God who asks nothing of us is not worth worshipping. However, instead of looking to reward and punishment, as Rabbi Elazar HaKappar does here, he saw the source of obligation for ethical behavior as coming from relationships, in particular what he called "I-Thou" relationships. In these relationships, we do not see the other person simply as an instrument, as an "it" to be used to further our ends. Instead, we have an open and honest relationship with the other person in which we are responsive not only to what he or she says, but also to who he or she is. In such dialogue and mutual responsiveness, Buber says, we can also sense God's presence as a "Thou." Such responsive interaction is the source of ethical responsibility, through which our awareness includes not only ourselves, but also others, and God as the eternal "Thou."

Buber thus sees the wellspring of ethics in feelings that arise in our interactions with others, feelings that include an awareness of the transcendent. Thus, Buber builds a religious foundation for ethics without any appeal to reward and punishment. This innovative grounding of ethics in religious experience is valuable, but it is also dangerously vulnerable.

An individual's interpretation of his or her experience is fallible, may be quite contrary to a good relationship, and may even be unethical. Thus, it is unwise to base ethics only on individual feelings. Buber's "Romantic" approach is vulnerable in the same way as past mystics could produce drastically bad ideas, as well as invaluable insights.

Here, the Sages' approach has more wisdom. The bridge from individual feelings to ethical guidelines is mediated by a social process lasting over many generations. In this way, individual capriciousness is filtered out, and though we can still feel the emotional basis of ethical guidelines, they are put on a sounder and more enduring footing.

Buber's rejection of *halakhah* as lifeless because it is based on set rules thus doesn't hold up. We need to transcend the self, and involve tradition, as well as other people, to identify the best ethical guidelines by which to live our lives.

Chapter Five

> *Ten things were created on the eve of Shabbat at twilight:*
> *the mouth of the earth, the mouth of the well,*
> *the mouth of the donkey, the rainbow, the manna,*
> *the staff, the shamir, the script, the stylus, the tablets.*
> *And some say: evil spirits, too, and the grave of Moses,*
> *and the ram of Abraham our father.*
> *And some say: also tongs made with tongs. (5:9)*

עֲשָׂרָה דְבָרִים נִבְרְאוּ בְּעֶרֶב שַׁבָּת בֵּין הַשְּׁמָשׁוֹת, וְאֵלּוּ הֵן, פִּי הָאָרֶץ, פִּי
הַבְּאֵר, פִּי הָאָתוֹן, הַקֶּשֶׁת, וְהַמָּן, וְהַמַּטֶּה, וְהַשָּׁמִיר, הַכְּתָב, וְהַמִּכְתָּב,
וְהַלֻּחוֹת, וְיֵשׁ אוֹמְרִים אַף הַמַּזִּיקִין וּקְבוּרָתוֹ שֶׁל מֹשֶׁה וְאֵילוֹ שֶׁל אַבְרָהָם
אָבִינוּ, וְיֵשׁ אוֹמְרִים אַף צְבָת בִּצְבָת עֲשׂוּיָה.

IN THIS fifth chapter of *Avot* most of the sayings are anonymous and are arranged in order of being about "ten things," "seven things," etc. The first eight of the "ten things" lists concern more minor biblical facts. (See the *Appendices* for the full text.) This final mishnah that lists "ten things" deals, however, with a key theological issue: the status of miracles.

Eve of Shabbat at twilight. The idea here is that all the events record-ed in the Torah that appear to be contrary to the normal order of nature were, in fact, especially arranged for by God in the last moments of the final day of Creation—at the "eve of Shabbat at twilight."

The mouth. "The mouth of the earth" refers to when the earth "opened its mouth" and swallowed Koraḥ and his band, rebels against Moses (NUM 16:32). "The mouth of the well" is Miriam's well (NUM 21:16, TA'AN 9a), which according to legend would miraculously reappear wherever the Israelites camped (SHAB 35a). The "mouth of the donkey" refers to Balaam's donkey (NUM 22:28), which had the power of human speech.

The rainbow. "The rainbow" is displayed for the first time to Noah (GEN 9:13), long after the creation. "The manna" miraculously appeared to feed the Israelites fleeing Egypt (EX 16:14). "The staff" is the staff God gave to Moses (EX 4:17), with which he performed miracles demon-strating God's power to Pharaoh, and later split the Red Sea (EX 14:16). "The *shamir*" is, according to legend, a miraculous worm that could split stones (SOT 48b). Solomon is said to have used such worms to cut stones for the Temple, so that no iron—the material of the sword—was used.

The script. Theologically speaking, the most important miracles in the Torah are Creation, which shows God as both the creator and the ruler of the world, and God personally giving the Ten Commandments, which authenticates the Torah and the covenant with the Jewish people. Here, the idea is that God had in the beginning created the tablets with the Commandments engraved on them, so Moses could receive them much later on Mount Sinai. To do this, God needed to create not only the stone tablets, but also a written script and a tool to engrave words on the tablets. It is somehow fitting that the Sages, who revered the written word, assert that God created the system of written language.

And some say. The folk belief in evil spirits was widespread in talmudic times. The Sages tended to minimize the influence of spirits, as they saw God as ruling all, and humans as having freedom of choice. "Tongs made with tongs" suggests that God made the first pair of tongs, as God would not need another pair of tongs to hold them, as a human blacksmith would.

There are three types of miracles in the Bible (cf. EJ, "Miracles"): events that go against the ordinary order of nature; "signs," or demonstrations of God's power consistent with nature; and "daily miracles," the wonders of love and beauty and of nature's bounty that we witness daily. The Sages, accepting the Greek idea of the "cosmos" or orderly nature, had difficulties only with the first category of miracles, which this mishnah addresses.

Modern Life

MODERN SCIENCE has led Jews to question the notion of God intervening against the order of nature. Such intervention is still possible within current scientific theory because of that randomness that exists within nature, but cannot be independently tested for and confirmed against alternative hypotheses, as in science.

Mordecai Kaplan argued that Jews should reject the idea of God's intentionality in the world, and see God as the natural powers within us that make for a better life. Eugene Borowitz has argued that the concept of the unity of God, expressed in the *Shema*, is central to Judaism, and missing from Kaplan's theology. Martin Buber has said that, if we are open to it, we can experience God's presence in nature and in loving relationships, and these are "signs" just as much as the biblical miracles were.

Seven things mark the crude, and seven the wise.
The wise do not speak before one who is greater in wisdom,
   nor interrupt the words of a colleague, nor rush to reply.
Their questions are relevant, their answers to the point.
They speak of first things first, and last things last.
Of things they have not understood they say,
   "I do not understand," and they acknowledge the truth.
The opposites mark the crude. (5:10)

שִׁבְעָה דְבָרִים בְּגוֹלֶם וְשִׁבְעָה בְּחָכָם, חָכָם אֵינוֹ מְדַבֵּר לִפְנֵי מִי שֶׁגָּדוֹל מִמֶּנּוּ
בְּחָכְמָה וּבְמִנְיָן, וְאֵינוֹ נִכְנָס לְתוֹךְ דִּבְרֵי חֲבֵרוֹ, וְאֵינוֹ נִבְהָל לְהָשִׁיב, שׁוֹאֵל
כְּעִנְיָן, וּמֵשִׁיב כַּהֲלָכָה, וְאוֹמֵר עַל רִאשׁוֹן רִאשׁוֹן וְעַל אַחֲרוֹן אַחֲרוֹן, וְעַל
מַה שֶּׁלֹּא שָׁמַע, אוֹמֵר לֹא שָׁמַעְתִּי, וּמוֹדֶה עַל הָאֱמֶת. וְחִלּוּפֵיהֶן בְּגוֹלֶם.

SEVEN THINGS *mark the crude.* Beginning with the Talmud, Jewish tradition has been taught and developed through discussion and debate over specific cases and issues. The idea that reasoned argument and debate can help us discover the truth comes from Socrates, and it entered into Judaism when Judea was part of a Hellenist empire, and was heavily influenced by ancient Greek culture. Discussion is difficult among those who disagree and who also have a personal stake in the outcome. Then anger, pride, and other emotions the Sages warn against can raise their heads and sabotage productive discussion.

In discussions among scholars, pride is the main obstacle. As we can see from the testimony of Shimon ben Gamliel (1:17) and Rabbi Eliezer (2:15), this was a serious problem even among some great Sages. Rules of respect and manners help tremendously to create discussions that are fruitful. Some of these rules are mentioned here. It is revealing that Hillel, the most revered of the Sages, systematized the principles of talmudic argument and was a model of good manners in discussion (see the commentary to 5:20).

The wise do not speak. This first guideline means that we should wait to speak until after more knowledgeable people finish what they have to say. Note that these guidelines give respect to the other person involved in a debate or discussion, check vanity in ourselves, and help the truth emerge—all at the same time.

MODERN LIFE

THESE GUIDELINES are evidently formulated with teachers, students, and scholars in mind. In the traditional style of Talmud study, students learn through discussion and debate about the passage they are studying, what its correct interpretation is, and how it applies in a contemporary context. Such a system of critical discussion is very powerful for understanding ideas in depth, and also for seeing their limitations. Indeed, as we have seen, one Sage, Rava, thought that we are all asked in heaven whether or not we have critically discussed wisdom (see 1:15). However, it is easy for the feelings of students and teachers to get bruised in such debate. Rules for proper conduct *(derekh eretz)* in study are vital so that everyone can progress with good feeling. Unfortunately, as the Talmud notes, scholars in the Land of Israel were very courteous—following the example of the school of Hillel—but when the center of learning moved to Babylonia, critical discussion became more brutal. Since then, the rules of courteous conduct unfortunately have been commonly violated.

In modern life, the process of discussing problems to try to get at the truth has moved from being a concern only of scholars, and has become central to personal relationships. Marriage has become an equal relationship, with flexible roles for each spouse. This means that couples must discuss what challenges they face, what is the best course of action for meeting these challenges, and who should be responsible for doing what in carrying out that course of action. Relationships between parents and teens also involve changing roles and responsibilities, going from relations based on dependence to those based on greater equality and independence. At work, employees often have more expertise about their work tasks than their bosses do, so that they need to negotiate the terms of their responsibilities and assignments. In all of these cases, disagreements are emotionally charged because each person has a stake in the outcome and the truth is important to both people involved.

After starting softly (see 4:23), the next step in crafting discussions to resolve problems is, according to modern psychologists, to listen with compassion to the other person's point of view. Compassionate listening does two critical things: it helps to reduce emotional tension and win cooperation, and it also brings to light information that may be critical to finding a good solution. The final steps in a discussion following Jewish values is to brainstorm kind and fair solutions, to assess the possible solutions, choose one, and develop a plan to implement it.

One who says:

Mine is mine and yours is yours—average
  (and some say—the character of Sodom);
Mine is yours and yours is mine—ignoramus;
Mine is yours, and yours is yours—saintly;
Yours is mine, and mine is mine—wicked. (5:13)

אַרְבַּע מִדּוֹת בָּאָדָם: הָאוֹמֵר שֶׁלִּי שֶׁלִּי וְשֶׁלְּךָ שֶׁלָּךְ–זוֹ מִדָּה בֵינוֹנִית, וְיֵשׁ
אוֹמְרִים זוֹ מִדַּת סְדוֹם. שֶׁלִּי שֶׁלָּךְ וְשֶׁלְּךָ שֶׁלִּי–עַם הָאָרֶץ, שֶׁלִּי שֶׁלָּךְ וְשֶׁלְּךָ
שֶׁלָּךְ–חָסִיד, שֶׁלְּךָ שֶׁלִּי וְשֶׁלִּי שֶׁלִּי–רָשָׁע.

Four types of temperament:

Easy to anger, easy to appease—the loss is canceled by the gain.
Hard to anger, hard to appease—the gain is canceled by the loss.
Hard to anger, easy to appease—saintly.
Easy to anger, hard to appease—wicked. (5:14)

אַרְבַּע מִדּוֹת בְּדֵעוֹת, נוֹחַ לִכְעוֹס וְנוֹחַ לִרְצוֹת–יָצָא הֶפְסֵדוֹ בִּשְׂכָרוֹ, קָשֶׁה
לִכְעוֹס וְקָשֶׁה לִרְצוֹת–יָצָא שְׂכָרוֹ בְּהֶפְסֵדוֹ, קָשֶׁה לִכְעוֹס וְנוֹחַ לִרְצוֹת–
חָסִיד, נוֹחַ לִכְעוֹס וְקָשֶׁה לִרְצוֹת–רָשָׁע.

Four types who give charity:

One wants to give, but does not want others to give—
  a bad eye on others' possessions.
One does not want to give, but wants others to give—
  a bad eye on his own possessions.
One wants to give,
  and wants others to give—saintly.
One does not want to give,
  and does not want others to give—wicked. (5:16)

אַרְבַּע מִדּוֹת בְּנוֹתְנֵי צְדָקָה, הָרוֹצֶה שֶׁיִּתֵּן וְלֹא יִתְּנוּ אֲחֵרִים–עֵינוֹ רָעָה בְּשֶׁל
אֲחֵרִים, יִתְּנוּ אֲחֵרִים וְהוּא לֹא יִתֵּן–עֵינוֹ רָעָה בְּשֶׁלּוֹ, יִתֵּן וְיִתְּנוּ אֲחֵרִים–
חָסִיד, לֹא יִתֵּן וְלֹא יִתְּנוּ אֲחֵרִים–רָשָׁע.

These texts view generosity and anger as keys to understanding character. Another such text: "By three things a person's character is revealed:

166

his cup, his purse and *his anger*; and some say, by *his laughter* also" (ER 65b). In Hebrew, the three things alliterate and rhyme: *koso, kiso, ka'aso.*

Mine is mine. The medieval commentators explain the comment "the character of Sodom" as follows: the "average" person avoids charity, and lack of charity was one of the characteristics of Sodom (EZEK 16:49).

Easy to anger. The Hebrew here for "types," *midot*, literally means "measures." The medieval commentator Rabbi Shimon ben Tzemaḥ said that these types of temperaments are not fixed, but rather are qualities that we have the power to improve or to make worse. A new feature of this mishnah is that it sees the quality of being easily placated, of letting go of anger, as a virtue in itself.

One wants to give. The "bad eye" means, as noted earlier, being stingy or looking at others with envy. As Maimonides points out, the interesting new idea in this mishnah is that it is best for a person not only to be generous, but also to promote an attitude of, and the practice of, generosity among others.

MODERN LIFE

THE CHARACTER of Sodom. A charitable attitude between people and a ready willingness to give charity are, in the view of some Sages, qualities that mark the difference between a good society and a bad one.

This thought-provoking aside on the importance of generosity has echoes throughout *Avot*. In *Avot* 2:13, Rabbi Eliezer says that the key to following a good path in life is "a good eye"—an open and generous nature. The good eye is closely connected to other Rabbinic values: we should be in the habit of judging others charitably (2:13); we should be "a good friend, a good neighbor," have a "good heart," and should "receive every person with joy" (3:16). The "bad eye," a possessive and envious nature, is condemned here (5:16), and indeed is said in an earlier text to "drive a person out of the world" (2:16).

The thread running through all of these sayings seems to be an awareness that there are critical moments when we can turn one way or the other: we can become suspicious and defensive, or keep our generous instincts alive and nurture them. This moment of choice is a point where people turn to either the *yetzer ha-ra*, "the bad inclination," or the *yetzer ha-tov,* "the good inclination." We can recognize the face of the good inclination by the openness and generosity it inspires.

FOUR CHARACTERS IN STUDENTS:

Quick to understand and quick to forget—
their gain is canceled by their loss.
Slow to understand and slow to forget—
their loss is canceled by their gain.
Quick to understand and slow to forget—
wise.
Slow to understand and quick to forget—
this is a misfortune. (5:15)

אַרְבַּע מִדּוֹת בְּתַלְמִידִים: מָהִיר לִשְׁמֹעַ וּמָהִיר לְאַבֵּד–יָצָא שְׂכָרוֹ בְּהֶפְסֵדוֹ,
קָשֶׁה לִשְׁמֹעַ וְקָשֶׁה לְאַבֵּד–יָצָא הֶפְסֵדוֹ בִּשְׂכָרוֹ, מָהִיר לִשְׁמֹעַ וְקָשֶׁה
לְאַבֵּד–זֶה חֵלֶק טוֹב, קָשֶׁה לִשְׁמֹעַ וּמָהִיר לְאַבֵּד–זֶה חֵלֶק רָע.

FOUR TYPES WHO GO TO THE HOUSE OF STUDY:

Those who attend, but do not practice—
they have the reward for attending.
Those who practice, but do not attend—
they have the reward for practice.
Those who attend and practice—saintly.
Those who neither attend nor practice—wicked. (5:17)

אַרְבַּע מִדּוֹת בְּהוֹלְכֵי בֵית הַמִּדְרָשׁ, הוֹלֵךְ וְאֵינוֹ עֹשֶׂה–שְׂכַר הֲלִיכָה בְּיָדוֹ,
עֹשֶׂה וְאֵינוֹ הוֹלֵךְ שְׂכַר מַעֲשֶׂה בְּיָדוֹ, הוֹלֵךְ וְעֹשֶׂה–חָסִיד, לֹא הוֹלֵךְ וְלֹא
עֹשֶׂה–רָשָׁע.

FOUR TYPES WHO SIT BEFORE THE WISE:

A sponge, a funnel, a strainer, and a sifter.
The sponge soaks up everything.
The funnel takes in at one end and lets out at the other.
The strainer lets out the wine, and keeps the dregs.
The sifter lets out the meal, and keeps the fine flour. (5:18)

אַרְבַּע מִדּוֹת בְּיוֹשְׁבִים לִפְנֵי חֲכָמִים: סְפוֹג, וּמַשְׁפֵּךְ מְשַׁמֶּרֶת, וְנָפָה. סְפוֹג,
שֶׁהוּא סוֹפֵג אֶת הַכֹּל; וּמַשְׁפֵּךְ, שֶׁמַּכְנִיס בְּזוֹ וּמוֹצִיא בְזוֹ; מְשַׁמֶּרֶת, שֶׁמּוֹצִיאָה
אֶת הַיַּיִן וְקוֹלֶטֶת אֶת הַשְּׁמָרִים; וְנָפָה, שֶׁמּוֹצִיאָה אֶת הַקֶּמַח וְקוֹלֶטֶת אֶת
הַסֹּלֶת.

THESE EXPLORE the qualities of good students—particularly interesting because Judaism established the first mass education system (BB 12a).

Quick to understand. Students were supposed to understand before memorizing, but memorization—and remembering exactly what your teachers said—was an important part of traditional Jewish education. The Oral Torah, including the sayings in this book, was originally memorized by students, and continued to be even after it was written down. The Talmud provides mnemonic devices to aid memorization.

Those who attend. "Practice" here means applying what you have learned in daily life through acts of kindness and justice. It is characteristic of the Rabbinic outlook that studying in itself is a merit.

The sponge soaks. Joseph ben Judah ibn Aknin, medieval commentator on *Avot*, says of these four types, "The first is a simpleton, the second is a fool, the third has an evil portion, and the fourth is wise."

The ability to judge what is important and to apply concepts in practice are greatly influenced by a student's attitude, by his or her goal in studying. In *Avot de-Rabbi Natan,* a commentary (ch. 40) says that what distinguishes the good student from the poor student is whether the student is truly interested in listening and learning, or is merely learning for the sake of getting ahead, for prestige. In my observation, a student's interest in applying ideas is also of critical importance.

MODERN LIFE
THE STUDENT who studies the practical application of concepts is more likely to get a good understanding of them, and particularly of their strengths and weaknesses—or in the terms used here, is more likely to be a "sifter" than a "sponge." The talmudic style of study, which is focused on applying ethical and legal ideas to case studies, if done correctly, fosters such a practical understanding.

To "add," as Hillel would have us do (*Avot* 1:13), students also need to bring into their inquiry their own life experiences and goals, and see how past ideas apply in their own generation. In other words, they need to have intellectual goals and problems that interest them, and to nurture their interests. Individuals growing up and interacting with their world are the wellspring of progress in every field. Our current educational system too often pours water on that precious spark of individuality; students must resist such forces for progress to be made.

> *All love that is dependent on a particular thing,*
> *when the thing ceases, the love ceases.*
> *All love that isn't dependent on a particular thing,*
> *it will never cease.*
> *Which is a love dependent on a particular thing?*
> *The love of Amnon and Tamar.*
> *Which is a love not dependent on a particular thing?*
> *The love of David and Jonathan. (5:19)*

כָּל אַהֲבָה שֶׁהִיא תְלוּיָה בְדָבָר, בָּטֵל דָּבָר בְּטֵלָה אַהֲבָה, וְשֶׁאֵינָה תְלוּיָה
בְדָבָר, אֵינָהּ בְּטֵלָה לְעוֹלָם. אֵיזוֹ הִיא אַהֲבָה שֶׁהִיא תְלוּיָה בְדָבָר? זוֹ אַהֲבַת
אַמְנוֹן וְתָמָר, וְשֶׁאֵינָהּ תְלוּיָה בְדָבָר? זוֹ אַהֲבַת דָּוִד וִיהוֹנָתָן.

AMNON AND Tamar. Amnon was the eldest son of King David. He became love-sick from desire for his half-sister Tamar. Feigning real illness, he lured her into his bedroom alone and raped her. Then, his love turned into great hatred, and "his loathing for her was greater than the passion he had felt for her" (II SAM 13:15).

David and Jonathan. David and Jonathan were comrades in battles against the Philistines. "The soul of Jonathan was knit with the soul of David, and Jonathan loved him as his own soul" (I SAM 1:18). They made a pact of friendship, and Jonathan gave his sword to David for battle. When King Saul, Jonathan's father, turned against David, Jonathan protected his friend. When Jonathan was killed in battle, David lamented, "My brother Jonathan, you were most dear to me. Your love was wonderful to me more than the love of women" (II SAM 1:26). Later, as king, David took care of Jonathan's crippled son and all of his descendents.

Dependent on a particular thing. The particular thing love can depend on can be, for example, an object of lust or a possession. Love will die when that object is not available. What kind of love is "not dependent on a particular thing?" David and Jonathan show a loyalty that transcends any personal advantage. Jonathan was willing to shield David from his own father's unjust wrath and vengeance, though his father was king, making such devotion a big risk for Jonathan. David took care of Jonathan's descendants, though Jonathan was dead and thus could not possibly reward him.

The two contrasting stories could exemplify Aristotle's distinction between friendships based on pleasure or advantage and friendships based on virtue and the mutual pursuit of the good. Jewish commentators, however, say that enduring love is based on goals that are "for the sake of Heaven." For example, the medieval commentator Joseph ben Judah ibn Aknin says that when a disciple loves his master in order to learn from him, or when scholars love to come together to study, such love will endure. Wisdom is "for the sake of Heaven" and never vanishes. In his commentary on this mishnah, Maimonides characteristically adds an Aristotelian twist, viewing every physical cause of love as transient, whereas, "If the cause of the love is a Godly matter, true knowledge, it is impossible that this love will ever be nullified, for its cause exists eternally."

MODERN LIFE

SEVENTEENTH-CENTURY philosopher Baruch Spinoza, the first "modern" in religious thought, built a whole philosophy of life on this mishnah, and on Maimonides' interpretation of it. He sought a way to "continuous, supreme, and unending happiness." According to the system he arrived at, everything is an aspect of God. When we attach our love to a particular person or place, we are bound to be disappointed, because people and things change. What we love in the person and place is, however, actually a part of God, and God is its cause. If we have true understanding, we will shift all of our love to God, who is eternal. This "intellectual love of God" gives supreme, unending happiness.

Spinoza's system reflects the mystic's disillusionment with the mundane and hunger for the infinite. Yet, as Rabbi Abraham Joshua Heschel pointed out, Judaism treasures and sanctifies time. Kohelet wrote, "God has made everything beautiful in its time" (ECCL 3:11). The love of a particular woman or man is sanctified by marriage. And seeing a beautiful sunset is noted with a blessing. For the Sages, the transient too is sacred.

Our love is, as a rule, neither merely the momentary passion of Amnon, nor the purely disinterested model of David and Jonathan, but rather partakes of both. Indeed, the more a moment becomes detached from what endures, the more it becomes meaningless; and eternity detached from life as it is lived is cold and indifferent. We find meaning in the wedding of hope and memory, the kiss of the moment.

On Controversy:

> *Any controversy for the sake of Heaven*
> *will in the end be preserved;*
> *And that not for the sake of Heaven*
> *will not in the end be preserved. (5:20)*

כָּל מַחֲלוֹקֶת שֶׁהִיא לְשֵׁם שָׁמַיִם סוֹפָהּ לְהִתְקַיֵּם, וְשֶׁאֵינָהּ לְשֵׁם שָׁמַיִם אֵין
סוֹפָהּ לְהִתְקַיֵּם, אֵיזוֹ הִיא מַחֲלוֹקֶת שֶׁהִיא לְשֵׁם שָׁמַיִם? זוֹ מַחֲלוֹקֶת הִלֵּל
וְשַׁמַּאי, וְשֶׁאֵינָהּ לְשֵׁם שָׁמַיִם? זוֹ מַחֲלוֹקֶת קֹרַח וְכָל עֲדָתוֹ.

Rabbi Yoḥanan HaSandlar:

> *Every assembly which is for the sake of*
> *Heaven will in the end be preserved;*
> *And those not for the sake of Heaven*
> *will not in the end be preserved. (4:14)*

רַבִּי יוֹחָנָן הַסַּנְדְּלָר אוֹמֵר: כָּל כְּנֵסִיָּה שֶׁהִיא לְשֵׁם שָׁמַיִם, סוֹפָהּ לְהִתְקַיֵּם,
וְשֶׁאֵינָהּ לְשֵׁם שָׁמַיִם, אֵין סוֹפָהּ לְהִתְקַיֵּם.

THE HEBREW of the first of these *mishnayot* continues with this discussion: "Which is a controversy for the sake of Heaven? That of Hillel and Shammai. Which is a controversy not for the sake of Heaven? That of Koraḥ and all his band [with Moses]."

Koraḥ and his followers rebelled against Moses' religious authority, and wanted to usurp it (NUM 16). Koraḥ's goal was personal power, rather than uncovering truths that would help the community at large. His rebellion also illustrates an assembly that is not "for the sake of Heaven." He did not argue for a point of view, but just tried to grab power. In the end, he and his band were punished when the earth opened up and swallowed them alive. The story of Koraḥ also illustrates that the critical tradition within Judaism was limited, as its starting point was an acceptance of the authority of Torah—even though the correct interpretation of Torah is left open to debate.

The example of Hillel and Shammai is not only an illustration, but also a historically important influence. The Talmud reports that there was a long running dispute between the followers of Hillel and Shammai. After three years a divine voice went forth saying:

☙ "These and these are indeed words of the living God, but *halakhah* follows the *Beit Hillel*." . . . For the *Beit Hillel* were gentle and modest, and studied both their opinions and those of the other school, and humbly mentioned the words of the other school before their own. (ER 13b)

As Menachem Fisch points out in *Rational Rabbis* (pp. 210–11), in nearly half of the disputes where the *Beit Shammai* (school of Shammai) had the last word, the *Beit Hillel* (school of Hillel) accepted the views of the *Beit Shammai*. But where the *Beit Hillel* had the last word, the *Beit Shammai* was not willing to accept the views of the *Beit Hillel* on a single issue. This key difference between the *Beit Hillel* and *Beit Shammai* dramatically illustrates that, for a critical tradition to be successful, those disagreeing must have not only the humility to listen to differing viewpoints, but also a willingness to change. Only then is the commitment to openness real, and can the critical tradition be kept alive. Lacking critical dialogue and creative responses to it, traditions tend to become rigid, stale, and unproductive.

MODERN LIFE

RECORDING AND studying contrary opinions is, according to Karl Popper, the defining characteristic of the critical tradition. He wrote that, for the first time in history, the pre-Socratic Greek philosophers actually discussed one another's differing theories without trying to suppress the opposition. The critical tradition matured through Socrates' view that argument is a way to arrive at the truth. This Socratic tradition profoundly influenced Judaism in Hellenistic times. (We do not see it in the Hebrew Bible.) The critical tradition is, Popper noted, key to the growth of science and to democratic social change. It is one of the great advances in the history of humanity. Within Jewish tradition, it has been the means of keeping a far-flung community both unified and evolving.

Avot 5:20 clearly sets the standard for Jewish studies being a critical tradition. For it says that minority opinions are also sacred and so they should be preserved. Thus, the Talmud not only records minority opinions, but also frequently leaves debates unresolved, anticipating further discussion and discovery. Menachem Fisch argues in *Rational Rabbis* that the Talmud also allows for changing past rulings. In other words, the next generation may discover something new, and a minority view may become the majority one. In the Middle Ages, Jewish tradition became less critical and more conservative, not permitting reversals of tradition. In modern times, however, we now have the opportunity to return to the more dynamic approach of the Sages of the Talmud.

ON MORAL LEADERSHIP:

Those who lead multitudes to virtue,
no sin will come through them.
Those who lead multitudes to sin, they will never be able
to do enough to make repentance. (5:21)

כָּל הַמְזַכֶּה אֶת הָרַבִּים, אֵין חֵטְא בָּא עַל יָדוֹ, וְכָל הַמַּחֲטִיא אֶת הָרַבִּים אֵין
מַסְפִּיקִין בְּיָדוֹ לַעֲשׂוֹת תְּשׁוּבָה. מֹשֶׁה זָכָה וְזִכָּה אֶת הָרַבִּים, זְכוּת הָרַבִּים
תָּלוּי בּוֹ, שֶׁנֶּאֱמַר: "צִדְקַת יְיָ עָשָׂה וּמִשְׁפָּטָיו עִם יִשְׂרָאֵל." יָרְבְעָם בֶּן נְבָט
חָטָא וְהֶחֱטִיא אֶת הָרַבִּים חֵטְא הָרַבִּים תָּלוּי בּוֹ, שֶׁנֶּאֱמַר: "עַל חַטֹּאת יָרְבְעָם
אֲשֶׁר חָטָא וַאֲשֶׁר הֶחֱטִיא אֶת יִשְׂרָאֵל."

RABBI MATIA BEN ḤARASH:

Be the first to greet every person;
And be a tail to lions, not a head to jackals. (4:20)

רַבִּי מַתְיָא בֶּן חָרָשׁ אוֹמֵר: הֱוֵי מַקְדִּים בִּשְׁלוֹם כָּל אָדָם, וֶהֱוֵי זָנָב לָאֲרָיוֹת,
וְאַל תְּהִי רֹאשׁ לַשֻּׁעָלִים.

THE FIRST mishnah continues with this explanation, with prooftexts included:

ɠ Moses was virtuous, led many to virtue, and the merit of the many is credited to him. As it is said: "He performed God's righteousness, and God's
ordinances together with Israel" (DEUT 33:21). Jeroboam, the son of Nebat,
sinned, caused many to sin, and he was blamed for the sins of the many. As
it is said: "For the sins of Jeroboam that he committed, and that he caused
Israel to commit" (1 KINGS 15:30).

Jeroboam was the king instrumental in splitting the united kingdom
of Solomon into the two kingdoms of Israel and Judah, the former led
by him, and the latter by Rehoboam, the son of Solomon. He also caused
his subjects to worship idols—two golden calves—and ordained many
priests to worship them. He did not repent, and his whole house suffered "annihilation from the face of the earth" (1 KINGS 13:33–34). The
kingdom of Israel eventually dissolved without a legacy, whereas Judah
endured and its legacy is today's Jewish people.

Be a tail to lions. This mishnah—the inverse of a popular Roman saying—relates to the choices we have as to whether to join ethical organizations or corrupt ones where we think we can get ahead. The jackal,

which follows the lion and scavenges its kill, is, like the lion, a social animal that lives in packs that have leaders. Better to be a follower in an organization with integrity and moral leadership, says Rabbi Matia ben Ḥarash, than a leader in a corrupt one.

MODERN LIFE

Those who lead multitudes to virtue. The concept in this mishnah is that we need to think not only about whether what we do is right, but also about the ennobling or corrupting effect that our actions can have on other people. Adults are normally in a position of having some power over others (customer, employee, child) and so are, in some aspect of their lives, leaders. In this day, when large organizations are prevalent, we regularly see the great power that leaders have for moral good or ill. When a leader makes decisions fairly on the bases of the goals of the organization and of respect for the needs of individuals, it sends a powerful message to subordinates. It says: "The way to get ahead in this organization is to serve its goals and respect others." Your advancement will be according to your contribution. If a leader is instead self-serving, putting his or her own selfish goals above serving the goals of the organization and respecting others, then it also sends a powerful message: "As long as you help me, by whatever means, I will reward you."

These messages propagate ethical behavior or corruption throughout an organization. With moral leadership, immediate subordinates will know that the way to get ahead is to be honest and do quality work. They will in turn ask the same from their subordinates, as that will help deliver for their boss and the organization as a whole. With corrupt leadership, the subordinates will know that the way ahead is to serve the personal needs of the boss, using lies and flattery, if need be. And again, this will propagate itself downward through the organization, putting corrupting pressures on everyone in it.

Those who lead multitudes to sin. A person who causes many others to sin, such as an unethical leader, will never be able to repair wrongs done by the many he or she has influenced, and hence will never able to do enough to make repentance. Of course, whether or not people are corrupt depends on them, as well as on their leaders. Still, the reality is that bad leaders bring out the worst in people, and good leaders bring out the best.

THREE QUALITIES:

All who possess these three things,
praise as disciples of our father Abraham.
But if these three other things,
they are disciples of the wicked Balaam.
A good eye, a humble spirit, and a forbearing soul—
a disciple of our father Abraham.
A bad eye, a haughty spirit, and a greedy soul—
a disciple of the wicked Balaam. (5:22)

כָּל מִי שֶׁיֵּשׁ בּוֹ שְׁלשָׁה דְבָרִים הַלָּלוּ, הוּא מִתַּלְמִידָיו שֶׁל אַבְרָהָם אָבִינוּ,
וּשְׁלשָׁה דְבָרִים אֲחֵרִים, הוּא מִתַּלְמִידָיו שֶׁל בִּלְעָם הָרָשָׁע: עַיִן טוֹבָה, וְרוּחַ
נְמוּכָה, וְנֶפֶשׁ שְׁפָלָה–תַּלְמִידָיו שֶׁל אַבְרָהָם אָבִינוּ; עַיִן רָעָה, וְרוּחַ גְּבוֹהָה,
וְנֶפֶשׁ רְחָבָה–תַּלְמִידָיו שֶׁל בִּלְעָם הָרָשָׁע, מַה בֵּין תַּלְמִידָיו שֶׁל אַבְרָהָם
אָבִינוּ לְתַלְמִידָיו שֶׁל בִּלְעָם הָרָשָׁע? תַּלְמִידָיו שֶׁל אַבְרָהָם אָבִינוּ אוֹכְלִין
בָּעוֹלָם הַזֶּה וְנוֹחֲלִין הָעוֹלָם הַבָּא, שֶׁנֶּאֱמַר: "לְהַנְחִיל אֹהֲבַי יֵשׁ וְאוֹצְרוֹתֵיהֶם
אֲמַלֵּא," אֲבָל תַּלְמִידָיו שֶׁל בִּלְעָם הָרָשָׁע יוֹרְשִׁין גֵּיהִנֹּם וְיוֹרְדִין לִבְאֵר שַׁחַת,
שֶׁנֶּאֱמַר: "וְאַתָּה אֱלֹהִים תּוֹרִדֵם לִבְאֵר שַׁחַת אַנְשֵׁי דָמִים וּמִרְמָה לֹא יֶחֱצוּ
יְמֵיהֶם וַאֲנִי אֶבְטַח בָּךְ."

THIS MISHNAH continues with a warning about the different rewards and punishments for the followers of Abraham and of Balaam:

What is the difference between the disciples of our father Abraham, and the disciples of the wicked Balaam? The disciples of our father Abraham enjoy this world and inherit the world to come. As it is said: "That I may cause those who love me to inherit substance, and that I may fill their treasuries" (PROV 8:21). The disciples of wicked Balaam inherit Gehinnom and descend to the deepest pit. As it is said: "For you, O God, will bring them down to the nethermost pit—those murderous, treacherous people; they will not live out half their days; but I will trust in you" (PS 55:24).

A good eye. As discussed in conjunction with *Avot* 2:13, "a good eye" means a generous nature: liberal in giving, not envious of others' possessions, and content with one's lot in life. The opposite, "a bad eye," in its non-superstitious version, means a grasping, envious, possessive nature.

A forbearing soul. The Hebrew here for "forbearing soul," *nefesh she-falah*, literally means "lowly soul (or spirit)." How is this different from the second trait, *ruaḥ nemukha*, "humble spirit?" The interpretation here

176

of "forbearing soul," following that of traditional commentators, is based on the contrast with the negative trait, "a greedy soul." A "forbearing soul," then, means having the restraint and self-control not to demand too much pleasure, status, power, and so on.

As noted earlier (*Avot* 1:2), there is another list of three character traits that are said to be signs of "membership in the Jewish nation: compassion, modesty, and acts of kindness" (YEV 79a). The parallels between that list and the one in this mishnah are interesting: compassion and a generous spirit—a good eye—are of a piece. Next, modesty and humility are also closely related. Finally, our willingness to do acts of kindness and restraint from greed seem to spring from the same source.

MODERN LIFE

THE TRAITS listed here as praiseworthy all run counter to the acquisitive pressures of modern commercial societies. A person with a "good eye," who takes pleasure in giving, is content with what they have, and is not envious of others, is not the best "mark" for advertisers.

Early in the 20th century, American philosopher William James wrote critically that Americans worship the "bitch goddess success." He meant "success" in a crass, monetary sense. A century earlier, at the beginning of the modern capitalist era, the Ḥasidic Rabbi Naḥman of Breslav wrote in similar terms of the devotion to money as a false god:

&❧ Money-worship, like idol worship stems from a lack of trust in God. The more it is uprooted, the more the world radiates with the blessing of the Holy One's love. (*ADVICE*, p. 139)

Rabbi Naḥman is not condemning wealth itself here, for Judaism does not have a tradition of holy poverty. There were, for example, annual prayers for prosperity at Rosh Hashanah in the ancient Temple. He is, rather, condemning money as an idol, and making money a prime goal in life instead of a means.

Interestingly, Rabbi Naḥman links money worship to anxiety about our future. If we do honest work and follow the other ethical commandments, then we need to trust that we will not see want. When we let go of desperate anxiety about money, it will change us, he believes, in a fundamental way: we will be open to feeling the radiant blessing of God's love. Of course, Rabbi Naḥman accepted the "old time religion" of Rabbi Akiva's God who listens and judges. But I think he speaks to us even if we have a more modern sense of the *shekhinah*.

Yehudah ben Teima:

At age five, ready for Scripture;
Age ten, for Mishnah; age thirteen, for mitzvot;
Age fifteen, for Talmud; age eighteen, for marriage;
Age twenty, for career; age thirty, for might;
Age forty, for understanding; age fifty, for giving counsel;
Age sixty, for old age; age seventy, for white hair;
Age eighty, for valor; age ninety, for bent back;
Age one hundred, as if dead,
   and already passed from the world. (5:24)

הוּא הָיָה אוֹמֵר: בֶּן חָמֵשׁ שָׁנִים לַמִּקְרָא, בֶּן עֶשֶׂר שָׁנִים לַמִּשְׁנָה, בֶּן שְׁלֹשׁ עֶשְׂרֵה xx לַמִּצְוֹת, בֶּן חֲמֵשׁ עֶשְׂרֵה לַגְּמָרָא, בֶּן שְׁמוֹנָה עֶשְׂרֵה לַחֻפָּה, בֶּן עֶשְׂרִים לִרְדּוֹף, בֶּן שְׁלֹשִׁים לַכֹּחַ, בֶּן אַרְבָּעִים לַבִּינָה, בֶּן חֲמִשִּׁים לָעֵצָה, בֶּן שִׁשִּׁים לְזִקְנָה, בֶּן שִׁבְעִים לְשֵׂיבָה, בֶּן שְׁמוֹנִים לִגְבוּרָה, בֶּן תִּשְׁעִים לָשׁוּחַ, בֶּן מֵאָה כְּאִלּוּ מֵת וְעָבַר וּבָטֵל מִן הָעוֹלָם:

This early version of Shakespeare's "ages of man" (*As You Like It*, II.7) is revealing both for how life has changed in 2000 years, and how it has not.

At age five, ready for Scripture. The youngest students are ready to study the Bible in Hebrew. After these beginning stages, Bible is studied through the lens of Talmud—the real meat of traditional studies.

Age thirteen, for mitzvot. This is the first mention of 13 as the age when a Jew is responsible for fulfilling the mitzvot—both the ethical and the ritual mitzvot—the bar mitzvah. Chapter 16 of *Avot de-Rabbi Natan* says that at age 13, a person has strong *yetzer ha-tov*, good impulses, as well as *yetzer ha-ra*, bad impulses—and so he or she can make free moral choices. Hence, this is the age of moral responsibility.

Modern Life

Age eighteen, for marriage. Of all the changes in personal relationships in the 2000 years since the time of the Sages, the changes in marriage in the past century are probably the most significant. The basic social changes have been: effective contraception; acceptance of the ideal of equal power between husband and wife; self-chosen matches, rather than arranged marriages; and greater opportunity for paid employment for women, including those who are unmarried.

178

These changes have fundamentally altered the conditions for marriage. Sexual partnership is possible without resulting in the conception of children. The economic benefits of marriage are no longer so vital to women. And women have gained more decision-making power in marriage. The results have been a reduction in family size, a great increase in the divorce rate, marriage at later ages (an average of up to 10 years later than the 18 years of age mentioned here), having multiple sexual partners before marriage, and widespread cohabitation before marriage.

When the full impact of these changes was first felt in the 1970s, it became fashionable to believe that there was no conflict of interest between parents and children on the issue of divorce. Children, it was thought, would be better off with divorced parents than with unhappy parents, so that both parents and children would benefit from divorce.

This consensus was first challenged in 1989 in Judith Wallerstein's *Second Chances*, which found that divorce had left deep scars on all children past infancy, and a significant number of those children performed worse socially and academically than children of intact marriages. Paul Amato subsequently found that in the case of divorce from "high-conflict" marriages (one-third of divorces in the United States), children were on average better off, but that in cases of divorce from low-conflict marriages (two-thirds of divorces), children were significantly worse off. While only a minority of children of divorce suffer major social or psychological problems, the percentage who suffer these problems is still double that of children raised in intact marriages. And the damage to children of the never-married is yet higher. Thus, traditional marriage has proven to be still by far the best institution for the welfare of children.

In Judaism, the rabbis interpreted "be fertile and increase" (GEN 1:22) as a commandment to marry and have children. One of the effects of contraception and late marriage has been a decline in the Jewish birthrate outside those families following the traditional, Orthodox pattern.

Marriage is thus caught between conflicting forces. The widespread desire for greater options in the areas of sexuality and childbearing supports current patterns, but the harm done to children militates against them. It is clear that we are in a time of great change for marriage. In 100 years, this period will be looked upon as one of transition to a new pattern of courtship, marriage, and family. Traditional marriage, though, still seems destined to remain the central institution around which the Jewish family will be built and Jewish children will be raised.

Turn it and turn it, for all is in it.
Reflect on it, grow old and gray with it, and do not leave it,
For you will have no better guide than it. (5:25)

בֶּן בַּג בַּג אוֹמֵר: הֲפָךְ בָּהּ וַהֲפָךְ בָּהּ דְּכֹלָּא בָהּ, וּבָהּ תֶּחֱזֵי וְסִיב וּבְלֵה בָהּ,
וּמִנָּהּ לָא תָזוּעַ, שֶׁאֵין לְךָ מִדָּה טוֹבָה הֵימֶנָּה.

Ben Hei Hei:

As the travail, so the reward. (5:26)

בֶּן הֵא הֵא אוֹמֵר: לְפוּם צַעֲרָא אַגְרָא.

THESE SAYINGS (in Aramaic) are attributed to Hillel in *Avot de-Rabbi Natan*, chapter 12. A number of commentators speculate that the names here, Ben Bag Bag and Ben Hei Hei, are acronyms, but it is not clear whom they refer to.

As the travail. "Travail" translates the Hebrew *tza'ara*, meaning troubles and pains that one has to endure in the struggles of life. Benjamin Franklin later put it this way: "No gains without pains" (*Poor Richard's Almanack*, 1745). Spinoza, at the end of his monumental *Ethics*, in apologizing for the difficulty of the work, said, "All things excellent are as difficult as they are rare." This is, alas, all too often confirmed. The promise in this mishnah is that if you put in the toil, it will make a difference. The travail and the reward refers no doubt to the effort of Torah study and its rewards, but it seems to hold equally for other efforts and their rewards, as well.

MODERN LIFE

TURN IT and turn it. Contrary to Ecclesiastes 1:9, there are, in fact, things "new under the sun:" airplanes, telephones, representative democracy, capitalism, contraception, computers, and so on. However, human nature has not changed since the time of the Talmud, and in fact, the Torah and the Talmud do enlighten us on almost every facet of human nature. Hopefully, the process of development of Jewish tradition, and of Oral Torah, is not done, and its guidance for our lives will become ever stronger. Then every new generation will turn anew for guidance to: "Moses received Torah from Sinai, and passed it on ..."

Appendices

Avot: Complete Text

THE FOLLOWING is the complete Hebrew text and English translation of *Avot* in traditional order. The *mishnayot* that appear out of order in the main text have their page numbers indicated in brackets. *Mishnayot* 5:1–8 and 5:12 are marked with an asterisk * to indicate that they are not included in the main text with the commentaries.

For completeness, the supplemental chapter *Kinyan Torah*, Chapter 6 to *Pirke Avot* in the siddur, follows, with a brief introduction.

THE FOLLOWING passages from the Talmud are traditionally recited before and after reading a chapter of *Pirke Avot* on Shabbat.

Before:

כָּל יִשְׂרָאֵל יֵשׁ לָהֶם חֵלֶק לָעוֹלָם הַבָּא, שֶׁנֶּאֱמַר: וְעַמֵּךְ כֻּלָּם
צַדִּיקִים לְעוֹלָם יִירְשׁוּ אָרֶץ. נֵצֶר מַטָּעַי מַעֲשֵׂה יָדַי לְהִתְפָּאֵר.

All Israel has a portion in the world to come. As it is said (IS 60:21): "And your people, all of them righteous, shall possess the land for all time. They are the shoot that I planted, my handiwork in which I glory." (SAN 90a)

After:

רַבִּי חֲנַנְיָא בֶּן עֲקַשְׁיָא אוֹמֵר, רָצָה הַקָּדוֹשׁ בָּרוּךְ הוּא לְזַכּוֹת אֶת
יִשְׂרָאֵל, לְפִיכָךְ הִרְבָּה לָהֶם תּוֹרָה וּמִצְוֹת, שֶׁנֶּאֱמַר: יְיָ חָפֵץ לְמַעַן
צִדְקוֹ יַגְדִּיל תּוֹרָה וְיַאְדִּיר.

Rabbi Ḥananiah ben Akashia said: The Holy One, blessed be He, wanted to make Israel worthy. Therefore He gave them a copious Torah and commandments. As it is said (IS 42:21): "The Lord was pleased, for the sake of its righteousness, to make the Torah great and glorious." (MAK 32b)

אבות: פרק א

א. מֹשֶׁה קִבֵּל תּוֹרָה מִסִּינַי וּמְסָרָהּ לִיהוֹשֻׁעַ, וִיהוֹשֻׁעַ לִזְקֵנִים, וּזְקֵנִים לִנְבִיאִים, וּנְבִיאִים מְסָרוּהָ לְאַנְשֵׁי כְנֶסֶת הַגְּדוֹלָה. הֵם אָמְרוּ שְׁלֹשָׁה דְבָרִים: הֱווּ מְתוּנִים בַּדִּין, וְהַעֲמִידוּ תַלְמִידִים הַרְבֵּה, וַעֲשׂוּ סְיָג לַתּוֹרָה.

ב. שִׁמְעוֹן הַצַּדִּיק הָיָה מִשְּׁיָרֵי כְנֶסֶת הַגְּדוֹלָה. הוּא הָיָה אוֹמֵר: עַל שְׁלֹשָׁה דְבָרִים הָעוֹלָם עוֹמֵד עַל הַתּוֹרָה, וְעַל הָעֲבוֹדָה, וְעַל גְּמִילוּת חֲסָדִים.

ג. אַנְטִיגְנוֹס אִישׁ סוֹכוֹ קִבֵּל מִשִּׁמְעוֹן הַצַּדִּיק. הוּא הָיָה אוֹמֵר: אַל תִּהְיוּ כַּעֲבָדִים הַמְשַׁמְּשִׁין אֶת הָרַב עַל מְנָת לְקַבֵּל פְּרָס, אֶלָּא הֱווּ כַּעֲבָדִים, הַמְשַׁמְּשִׁין אֶת הָרַב שֶׁלֹּא עַל מְנָת לְקַבֵּל פְּרָס, וִיהִי מוֹרָא שָׁמַיִם עֲלֵיכֶם.

ד. יוֹסֵי בֶּן יוֹעֶזֶר אִישׁ צְרֵדָה וְיוֹסֵי בֶּן יוֹחָנָן אִישׁ יְרוּשָׁלַיִם קִבְּלוּ מֵהֶם. יוֹסֵי בֶּן יוֹעֶזֶר אִישׁ צְרֵדָה אוֹמֵר: יְהִי בֵיתְךָ בֵּית וַעַד לַחֲכָמִים, וֶהֱוֵי מִתְאַבֵּק בַּעֲפַר רַגְלֵיהֶם, וֶהֱוֵי שׁוֹתֶה בַצָּמָא אֶת דִּבְרֵיהֶם.

ה. יוֹסֵי בֶּן יוֹחָנָן אִישׁ יְרוּשָׁלַיִם אוֹמֵר: יְהִי בֵיתְךָ פָּתוּחַ לָרְוָחָה, וְיִהְיוּ עֲנִיִּים בְּנֵי בֵיתֶךָ, וְאַל תַּרְבֶּה שִׂיחָה עִם הָאִשָּׁה. בְּאִשְׁתּוֹ אָמְרוּ, קַל וָחֹמֶר בְּאֵשֶׁת חֲבֵרוֹ. מִכָּאן אָמְרוּ חֲכָמִים: כָּל הַמַּרְבֶּה שִׂיחָה עִם הָאִשָּׁה–גּוֹרֵם רָעָה לְעַצְמוֹ, וּבוֹטֵל מִדִּבְרֵי תוֹרָה, וְסוֹפוֹ יוֹרֵשׁ גֵּיהִנָּם.

ו. יְהוֹשֻׁעַ בֶּן פְּרַחְיָה וְנִתַּאי הָאַרְבֵּלִי קִבְּלוּ מֵהֶם. יְהוֹשֻׁעַ בֶּן פְּרַחְיָה אוֹמֵר: עֲשֵׂה לְךָ רַב, וּקְנֵה לְךָ חָבֵר, וֶהֱוֵי דָן אֶת כָּל הָאָדָם לְכַף זְכוּת.

ז. נִתַּאי הָאַרְבֵּלִי אוֹמֵר: הַרְחֵק מִשָּׁכֵן רָע, וְאַל תִּתְחַבֵּר לָרָשָׁע, וְאַל תִּתְיָאֵשׁ מִן הַפּוּרְעָנוּת.

ח. יְהוּדָה בֶּן טַבַּאי וְשִׁמְעוֹן בֶּן שָׁטַח קִבְּלוּ מֵהֶם. יְהוּדָה בֶּן טַבַּאי אוֹמֵר: אַל תַּעַשׂ עַצְמְךָ כְּעוֹרְכֵי הַדַּיָּנִין, וּכְשֶׁיִּהְיוּ בַּעֲלֵי הַדִּין עוֹמְדִים לְפָנֶיךָ, יִהְיוּ בְעֵינֶיךָ כִּרְשָׁעִים, וּכְשֶׁנִּפְטָרִים מִלְּפָנֶיךָ, יִהְיוּ בְעֵינֶיךָ כְּזַכָּאִין כְּשֶׁקִּבְּלוּ עֲלֵיהֶם אֶת הַדִּין.

ט. שִׁמְעוֹן בֶּן שָׁטַח אוֹמֵר: הֱוֵי מַרְבֶּה לַחֲקוֹר אֶת הָעֵדִים, וֶהֱוֵי זָהִיר בִּדְבָרֶיךָ, שֶׁמָּא מִתּוֹכָם יִלְמְדוּ לְשַׁקֵּר.

י. שְׁמַעְיָה וְאַבְטַלְיוֹן קִבְּלוּ מֵהֶם. שְׁמַעְיָה אוֹמֵר: אֱהַב אֶת הַמְּלָאכָה, וּשְׂנָא אֶת הָרַבָּנוּת, וְאַל תִּתְוַדַּע לָרָשׁוּת.

יא. אַבְטַלְיוֹן אוֹמֵר: חֲכָמִים הִזָּהֲרוּ בְדִבְרֵיכֶם, שֶׁמָּא תָחוּבוּ חוֹבַת גָּלוּת וְתִגְלוּ לִמְקוֹם מַיִם הָרָעִים, וְיִשְׁתּוּ הַתַּלְמִידִים הַבָּאִים אַחֲרֵיכֶם וְיָמוּתוּ, וְנִמְצָא שֵׁם שָׁמַיִם מִתְחַלֵּל.

184

1:1   Moses received Torah from Sinai, and passed it on to Joshua, and Joshua to the elders, and the elders to the prophets, and the prophets passed it on to men of the Great Assembly. They had three sayings: Be deliberate in judging; educate many students; make a fence around the Torah.

1:2   Shimon the Righteous was one of the last from the Great Assembly. He used to say: Upon three things the world stands: upon the Torah, upon worship, and upon acts of kindness.

1:3   Antigonos of Sokho received from Shimon the Righteous. He used to say: Be not as servants who serve the master on condition of receiving a reward; be rather as servants who serve the master without condition of receiving a reward; and let the fear of Heaven be upon you.

1:4   Yose ben Yo'ezer of Tzeredah and Yose ben Yohanan of Jerusalem received from them. Yose ben Yo'ezer of Tzeredah said: Let your house be a meetinghouse for the wise; sit in the dust at their feet, and drink in their words with thirst.

1:5   Yose ben Yohanan of Jerusalem said: Let your house be open wide; let the poor be members of your household; and don't talk too much with the wife. This being said of one's own wife, so much more so of a friend's wife. Thus sages have said: So long as a man talks a lot with the woman, he causes evil to himself, neglects the study of the Torah, and in the end will inherit Gehinnom.

1:6   Yehoshua ben Perahiah and Nittai of Arbel received from them. Yehoshua ben Perahiah said: Choose for yourself a mentor; acquire for yourself a friend; and judge every person in a favorable light.

1:7   Nittai of Arbel said: Keep away from a bad neighbor; do not fraternize with the wicked; and do not despair about calamity.

1:8   Yehudah ben Tabbai and Shimon ben Shatah received from them. Yehudah ben Tabbai said: While a judge, do not act as an advocate; while the litigants stand before you, regard them both as guilty; but when they leave, having accepted the judgment, regard them both as innocent.

1:9   Shimon ben Shatah said: Examine the witnesses thoroughly, and be careful in your words, lest they learn from them to lie.

1:10   Shemaiah and Avtalion received from them. Shemaiah said: Love work, hate domination, and do not become familiar with the authorities.

1:11   Avtalion said: O sages, be careful with your words; for you may incur the penalty of exile, and be banished to a place of evil waters; the disciples who come after you will drink of them and die, and the Name of Heaven be profaned.

יב. הִלֵּל וְשַׁמַּאי קִבְּלוּ מֵהֶם. הִלֵּל אוֹמֵר: הֱוֵי מִתַּלְמִידָיו שֶׁל אַהֲרֹן, אוֹהֵב שָׁלוֹם וְרוֹדֵף שָׁלוֹם, אוֹהֵב אֶת הַבְּרִיּוֹת וּמְקָרְבָן לַתּוֹרָה.

יג. הוּא הָיָה אוֹמֵר: נְגִיד שְׁמָא אֲבַד שְׁמֵהּ, וּדְלָא מוֹסִיף יָסֵף, וּדְלָא יָלִיף קְטָלָא חַיָּב, וּדְאִשְׁתַּמֵּשׁ בְּתַגָּא חֲלָף.

יד. הוּא הָיָה אוֹמֵר: אִם אֵין אֲנִי לִי מִי לִי, וּכְשֶׁאֲנִי לְעַצְמִי מָה אֲנִי, וְאִם לֹא עַכְשָׁו אֵימָתָי.

טו. שַׁמַּאי אוֹמֵר: עֲשֵׂה תוֹרָתְךָ קֶבַע, אֱמוֹר מְעַט וַעֲשֵׂה הַרְבֵּה, וֶהֱוֵי מְקַבֵּל אֶת כָּל הָאָדָם בְּסֵבֶר פָּנִים יָפוֹת.

טז. רַבָּן גַּמְלִיאֵל הָיָה אוֹמֵר: עֲשֵׂה לְךָ רַב, וְהִסְתַּלֵּק מִן הַסָּפֵק, וְאַל תַּרְבֶּה לְעַשֵּׂר אֹמָדוֹת.

יז. שִׁמְעוֹן בְּנוֹ אוֹמֵר: כָּל יָמַי גָּדַלְתִּי בֵּין הַחֲכָמִים, וְלֹא מָצָאתִי לַגּוּף טוֹב מִשְּׁתִיקָה. וְלֹא הַמִּדְרָשׁ עִקָּר, אֶלָּא הַמַּעֲשֶׂה. וְכָל הַמַּרְבֶּה דְּבָרִים מֵבִיא חֵטְא.

יח. רַבָּן שִׁמְעוֹן בֶּן גַּמְלִיאֵל אוֹמֵר: עַל שְׁלֹשָׁה דְּבָרִים הָעוֹלָם קַיָּם, עַל הָאֱמֶת, וְעַל הַדִּין, וְעַל הַשָּׁלוֹם, שֶׁנֶּאֱמַר: "אֱמֶת וּמִשְׁפַּט שָׁלוֹם שִׁפְטוּ בְּשַׁעֲרֵיכֶם."

א. רַבִּי אוֹמֵר: אֵיזוֹ הִיא דֶּרֶךְ יְשָׁרָה שֶׁיָּבוֹר לוֹ הָאָדָם? כָּל שֶׁהִיא תִּפְאֶרֶת לְעֹשֶׂיהָ וְתִפְאֶרֶת לוֹ מִן הָאָדָם. וֶהֱוֵי זָהִיר בְּמִצְוָה קַלָּה כְּבַחֲמוּרָה, שֶׁאֵין אַתָּה יוֹדֵעַ מַתַּן שְׂכָרָן שֶׁל מִצְווֹת. וֶהֱוֵי מְחַשֵּׁב הֶפְסֵד מִצְוָה כְּנֶגֶד שְׂכָרָהּ, וּשְׂכַר עֲבֵרָה כְּנֶגֶד הֶפְסֵדָהּ. הִסְתַּכֵּל בִּשְׁלֹשָׁה דְּבָרִים, וְאֵין אַתָּה בָּא לִידֵי עֲבֵרָה. דַּע מַה לְּמַעְלָה מִמְּךָ, עַיִן רוֹאָה, וְאֹזֶן שׁוֹמַעַת, וְכָל מַעֲשֶׂיךָ בַּסֵּפֶר נִכְתָּבִים.

ב. רַבָּן גַּמְלִיאֵל בְּנוֹ שֶׁל רַבִּי יְהוּדָה הַנָּשִׂיא אוֹמֵר: יָפֶה תַלְמוּד תּוֹרָה עִם דֶּרֶךְ אֶרֶץ, שֶׁיְּגִיעַת שְׁנֵיהֶם מַשְׁכַּחַת עָוֹן, וְכָל תּוֹרָה שֶׁאֵין עִמָּהּ מְלָאכָה סוֹפָהּ בְּטֵלָה וְגוֹרֶרֶת עָוֹן. וְכָל הָעוֹסְקִים עִם הַצִּבּוּר, יִהְיוּ עוֹסְקִים עִמָּהֶם לְשֵׁם שָׁמַיִם, שֶׁזְּכוּת אֲבוֹתָם מְסַיַּעְתָּם, וְצִדְקָתָם עוֹמֶדֶת לָעַד, וְאַתֶּם מַעֲלֶה אֲנִי עֲלֵיכֶם שָׂכָר הַרְבֵּה כְּאִלּוּ עֲשִׂיתֶם.

ג. הֱווּ זְהִירִין בָּרָשׁוּת, שֶׁאֵין מְקָרְבִין לוֹ לְאָדָם אֶלָּא לְצֹרֶךְ עַצְמָן, נִרְאִין כְּאוֹהֲבִין בְּשְׁעַת הֲנָאָתָן, וְאֵין עוֹמְדִין לוֹ לְאָדָם בִּשְׁעַת דָּחֳקוֹ.

ד. הוּא הָיָה אוֹמֵר: עֲשֵׂה רְצוֹנוֹ כִּרְצוֹנֶךָ, כְּדֵי שֶׁיַּעֲשֶׂה רְצוֹנְךָ כִּרְצוֹנוֹ. בַּטֵּל רְצוֹנְךָ מִפְּנֵי רְצוֹנוֹ, כְּדֵי שֶׁיְּבַטֵּל רְצוֹן אֲחֵרִים מִפְּנֵי רְצוֹנֶךָ.

1:12 Hillel and Shammai received from them. Hillel said: Be among the disciples of Aaron: a lover of peace and pursuer of peace; love all fellow creatures, and bring them near to the Torah.

1:13 He used to say: Promote your name—lose your name; fail to add—you diminish; fail to study—you deserve to die; and exploit the crown—you perish.

1:14 He used to say: If I am not for myself, who is for me? And when I am for myself, what am I? And if not now, when?

1:15 Shammai said: Make your Torah a set priority; say little and do much; and receive every person with a pleasant face.

1:16 Rabban Gamliel used to say: Choose for yourself a mentor; remove yourself from the doubtful; and do not tithe by estimation excessively.

1:17 Shimon, his son, said: All my days I grew up among the sages, and I have found nothing better for a person than silence; and the main thing is not the learning, but the doing; and all who speak too much bring on sin.

1:18 Rabban Shimon ben Gamliel said: By three things is the world sustained: by justice, by truth and by peace. As it is said: "Judge you truthfully and a judgment of peace in your gates" (ZECH 8:16).

2:1 Rabbi said: Which is the right path that you should choose for yourself? One that is admirable in your own eyes, and admirable in the eyes of others. Be as careful with a minor commandment as with a major one, for you do not know the rewards of the commandments. Weigh the losses in doing the right thing against the gains, and the gains from committing a sin against the losses. Reflect on three things and you will not come into the grip of sin: know that above you are an eye that sees, an ear that hears, and all your deeds written in a book.

2:2 Rabban Gamliel, the son of Rabbi Yehuda haNasi said: Excellent is the study of Torah along with worldly activities, for toil in both causes sin to be forgotten. All Torah unaccompanied by labor ends in idleness and causes sin. Let all who work with the community work with them for the sake of Heaven. Then the merit of their ancestors will aid them, and their righteousness will endure forever. "And upon you, I will bestow a great reward, as if you had accomplished it."

2:3 Be wary of the authorities, for they befriend a person only for their own advantage. They appear as friend when it suits them, but do not stand by a man in his hour of need.

2:4 He used to say: Do His will as if it were your will, so that He may do your will as His will. Nullify your will before His will, so that He may nullify the will of others before your will.

ה. הִלֵּל אוֹמֵר: אַל תִּפְרוֹשׁ מִן הַצִּבּוּר, וְאַל תַּאֲמִין בְּעַצְמְךָ עַד יוֹם מוֹתְךָ, וְאַל
    תָּדִין אֶת חֲבֵרְךָ עַד שֶׁתַּגִּיעַ לִמְקוֹמוֹ, וְאַל תֹּאמַר דָּבָר שֶׁאִי אֶפְשָׁר לִשְׁמֹעַ,
    שֶׁסּוֹפוֹ לְהִשָּׁמַע, וְאַל תֹּאמַר לִכְשֶׁאֶפָּנֶה אֶשְׁנֶה, שֶׁמָּא לֹא תִּפָּנֶה.

ו. הוּא הָיָה אוֹמֵר: אֵין בּוּר יְרֵא חֵטְא, וְלֹא עַם הָאָרֶץ חָסִיד, וְלֹא הַבַּיְשָׁן
    לָמֵד, וְלֹא כָּל הַקַּפְדָן מְלַמֵּד, וְלֹא כָּל הַמַּרְבֶּה בִסְחוֹרָה מַחְכִּים. וּבְמָקוֹם
    שֶׁאֵין אֲנָשִׁים הִשְׁתַּדֵּל לִהְיוֹת אִישׁ.

ז. אַף הוּא רָאָה גֻלְגֹּלֶת אַחַת שֶׁצָּפָה עַל פְּנֵי הַמָּיִם, אָמַר לָהּ: עַל דְּאַטֵּפְתְּ
    אַטְּפוּךְ, וְסוֹף מְטַיְּפָיִךְ יְטוּפוּן.

ח. הוּא הָיָה אוֹמֵר: מַרְבֶּה בָשָׂר–מַרְבֶּה רִמָּה, מַרְבֶּה נְכָסִים–מַרְבֶּה דְאָגָה,
    מַרְבֶּה נָשִׁים–מַרְבֶּה כְשָׁפִים, מַרְבֶּה שְׁפָחוֹת–מַרְבֶּה זִמָּה, מַרְבֶּה עֲבָדִים–
    מַרְבֶּה גָזֵל, מַרְבֶּה תוֹרָה–מַרְבֶּה חַיִּים, מַרְבֶּה יְשִׁיבָה–מַרְבֶּה חָכְמָה, מַרְבֶּה
    עֵצָה–מַרְבֶּה תְבוּנָה, מַרְבֶּה צְדָקָה–מַרְבֶּה שָׁלוֹם. קָנָה שֵׁם טוֹב–קָנָה
    לְעַצְמוֹ, קָנָה לוֹ דִבְרֵי תוֹרָה–קָנָה לוֹ חַיֵּי הָעוֹלָם הַבָּא.

ט. רַבָּן יוֹחָנָן בֶּן זַכַּאי קִבֵּל מֵהִלֵּל וּמִשַּׁמַּאי, הוּא הָיָה אוֹמֵר: אִם לָמַדְתָּ תּוֹרָה
    הַרְבֵּה, אַל תַּחֲזִיק טוֹבָה לְעַצְמְךָ, כִּי לְכַךְ נוֹצָרְתָּ.

י. חֲמִשָּׁה תַלְמִידִים הָיוּ לוֹ לְרַבָּן יוֹחָנָן בֶּן זַכַּאי, וְאֵלּוּ הֵן: רַבִּי אֱלִיעֶזֶר בֶּן
    הוֹרְקָנוֹס, רַבִּי יְהוֹשֻׁעַ בֶּן חֲנַנְיָא, רַבִּי יוֹסֵי הַכֹּהֵן, רַבִּי שִׁמְעוֹן בֶּן נְתַנְאֵל,
    וְרַבִּי אֶלְעָזָר בֶּן עֲרָךְ.

יא. הוּא הָיָה מוֹנֶה שְׁבָחָם: אֱלִיעֶזֶר בֶּן הוֹרְקָנוֹס–בּוֹר סוּד שֶׁאֵינוֹ מְאַבֵּד טִפָּה,
    יְהוֹשֻׁעַ בֶּן חֲנַנְיָה–אַשְׁרֵי יוֹלַדְתּוֹ, יוֹסֵי הַכֹּהֵן–חָסִיד, שִׁמְעוֹן בֶּן נְתַנְאֵל–יְרֵא
    חֵטְא, אֶלְעָזָר בֶּן עֲרָךְ–כְּמַעְיָן הַמִּתְגַּבֵּר.

יב. הוּא הָיָה אוֹמֵר: אִם יִהְיוּ כָּל חַכְמֵי יִשְׂרָאֵל בְּכַף מֹאזְנַיִם, וֶאֱלִיעֶזֶר בֶּן
    הוֹרְקָנוֹס בְּכַף שְׁנִיָּה, מַכְרִיעַ אֶת כֻּלָּם. אַבָּא שָׁאוּל אוֹמֵר מִשְּׁמוֹ: אִם יִהְיוּ
    כָּל חַכְמֵי יִשְׂרָאֵל בְּכַף מֹאזְנַיִם, וֶאֱלִיעֶזֶר בֶּן הוֹרְקָנוֹס אַף עִמָּהֶם, וְאֶלְעָזָר
    בֶּן עֲרָךְ בְּכַף שְׁנִיָּה, מַכְרִיעַ אֶת כֻּלָּם.

יג. אָמַר לָהֶם: צְאוּ וּרְאוּ אֵיזוֹ הִיא דֶרֶךְ טוֹבָה שֶׁיִּדְבַּק בָּהּ הָאָדָם. רַבִּי אֱלִיעֶזֶר
    אוֹמֵר: עַיִן טוֹבָה. רַבִּי יְהוֹשֻׁעַ אוֹמֵר: חָבֵר טוֹב. רַבִּי יוֹסֵי אוֹמֵר: שָׁכֵן טוֹב. רַבִּי
    שִׁמְעוֹן אוֹמֵר: הָרוֹאֶה אֶת הַנּוֹלָד. רַבִּי אֶלְעָזָר אוֹמֵר: לֵב טוֹב. אָמַר לָהֶם:
    רוֹאֶה אֲנִי אֶת דִּבְרֵי אֶלְעָזָר בֶּן עֲרָךְ מִדִּבְרֵיכֶם, שֶׁבִּכְלַל דְּבָרָיו דִּבְרֵיכֶם:

2:5 Hillel said: Do not separate yourself from the community. Do not trust yourself until the day of your death. Do not judge your comrade until you have come into his place. Do not say a thing that should not be heard, for in the end it will be heard. Do not say: "When I am free, I will study"; perhaps you will never be free.

2:6 He used to say: The crude do not fear sin, and the ignorant cannot be models of piety. The bashful do not learn, and the short-tempered cannot teach. And not all who succeed in business are wise. In a place where there is no person to make a difference, strive to be that person.

2:7 Hillel saw a lone skull floating in the water. He spoke to it: because you drowned others, you were drowned; and in the end those who drowned you will be drowned.

2:8 He used to say: More flesh, more worms; more wealth, more worry; more wives, more witchcraft; more maidservants, more lechery; more manservants, more robbery. More Torah, more life; more study, more wisdom; more counsel, more understanding; more charity, more peace. If you gain a good name, you gain for yourself. If you gain knowledge of Torah, you gain for yourself life in the world to come.

2:9 Rabban Yoḥanan ben Zakkai received from Hillel and from Shammai. He used to say: If you have learned much Torah, do not flatter yourself, because for this you were created.

2:10 Rabban Yoḥanan ben Zakkai had five students and they were: Rabbi Eliezer ben Hyrcanus, Rabbi Yehoshua ben Ḥanania, Rabbi Yose, the priest, Rabbi Shimon ben Netanel and Rabbi Elazar ben Arach.

2:11 He used to recount their praises: Eliezer ben Hyrcanus is a plastered cistern which does not lose a drop; Yehoshua ben Ḥanania —happy is she who bore him; Yose, the priest, is a pious man; Shimon ben Netanel fears sin; and Elazar ben Arach is an ever-flowing fountain.

2:12 He used to say: if all the sages of Israel were in one pan of the scales and Eliezer ben Hyrcanus in the other pan, he would outweigh them all. Abba Shaul said in his name: If all the sages of Israel were in one pan of the scales, and Rabbi Eliezer ben Hyrcanus also with them, and Rabbi Elazar ben Arach in the other pan, he would outweigh them all.

2:13 He said to his students: Go out and see which is the good path that a person should stick to. Rabbi Eliezer said, a good eye; Rabbi Yehoshua said, a good friend; Rabbi Yose said, a good neighbor; Rabbi Shimon said, one who foresees consequences. Rabbi Elazar said, a good heart. He said to them: From among your sayings, I recognize that of Elazar ben Arach, for within his words yours are included.

יד. אָמַר לָהֶם: צְאוּ וּרְאוּ אֵיזוֹ הִיא דֶּרֶךְ רָעָה שֶׁיִּתְרַחֵק מִמֶּנָּה הָאָדָם. רַבִּי
אֱלִיעֶזֶר אוֹמֵר: עַיִן רָעָה. רַבִּי יְהוֹשֻׁעַ אוֹמֵר: חָבֵר רָע. רַבִּי יוֹסֵי אוֹמֵר: שָׁכֵן
רָע. רַבִּי שִׁמְעוֹן אוֹמֵר: הַלֹּוֶה וְאֵינוֹ מְשַׁלֵּם, אֶחָד הַלֹּוֶה מִן הָאָדָם כְּלֹּוֶה מִן
הַמָּקוֹם, שֶׁנֶּאֱמַר: "לֹוֶה רָשָׁע וְלֹא יְשַׁלֵּם, וְצַדִּיק חוֹנֵן וְנוֹתֵן" . רַבִּי אֶלְעָזָר
אוֹמֵר: לֵב רָע. אָמַר לָהֶם: רוֹאֶה אֲנִי אֶת דִּבְרֵי אֶלְעָזָר בֶּן עֲרָךְ מִדִּבְרֵיכֶם,
שֶׁבִּכְלַל דְּבָרָיו דִּבְרֵיכֶם.

טו. הֵם אָמְרוּ שְׁלֹשָׁה דְּבָרִים: רַבִּי אֱלִיעֶזֶר אוֹמֵר: יְהִי כְבוֹד חֲבֵרְךָ חָבִיב עָלֶיךָ
כְּשֶׁלָּךְ, וְאַל תְּהִי נוֹחַ לִכְעוֹס, וְשׁוּב יוֹם אֶחָד לִפְנֵי מִיתָתְךָ. וֶהֱוֵי מִתְחַמֵּם
כְּנֶגֶד אוּרָן שֶׁל חֲכָמִים, וֶהֱוֵי זָהִיר בְּגַחַלְתָּן שֶׁלֹּא תִכָּוֶה, שֶׁנְּשִׁיכָתָן נְשִׁיכַת
שׁוּעָל, וַעֲקִיצָתָן עֲקִיצַת עַקְרָב, וּלְחִישָׁתָן לְחִישַׁת שָׂרָף, וְכָל דִּבְרֵיהֶם כְּגַחֲלֵי
אֵשׁ.

טז. רַבִּי יְהוֹשֻׁעַ אוֹמֵר: עַיִן הָרָע, וְיֵצֶר הָרָע, וְשִׂנְאַת הַבְּרִיּוֹת, מוֹצִיאִין אֶת
הָאָדָם מִן הָעוֹלָם.

יז. רַבִּי יוֹסֵי אוֹמֵר: יְהִי מָמוֹן חֲבֵרְךָ חָבִיב עָלֶיךָ כְּשֶׁלָּךְ. וְהַתְקֵן עַצְמְךָ לִלְמוֹד
תּוֹרָה, שֶׁאֵינָהּ יְרֻשָּׁה לָךְ, וְכָל מַעֲשֶׂיךָ יִהְיוּ לְשֵׁם שָׁמָיִם.

יח. רַבִּי שִׁמְעוֹן אוֹמֵר: הֱוֵי זָהִיר בִּקְרִיאַת שְׁמַע וּבִתְפִלָּה, וּכְשֶׁאַתָּה מִתְפַּלֵּל,
אַל תַּעַשׂ תְּפִלָּתְךָ קֶבַע, אֶלָּא רַחֲמִים וְתַחֲנוּנִים לִפְנֵי הַמָּקוֹם, שֶׁנֶּאֱמַר:
"כִּי־חַנּוּן וְרַחוּם הוּא אֶרֶךְ אַפַּיִם וְרַב־חֶסֶד וְנִחָם עַל־הָרָעָה." וְאַל תְּהִי
רָשָׁע בִּפְנֵי עַצְמֶךָ.

יט. רַבִּי אֶלְעָזָר אוֹמֵר: הֱוֵי שָׁקוּד לִלְמוֹד תּוֹרָה, וְדַע מַה שֶּׁתָּשִׁיב לְאֶפִּיקוֹרוֹס,
וְדַע לִפְנֵי מִי אַתָּה עָמֵל, וּמִי הוּא בַּעַל מְלַאכְתְּךָ, שֶׁיְּשַׁלֵּם לְךָ שְׂכַר פְּעֻלָּתֶךָ.

כ. רַבִּי טַרְפוֹן אוֹמֵר: הַיּוֹם קָצֵר, וְהַמְּלָאכָה מְרֻבָּה, וְהַפּוֹעֲלִים עֲצֵלִים, וְהַשָּׂכָר
הַרְבֵּה, וּבַעַל הַבַּיִת דּוֹחֵק:

כא. הוּא הָיָה אוֹמֵר: לֹא עָלֶיךָ הַמְּלָאכָה לִגְמוֹר וְלֹא אַתָּה בֶן חוֹרִין לְהִבָּטֵל
מִמֶּנָּה; אִם לָמַדְתָּ תּוֹרָה הַרְבֵּה, נוֹתְנִין לְךָ שָׂכָר הַרְבֵּה, וְנֶאֱמָן הוּא בַּעַל
מְלַאכְתְּךָ, שֶׁיְּשַׁלֵּם לְךָ שְׂכַר פְּעֻלָּתֶךָ. וְדַע שֶׁמַּתַּן שְׂכָרָן שֶׁל צַדִּיקִים לֶעָתִיד
לָבוֹא.

2:14 He said to them: Go out and see which is the bad path that a person should stay far from. Rabbi Eliezer said, a bad eye; Rabbi Yehoshua said, a bad friend; Rabbi Yose said, a bad neighbor; Rabbi Shimon said, one who borrows and doesn't repay. One who borrows from man is as one who borrows from God, as it is said: "The wicked borrow and do not repay; but the righteous are gracious and give" (PS 37:21). Rabbi Elazar said, a bad heart. He said to them: From among your sayings, I recognize that of Elazar ben Arach, for within his words yours are included.

2:15 They said three things. Rabbi Eliezer said: Let the honor of your colleague be as dear to you as your own; do not be easy to anger; and repent one day before your death. Warm yourself at the fire of the wise, but be careful of their glowing coals, lest you be burned; for their bite is the bite of a jackal, their sting is the sting of a scorpion, their hiss is the hiss of a serpent, and all their words are like burning coals.

2:16 Rabbi Yehoshua said: The evil eye, the evil inclination, and hatred of humanity drive a person from the world.

2:17 Rabbi Yose said: Let the money of your associate be as dear to you as your own. Prepare yourself to study Torah, for it isn't yours by inheritance. And let all you do be for the sake of Heaven.

2:18 Rabbi Shimon said: Be mindful in the reciting of the *Shema* and the *Tefillah*, and when you pray, make your prayer not a set task, but a plea for compassion and grace before the Blessed Presence. As it is said (JOEL 2:13): "For He is gracious and compassionate, long-suffering and abundant in loving-kindness, and relenting of an evil decree." And do not be wicked in your own eyes.

2:19 Rabbi Elazar said: Be diligent in studying Torah, and know what to answer to an Epicurean. Know before whom you toil, and that your Employer can be trusted to pay you the wages for your labor.

2:20 Rabbi Tarfon said: The day is short and the work much; the workers are lazy and the wages high; and the Master of the house presses.

2:21 He used to say: You are not obliged to complete the work, but you are not free to neglect it; if you have learned much Torah, you will be given much reward; your Employer is trustworthy and will pay you the reward for your labor. And know that the granting of rewards to the righteous is in the time to come.

א. עֲקַבְיָא בֶּן מַהֲלַלְאֵל אוֹמֵר: הִסְתַּכֵּל בִּשְׁלשָׁה דְבָרִים וְאֵין אַתָּה בָא לִידֵי
עֲבֵרָה: דַּע מֵאַיִן בָּאתָ, וּלְאָן אַתָּה הוֹלֵךְ, וְלִפְנֵי מִי אַתָּה עָתִיד לִתֵּן דִּין
וְחֶשְׁבּוֹן. מֵאַיִן בָּאתָ? מִטִּפָּה סְרוּחָה. וּלְאָן אַתָּה הוֹלֵךְ? לִמְקוֹם עָפָר וְרִמָּה
וְתוֹלֵעָה. וְלִפְנֵי מִי אַתָּה עָתִיד לִתֵּן דִּין וְחֶשְׁבּוֹן? לִפְנֵי מֶלֶךְ מַלְכֵי הַמְּלָכִים
הַקָּדוֹשׁ בָּרוּךְ הוּא.

ב. רַבִּי חֲנִינָא סְגַן הַכֹּהֲנִים אוֹמֵר: הֱוֵי מִתְפַּלֵּל בִּשְׁלוֹמָהּ שֶׁל מַלְכוּת, שֶׁאִלְמָלֵא
מוֹרָאָהּ, אִישׁ אֶת רֵעֵהוּ חַיִּים בְּלָעוֹ.

ג. רַבִּי חֲנִינָא בֶּן תְּרַדְיוֹן אוֹמֵר: שְׁנַיִם שֶׁיּוֹשְׁבִין וְאֵין בֵּינֵיהֶם דִּבְרֵי תוֹרָה הֲרֵי
זֶה מוֹשַׁב לֵצִים. שֶׁנֶּאֱמַר: "וּבְמוֹשַׁב לֵצִים לֹא יָשָׁב." אֲבָל שְׁנַיִם שֶׁיּוֹשְׁבִין
וְיֵשׁ בֵּינֵיהֶם דִּבְרֵי תוֹרָה, שְׁכִינָה שְׁרוּיָה בֵינֵיהֶם. שֶׁנֶּאֱמַר: "אָז נִדְבְּרוּ יִרְאֵי
יְיָ אִישׁ אֶל רֵעֵהוּ, וַיַּקְשֵׁב יְיָ וַיִּשְׁמָע, וַיִּכָּתֵב סֵפֶר זִכָּרוֹן לְפָנָיו לְיִרְאֵי יְיָ
וּלְחשְׁבֵי שְׁמוֹ". אֵין לִי אֶלָּא שְׁנַיִם, מִנַּיִן אֲפִלּוּ אֶחָד שֶׁיּוֹשֵׁב וְעוֹסֵק בַּתּוֹרָה
שֶׁהַקָּדוֹשׁ-בָּרוּךְ-הוּא קוֹבֵעַ לוֹ שָׂכָר? שֶׁנֶּאֱמַר: "יֵשֵׁב בָּדָד וְיִדֹּם כִּי נָטַל
עָלָיו."

ד. רַבִּי שִׁמְעוֹן אוֹמֵר: שְׁלשָׁה שֶׁאָכְלוּ עַל שֻׁלְחָן אֶחָד וְלֹא אָמְרוּ עָלָיו דִּבְרֵי
תוֹרָה, כְּאִלּוּ אָכְלוּ מִזִּבְחֵי מֵתִים, שֶׁנֶּאֱמַר: "כִּי כָּל-שֻׁלְחָנוֹת מָלְאוּ קִיא
צֹאָה, בְּלִי מָקוֹם." אֲבָל שְׁלשָׁה שֶׁאָכְלוּ עַל שֻׁלְחָן אֶחָד וְאָמְרוּ עָלָיו דִּבְרֵי
תוֹרָה, כְּאִלּוּ אָכְלוּ מִשֻּׁלְחָנוֹ שֶׁל מָקוֹם. שֶׁנֶּאֱמַר: "וַיְדַבֵּר אֵלַי זֶה הַשֻּׁלְחָן
אֲשֶׁר לִפְנֵי יְיָ."

ה. רַבִּי חֲנִינָא בֶּן חֲכִינַאי אוֹמֵר: הַנֵּעוֹר בַּלַּיְלָה, וְהַמְהַלֵּךְ בַּדֶּרֶךְ יְחִידִי, וּמְפַנֶּה
לִבּוֹ לְבַטָּלָה, הֲרֵי זֶה מִתְחַיֵּב בְּנַפְשׁוֹ.

ו. רַבִּי נְחוּנְיָא בֶּן הַקָּנָה אוֹמֵר: כָּל הַמְקַבֵּל עָלָיו עוֹל תּוֹרָה, מַעֲבִירִין מִמֶּנּוּ
עוֹל מַלְכוּת וְעוֹל דֶּרֶךְ אֶרֶץ, וְכָל הַפּוֹרֵק מִמֶּנּוּ עוֹל תּוֹרָה, נוֹתְנִין עָלָיו עוֹל
מַלְכוּת וְעוֹל דֶּרֶךְ אֶרֶץ.

ז. רַבִּי חֲלַפְתָּא בֶּן דּוֹסָא אִישׁ כְּפַר חֲנַנְיָא אוֹמֵר: עֲשָׂרָה שֶׁיּוֹשְׁבִין וְעוֹסְקִין
בַּתּוֹרָה שְׁכִינָה שְׁרוּיָה בֵינֵיהֶם, שֶׁנֶּאֱמַר: "אֱלֹהִים נִצָּב בַּעֲדַת-אֵל". וּמִנַּיִן
אֲפִלּוּ חֲמִשָּׁה? שֶׁנֶּאֱמַר: "וַאֲגֻדָּתוֹ עַל-אֶרֶץ יְסָדָהּ." וּמִנַּיִן אֲפִלּוּ שְׁלשָׁה?
שֶׁנֶּאֱמַר: "בְּקֶרֶב אֱלֹהִים יִשְׁפֹּט." וּמִנַּיִן אֲפִלּוּ שְׁנַיִם? שֶׁנֶּאֱמַר: "אָז נִדְבְּרוּ
יִרְאֵי יְיָ אִישׁ אֶל רֵעֵהוּ, וַיַּקְשֵׁב יְיָ וַיִּשְׁמָע." וּמִנַּיִן אֲפִלּוּ אֶחָד? שֶׁנֶּאֱמַר:
"בְּכָל-הַמָּקוֹם אֲשֶׁר אַזְכִּיר אֶת-שְׁמִי אָבוֹא אֵלֶיךָ וּבֵרַכְתִּיךָ."

3:1 Akavia ben Mahalalel said: Reflect upon three things and you will not come into the grip of sin. Know where you came from, where you are going, and before whom you must give account. Where you came from: a fetid drop. Where you are going: to a place of dust, worm, and maggot. And before whom you must give account: the Supreme King of kings, the Holy One, blessed be he. [p.57]

3:2 Rabbi Ḥanina, Deputy High Priest, said: Pray for the welfare of the regime; but for fear of it people would swallow one another alive. [p. 60]

3:3 Rabbi Ḥanania ben Teradion said: When two people sit together and exchange no words of Torah, this is a "meeting of scoffers." As it is said: "Happy the man who … does not sit in a meeting of scoffers" (PS 1:1). When two people sit together and exchange words of Torah, the Divine Presence rests between them. As it is said: "Then the God-fearing spoke to one another and a book of remembrance was written before Him for those who feared God and meditated upon his name" (MAL 3:16). This would seem only to apply to two. How do we know that the Holy One, blessed be he, has fixed a reward even for a single person who occupies himself with Torah? It is said: "Let him sit alone and be quiet, because He has laid it upon him" (LAM 3:27).

3:4 Rabbi Shimon said: If three people eat at a table and say there no words of Torah, it is as if they eat from offerings to idols. As it is said: "For all tables are full of filthy vomit without the Blessed Presence" (IS 28:8). But if three people eat at a table and say there words of Torah, it is as if they eat at the table of the Lord. As it is said: And he said to me, "This is the table that is before the Lord" (EZEK 41:22).

3:5 Rabbi Ḥanina ben Ḥakhinai said: He who wakes in the night, or goes about on the road alone and turns his heart to idle matters, puts himself in mortal danger.

3:6 Rabbi Neḥunia ben Hakanah said: All who accept the yoke of the Torah are relieved of the yoke of the government and the yoke of worldly affairs. All who cast off the yoke of Torah, the yoke of the government and the yoke of worldly affairs is put upon them.

3:7 Rabbi Ḥalafta ben Dosa of the village of Ḥanania said: If ten people sit and occupy themselves with Torah, the Divine Presence rests among them. As it is said: "God stands in the assembly of the Lord" (PS 82:1). How do we know this is true even for five people? It is said: "He has founded his band upon the earth" (AMOS 9:6). Even for three? It is said: "Among judges he renders judgment" (PS 82:1). Even for two? It is said: "Then the God-fearing spoke to one another and a book of remembrance was written before Him for those who feared God and meditated upon his name" (MAL 3:16). Even for one? It is said: "Every place where my name is mentioned I will come to you and bless you" (EX 20:21). [p. 106]

ח. רַבִּי אֶלְעָזָר אִישׁ בַּרְתּוֹתָא אוֹמֵר: תֶּן לוֹ מִשֶּׁלּוֹ, שֶׁאַתָּה וְשֶׁלְּךָ שֶׁלּוֹ, וְכֵן בְּדָוִד הוּא אוֹמֵר: "כִּי־מִמְּךָ הַכֹּל וּמִיָּדְךָ נָתַנּוּ לָךְ."

ט. רַבִּי יַעֲקֹב אוֹמֵר: הַמְהַלֵּךְ בַּדֶּרֶךְ וְשׁוֹנֶה, וּמַפְסִיק מִמִּשְׁנָתוֹ וְאוֹמֵר: מַה נָּאֶה אִילָן זֶה, מַה נָּאֶה נִיר זֶה, מַעֲלֶה עָלָיו הַכָּתוּב כְּאִלּוּ מִתְחַיֵּב בְּנַפְשׁוֹ.

י. רַבִּי דּוֹסְתַּאי בַּר יַנַּאי מִשּׁוּם רַבִּי מֵאִיר אוֹמֵר: כָּל הַשּׁוֹכֵחַ דָּבָר אֶחָד מִמִּשְׁנָתוֹ, מַעֲלֶה עָלָיו הַכָּתוּב כְּאִלּוּ מִתְחַיֵּב בְּנַפְשׁוֹ, שֶׁנֶּאֱמַר: "רַק הִשָּׁמֶר לְךָ וּשְׁמֹר נַפְשְׁךָ מְאֹד פֶּן־תִּשְׁכַּח אֶת־הַדְּבָרִים אֲשֶׁר־רָאוּ עֵינֶיךָ." יָכוֹל אֲפִלּוּ תָקְפָה עָלָיו מִשְׁנָתוֹ? תַּלְמוּד לוֹמַר: "וּפֶן־יָסוּרוּ מִלְּבָבְךָ כֹּל יְמֵי חַיֶּיךָ," הָא אֵינוֹ מִתְחַיֵּב בְּנַפְשׁוֹ עַד שֶׁיֵּשֵׁב וִיסִירֵם מִלִּבּוֹ.

יא. רַבִּי חֲנִינָא בֶּן דּוֹסָא אוֹמֵר: כָּל שֶׁיִּרְאַת חֶטְאוֹ קוֹדֶמֶת לְחָכְמָתוֹ, חָכְמָתוֹ מִתְקַיֶּמֶת. וְכָל שֶׁחָכְמָתוֹ קוֹדֶמֶת לְיִרְאַת חֶטְאוֹ, אֵין חָכְמָתוֹ מִתְקַיֶּמֶת:

יב. הוּא הָיָה אוֹמֵר: כָּל שֶׁמַּעֲשָׂיו מְרֻבִּין מֵחָכְמָתוֹ, חָכְמָתוֹ מִתְקַיֶּמֶת. וְכָל שֶׁחָכְמָתוֹ מְרֻבָּה מִמַּעֲשָׂיו, אֵין חָכְמָתוֹ מִתְקַיֶּמֶת:

יג. הוּא הָיָה אוֹמֵר: כָּל שֶׁרוּחַ הַבְּרִיּוֹת נוֹחָה הֵימֶנּוּ, רוּחַ הַמָּקוֹם נוֹחָה הֵימֶנּוּ, וְכֹל שֶׁאֵין רוּחַ הַבְּרִיּוֹת נוֹחָה הֵימֶנּוּ, אֵין רוּחַ הַמָּקוֹם נוֹחָה הֵימֶנּוּ.

יד. רַבִּי דּוֹסָא בֶּן הָרְכִּינַס אוֹמֵר: שֵׁנָה שֶׁל שַׁחֲרִית, וְיַיִן שֶׁל צָהֳרַיִם, וְשִׂיחַת הַיְלָדִים, וִישִׁיבַת בָּתֵּי כְנֵסִיּוֹת שֶׁל עַמֵּי הָאָרֶץ, מוֹצִיאִין אֶת הָאָדָם מִן הָעוֹלָם.

טו. רַבִּי אֶלְעָזָר הַמּוֹדָעִי אוֹמֵר: הַמְחַלֵּל אֶת הַקֳּדָשִׁים, וְהַמְבַזֶּה אֶת הַמּוֹעֲדוֹת, וְהַמַּלְבִּין פְּנֵי חֲבֵרוֹ בָּרַבִּים, וְהַמֵּפֵר בְּרִיתוֹ שֶׁל אַבְרָהָם אָבִינוּ, וְהַמְגַלֶּה פָנִים בַּתּוֹרָה שֶׁלֹּא כַהֲלָכָה, אַף עַל פִּי שֶׁיֵּשׁ בְּיָדוֹ תּוֹרָה וּמַעֲשִׂים טוֹבִים, אֵין לוֹ חֵלֶק לָעוֹלָם הַבָּא.

טז. רַבִּי יִשְׁמָעֵאל אוֹמֵר: הֱוֵי קַל לְרֹאשׁ, וְנוֹחַ לְתִשְׁחֹרֶת, וֶהֱוֵי מְקַבֵּל אֶת כָּל הָאָדָם בְּשִׂמְחָה.

יז. רַבִּי עֲקִיבָא אוֹמֵר: שְׂחוֹק וְקַלּוּת רֹאשׁ מַרְגִּילִין אֶת הָאָדָם לְעֶרְוָה. מָסֹרֶת־סְיָג לַתּוֹרָה, מַעַשְׂרוֹת־סְיָג לָעֹשֶׁר, נְדָרִים־סְיָג לַפְּרִישׁוּת, סְיָג לַחָכְמָה־שְׁתִיקָה.

3:8 Rabbi Elazar of Bartota said: Give Him of what is His, for you and yours are His. Thus David said: "For all things are from You, and from Your own hand have we given you" (1 CHRON 29:14).

3:9 Rabbi Ya'akov said: If a person is walking by the way reviewing his Torah, and ceases, and says "How beautiful is this tree! How beautiful is this field!" Scripture regards him as in mortal danger. [p. 108]

3:10 Rabbi Dostai bar Yanai said in the name of Rabbi Meir: A person who forgets one word of his study, the scripture regards him as in mortal danger. As it is written: "Only take you care, take exceeding care for your self, lest you forget the things your eyes saw" (DEUT 4:9). Could this be so even when the lesson is too much for him? To this scripture answers: "Lest you turn aside in your heart all the days of our life" (DEUT 4:9). That is to say: one is not in mortal danger unless he sits and drives the words from his heart. [p. 108]

3:11 Rabbi Ḥanina ben Dosa said: All whose fear of sin comes before their wisdom, their wisdom will live on. All whose wisdom comes before their fear of sin, their wisdom will not live on.

3:12 He used to say: All whose deeds are greater than their wisdom, their wisdom will live on. All whose wisdom is greater than their deeds, their wisdom will not live on.

3:13 He used to say: if the spirit of your fellow man finds you pleasing, the spirit of the Holy One finds you pleasing. If the spirit of your fellow man does not find you pleasing, the spirit of the Holy One does not find you pleasing. [p. 55]

3:14 Rabbi Dosa ben Harkinas said: Morning sleep, midday wine, childish talk, and sitting in the gathering places of the ignorant drive a person from the world.

3:15 Rabbi Elazar of Modin said: Whoever profanes sacred things, desecrates the festivals, humiliates his colleague in public, annuls the covenant of Abraham our father, or perverts the meaning of Torah, even if he has Torah and good deeds, he will not have a share in the world to come.

3:16 Rabbi Ishmael said: Be deferential to your seniors, affable to your juniors and receive every person with joy. [p. 90]

3:17 Rabbi Akiva said: Joking and frivolity accustom a person to lewdness. Tradition is a fence for the Torah; tithes are a fence for riches; vows are a fence for abstinence; a fence for wisdom—silence.

יח. הוּא הָיָה אוֹמֵר: חָבִיב אָדָם שֶׁנִּבְרָא בְצֶלֶם. חִבָּה יְתֵרָה נוֹדַעַת לוֹ שֶׁנִּבְרָא בְצֶלֶם, שֶׁנֶּאֱמַר: "כִּי בְּצֶלֶם אֱלֹהִים עָשָׂה אֶת־הָאָדָם." חֲבִיבִין יִשְׂרָאֵל שֶׁנִּקְרְאוּ בָנִים לַמָּקוֹם. חִבָּה יְתֵרָה נוֹדַעַת לָהֶם שֶׁנִּקְרְאוּ בָנִים לַמָּקוֹם, שֶׁנֶּאֱמַר: "בָּנִים אַתֶּם לַיָי אֱלֹהֵיכֶם." חֲבִיבִין יִשְׂרָאֵל שֶׁנִּתַּן לָהֶם כְּלִי חֶמְדָּה. חִבָּה יְתֵרָה נוֹדַעַת לָהֶם, שֶׁנִּתַּן לָהֶם כְּלִי חֶמְדָּה, שֶׁבּוֹ נִבְרָא הָעוֹלָם. שֶׁנֶּאֱמַר: "כִּי לֶקַח טוֹב נָתַתִּי לָכֶם, תּוֹרָתִי אַל־תַּעֲזֹבוּ."

יט. הַכֹּל צָפוּי, וְהָרְשׁוּת נְתוּנָה, וּבְטוֹב הָעוֹלָם נִדּוֹן, וְהַכֹּל לְפִי רוֹב הַמַּעֲשֶׂה:

כ. הוּא הָיָה אוֹמֵר: הַכֹּל נָתוּן בָּעֵרָבוֹן, וּמְצוּדָה פְרוּסָה עַל כָּל הַחַיִּים, הֶחָנוּת פְּתוּחָה, וְהַחֶנְוָנִי מַקִּיף, וְהַפִּנְקָס פָּתוּחַ, וְהַיָּד כּוֹתֶבֶת, וְכָל הָרוֹצֶה לִלְוֹת, יָבוֹא וְיִלְוֶה, וְהַגַּבָּאִים מַחֲזִירִין תָּדִיר בְּכָל יוֹם, וְנִפְרָעִין מִן הָאָדָם מִדַּעְתּוֹ וְשֶׁלֹּא מִדַּעְתּוֹ, וְיֵשׁ לָהֶם עַל מַה שֶּׁיִּסְמֹכוּ, וְהַדִּין דִּין אֱמֶת, וְהַכֹּל מְתֻקָּן לִסְעוּדָה.

כא. רַבִּי אֶלְעָזָר בֶּן עֲזַרְיָה אוֹמֵר: אִם אֵין תּוֹרָה, אֵין דֶּרֶךְ אֶרֶץ; אִם אֵין דֶּרֶךְ אֶרֶץ אֵין תּוֹרָה. אִם אֵין חָכְמָה, אֵין יִרְאָה; אִם אֵין יִרְאָה, אֵין חָכְמָה. אִם אֵין דַּעַת, אֵין בִּינָה; אִם אֵין בִּינָה, אֵין דַּעַת. אִם אֵין קֶמַח, אֵין תּוֹרָה; אִם אֵין תּוֹרָה, אֵין קֶמַח.

כב. הוּא הָיָה אוֹמֵר: כָּל שֶׁחָכְמָתוֹ מְרֻבָּה מִמַּעֲשָׂיו, לְמָה הוּא דוֹמֶה? לְאִילָן שֶׁעֲנָפָיו מְרֻבִּין, וְשָׁרָשָׁיו מוּעָטִין, וְהָרוּחַ בָּאָה וְעוֹקַרְתּוֹ, וְהוֹפַכְתּוֹ עַל פָּנָיו, שֶׁנֶּאֱמַר: "וְהָיָה כְּעַרְעָר בָּעֲרָבָה וְלֹא יִרְאֶה כִּי־יָבוֹא טוֹב, וְשָׁכַן חֲרֵרִים בַּמִּדְבָּר, אֶרֶץ מְלֵחָה וְלֹא תֵשֵׁב." אֲבָל כָּל שֶׁמַּעֲשָׂיו מְרֻבִּין מֵחָכְמָתוֹ, לְמָה הוּא דוֹמֶה? לְאִילָן שֶׁעֲנָפָיו מוּעָטִין, וְשָׁרָשָׁיו מְרֻבִּין, שֶׁאֲפִלּוּ כָּל הָרוּחוֹת שֶׁבָּעוֹלָם בָּאוֹת וְנוֹשְׁבוֹת בּוֹ אֵין מְזִיזִין אוֹתוֹ מִמְּקוֹמוֹ, שֶׁנֶּאֱמַר: "וְהָיָה כְּעֵץ שָׁתוּל עַל־מַיִם וְעַל־יוּבַל יְשַׁלַּח שָׁרָשָׁיו וְלֹא יִרְאֶה כִּי־יָבֹא חֹם וְהָיָה עָלֵהוּ רַעֲנָן, וּבִשְׁנַת בַּצֹּרֶת לֹא יִדְאָג, וְלֹא יָמִישׁ מֵעֲשׂוֹת פֶּרִי."

כג. רַבִּי אֶלְעָזָר (בֶּן) חִסְמָא אוֹמֵר: קִנִּין וּפִתְחֵי נִדָּה הֵן הֵן גּוּפֵי הֲלָכוֹת; תְּקוּפוֹת וְגִימַטְרִיָּאוֹת–פַּרְפְּרָאוֹת לַחָכְמָה.

3:18 He used to say: Beloved is humanity, for it is created in the image of God; still more beloved, that it was made known to humanity that it is created in the image of God. As it is said: "In the image of God He made Man" (GEN 9:6). Beloved is Israel, for they were called children of God. Still more beloved, that it was made known to them that they were called children of God. As it is said: "Children are you to the Lord, your God" (DEUT 14:1). Beloved is Israel, for they were given a precious implement; still more beloved, that it was made known to them that they were given a precious implement through which the world was created. As it is said: "For I have given you a good teaching; do not forsake my Torah" (PROV 4:2).

3:19 All is foreseen, and freedom of choice is granted. With goodness the world is judged, and all is according to the preponderance of deeds.

3:20 He used to say: Everything is given on pledge, and a net is spread out over all who live. The shop is open, and the shopkeeper gives credit. The ledger is open, the hand writes, and all who want to borrow, come and borrow. The collectors go around regularly every day and settle accounts, whether the person knows it or not. They have reliable information, and the judgment is true. And all is arranged for the banquet. [p. 122]

3:21 Rabbi Elazar ben Azariah said: Without Torah, there is no proper worldly conduct; without proper worldly conduct, there is no Torah. Without wisdom, there is no awe of God; without awe of God, there is no wisdom. Without understanding, there is no knowledge; without knowledge, there is no understanding. Without flour, there is no Torah; without Torah, there is no flour.

3:22 He used to say: One whose wisdom exceeds his deeds, what is he like? Like a tree whose branches are many, and roots are few. The wind comes and uproots and overturns it. As it is said: "And he shall be like a bush in the desert, which does not sense when good will come; he shall dwell in a parched land in the wilderness, a salt land, not habitable" (JER 17:6). And one whose deeds exceed his wisdom, what is he like? Like a tree whose branches are few, and roots are many. Even if all the winds of the earth come and blow on it, it will not be moved from its place. As it is said: "He shall be like a tree planted by waters, sending forth its roots by a stream: it does not sense the coming of heat, its leaves are ever fresh; it has no care in a year of drought, it does not cease to yield its fruit" (JER 17:8). [p. 115]

3:23 Rabbi Eliezar Ḥisma said: The reckoning of bird sacrifices and the onset of a woman's unclean period—these, these are the body of Torah law; the calculations of heavenly cycles and geometry are side dishes for wisdom.

א. בֶּן זוֹמָא אוֹמֵר: אֵיזֶהוּ חָכָם? הַלּוֹמֵד מִכָּל אָדָם, שֶׁנֶּאֱמַר: "מִכָּל־מְלַמְּדַי הִשְׂכַּלְתִּי." אֵיזֶהוּ גִבּוֹר? הַכּוֹבֵשׁ אֶת יִצְרוֹ, שֶׁנֶּאֱמַר: "טוֹב אֶרֶךְ אַפַּיִם מִגִּבּוֹר, וּמֹשֵׁל בְּרוּחוֹ מִלֹּכֵד עִיר." אֵיזֶהוּ עָשִׁיר? הַשָּׂמֵחַ בְּחֶלְקוֹ, שֶׁנֶּאֱמַר: "יְגִיעַ כַּפֶּיךָ כִּי תֹאכֵל אַשְׁרֶיךָ וְטוֹב לָךְ." אַשְׁרֶיךָ–בָּעוֹלָם הַזֶּה, וְטוֹב לָךְ–לָעוֹלָם הַבָּא: אֵיזֶהוּ מְכֻבָּד? הַמְכַבֵּד אֶת הַבְּרִיּוֹת, שֶׁנֶּאֱמַר: "כִּי־מְכַבְּדַי אֲכַבֵּד וּבֹזַי יֵקָלּוּ."

ב. בֶּן עַזַּאי אוֹמֵר: הֱוֵי רָץ לְמִצְוָה קַלָּה, וּבוֹרֵחַ מִן הָעֲבֵרָה. שֶׁמִּצְוָה גוֹרֶרֶת מִצְוָה, וַעֲבֵרָה גוֹרֶרֶת עֲבֵרָה, שֶׁשְּׂכַר מִצְוָה מִצְוָה, וּשְׂכַר עֲבֵרָה עֲבֵרָה.

ג. הוּא הָיָה אוֹמֵר: אַל תְּהִי בָז לְכָל אָדָם, וְאַל תְּהִי מַפְלִיג לְכָל דָּבָר, שֶׁאֵין לְךָ אָדָם שֶׁאֵין לוֹ שָׁעָה, וְאֵין לְךָ דָבָר שֶׁאֵין לוֹ מָקוֹם.

ד. רַבִּי לְוִיטַס אִישׁ יַבְנֶה אוֹמֵר: מְאֹד מְאֹד הֱוֵי שְׁפַל רוּחַ, שֶׁתִּקְוַת אֱנוֹשׁ רִמָּה.

ה. רַבִּי יוֹחָנָן בֶּן בְּרוֹקָא אוֹמֵר: כָּל הַמְחַלֵּל שֵׁם שָׁמַיִם בַּסֵּתֶר, נִפְרָעִין מִמֶּנּוּ בְּגָלוּי, אֶחָד שׁוֹגֵג וְאֶחָד מֵזִיד בְּחִלּוּל הַשֵּׁם.

ו. רַבִּי יִשְׁמָעֵאל בַּר רַבִּי יוֹסֵי אוֹמֵר: הַלּוֹמֵד עַל מְנָת לְלַמֵּד, מַסְפִּיקִין בְּיָדוֹ לִלְמוֹד וּלְלַמֵּד, וְהַלּוֹמֵד עַל מְנָת לַעֲשׂוֹת, מַסְפִּיקִין בְּיָדוֹ לִלְמוֹד, וּלְלַמֵּד, לִשְׁמוֹר, וְלַעֲשׂוֹת.

ז. רַבִּי צָדוֹק אוֹמֵר: אַל תִּפְרוֹשׁ מִן הַצִּבּוּר, וְאַל תַּעַשׂ עַצְמְךָ כְּעוֹרְכֵי הַדַּיָּנִין, וְאַל תַּעֲשֶׂהָ עֲטָרָה לְהִתְגַּדֵּל בָּה, וְלֹא קַרְדּוֹם לַחְפּוֹר בָּה, וְכָךְ הָיָה הִלֵּל אוֹמֵר: וּדְאִשְׁתַּמֵּשׁ בְּתָגָא חֲלָף. הָא לָמַדְתָּ, כָּל הַנֶּהֱנֶה מִדִּבְרֵי תוֹרָה נוֹטֵל חַיָּיו מִן הָעוֹלָם.

ח. רַבִּי יוֹסֵי אוֹמֵר: כָּל הַמְכַבֵּד אֶת הַתּוֹרָה, גוּפוֹ מְכֻבָּד עַל הַבְּרִיּוֹת, וְכָל הַמְחַלֵּל אֶת הַתּוֹרָה, גוּפוֹ מְחֻלָּל עַל הַבְּרִיּוֹת.

ט. רַבִּי יִשְׁמָעֵאל בְּנוֹ אוֹמֵר: הַחֹשֵׂךְ עַצְמוֹ מִן הַדִּין, פּוֹרֵק מִמֶּנּוּ אֵיבָה, וְגָזֵל, וּשְׁבוּעַת שָׁוְא, וְהַגַּס לִבּוֹ בְּהוֹרָאָה, שׁוֹטֶה, רָשָׁע, וְגַס רוּחַ.

י. הוּא הָיָה אוֹמֵר: אַל תְּהִי דָן יְחִידִי, שֶׁאֵין דָּן יְחִידִי אֶלָּא אֶחָד. וְאַל תֹּאמַר: קַבְּלוּ דַעְתִּי שֶׁהֵן רַשָּׁאִין וְלֹא אָתָּה.

4:1 Ben Zoma said: Who is wise? One who learns from every person. As it is said: "From all my teachers have I gained wisdom" (PS 119:99). Who is valiant? One who conquers his impulses. As it is said: "He that is slow to anger is better than the mighty, and he that rules over his spirit than he who captures a city" (PROV 16:32). Who is rich? One who rejoices in his portion. As it is said: "When you eat the labor of your hands, you are happy, and it will be well with you" (PS 128:2). "You are happy"—in this world. And "it will be well with you"—in the world to come. Who is honored? One who honors others. As it is said: "Those who honor me will I honor and those who despise me will be put to shame" (I SAMUEL 2:30).

4:2 Ben Azzai said: Run to do a small mitzvah, and flee from sin. For mitzvah leads to mitzvah, and sin leads to sin. For the reward of a mitzvah is a mitzvah and the punishment of a sin is a sin.

4:3 He used to say: despise no man and dismiss no thing; for there is no man who does not have his hour, and no thing that does not have its place.

4:4 Rabbi Levitas of Yavneh said: Be very, very humble, for the hope of Man is the worm.

4:5 Rabbi Yoḥanan ben Berokah said: All who profane the Name of Heaven in secret, they will be punished in public. Unwittingly or wittingly—it is all the same for profanation of the Name. [p. 118]

4:6 Rabbi Ishmael his son said: All who learn in order to teach: they will be granted enough to learn and to teach; all who learn in order to do: they will be granted enough to learn and to teach, to keep the commandments and to do them.

4:7 Rabbi Tzadok said: Don't separate yourself from the community and [while a judge] do not act as an advocate. Do not make of it a crown to glorify yourself, nor a spade to dig with. Hillel, too, used to say: "He who exploits the crown shall perish." Thus you learn: anyone who uses the words of Torah for material gain removes his life from the world.

4:8 Rabbi Yose said: All who honor the Torah will be honored by their fellow men, and all who dishonor the Torah will be dishonored by their fellow men.

4:9 Rabbi Ishmael his son said: He who refrains from judging saves himself from animosity, robbery, and false oaths; he who brashly issues judgments is foolish, wicked, and arrogant.

4:10 He used to say: Do not judge alone, for none can judge alone except One. And do not say: "Accept my opinion!" for they are entitled, not you.

יא. רַבִּי יוֹנָתָן אוֹמֵר: כָּל הַמְקַיֵּם אֶת הַתּוֹרָה מֵעֹנִי, סוֹפוֹ לְקַיְּמָהּ מֵעֹשֶׁר, וְכָל הַמְבַטֵּל אֶת הַתּוֹרָה מֵעֹשֶׁר, סוֹפוֹ לְבַטְּלָהּ מֵעֹנִי.

יב. רַבִּי מֵאִיר אוֹמֵר: הֱוֵי מְמַעֵט בְּעֵסֶק, וַעֲסֹק בַּתּוֹרָה, וֶהֱוֵי שְׁפַל רוּחַ בִּפְנֵי כָל אָדָם, וְאִם בָּטַלְתָּ מִן הַתּוֹרָה, יֶשׁ לָךְ בְּטֵלִים הַרְבֵּה כְּנֶגְדָּךְ, וְאִם עָמַלְתָּ בַּתּוֹרָה, יֶשׁ לוֹ שָׂכָר הַרְבֵּה לִתֵּן לָךְ.

יג. רַבִּי אֱלִיעֶזֶר בֶּן יַעֲקֹב אוֹמֵר: הָעוֹשֶׂה מִצְוָה אַחַת, קוֹנֶה לוֹ פְּרַקְלִיט אֶחָד, וְהָעוֹבֵר עֲבֵרָה אַחַת, קוֹנֶה לוֹ קַטֵּגוֹר אֶחָד, תְּשׁוּבָה וּמַעֲשִׂים טוֹבִים כִּתְרִיס בִּפְנֵי הַפֻּרְעָנוּת.

יד. רַבִּי יוֹחָנָן הַסַּנְדְּלָר אוֹמֵר: כָּל כְּנֵסִיָּה שֶׁהִיא לְשֵׁם שָׁמַיִם, סוֹפָהּ לְהִתְקַיֵּם, וְשֶׁאֵינָהּ לְשֵׁם שָׁמַיִם, אֵין סוֹפָהּ לְהִתְקַיֵּם.

טו. רַבִּי אֶלְעָזָר בֶּן שַׁמּוּעַ אוֹמֵר: יְהִי כְבוֹד תַּלְמִידְךָ חָבִיב עָלֶיךָ כְּשֶׁלָּךְ, וּכְבוֹד חֲבֵרְךָ כְּמוֹרָא רַבָּךְ, וּמוֹרָא רַבָּךְ כְּמוֹרָא שָׁמָיִם.

טז. רַבִּי יְהוּדָה אוֹמֵר: הֱוֵי זָהִיר בְּתַלְמוּד, שֶׁשִּׁגְגַת תַּלְמוּד עוֹלָה זָדוֹן.

יז. רַבִּי שִׁמְעוֹן אוֹמֵר: שְׁלֹשָׁה כְתָרִים הֵן: כֶּתֶר תּוֹרָה, וְכֶתֶר כְּהֻנָּה, וְכֶתֶר מַלְכוּת, וְכֶתֶר שֵׁם טוֹב עוֹלֶה עַל גַּבֵּיהֶן.

יח. רַבִּי נְהוֹרַאי אוֹמֵר: הֱוֵי גוֹלֶה לִמְקוֹם תּוֹרָה, וְאַל תֹּאמַר שֶׁהִיא תָבוֹא אַחֲרֶיךָ שֶׁחֲבֵרֶיךָ יְקַיְּמוּהָ בְּיָדֶךָ, וְאֶל בִּינָתְךָ אַל תִּשָּׁעֵן.

יט. רַבִּי יַנַּאי אוֹמֵר: אֵין בְּיָדֵינוּ לֹא מִשַּׁלְוַת הָרְשָׁעִים וְאַף לֹא מִיִּסּוּרֵי הַצַּדִּיקִים.

כ. רַבִּי מַתְיָא בֶּן חָרָשׁ אוֹמֵר: הֱוֵי מַקְדִּים בִּשְׁלוֹם כָּל אָדָם, וֶהֱוֵי זָנָב לָאֲרָיוֹת, וְאַל תְּהִי רֹאשׁ לַשּׁוּעָלִים.

כא. רַבִּי יַעֲקֹב אוֹמֵר: הָעוֹלָם הַזֶּה דּוֹמֶה לִפְרוֹזְדוֹר בִּפְנֵי הָעוֹלָם הַבָּא. הַתְקֵן עַצְמְךָ בִּפְרוֹזְדוֹר, כְּדֵי שֶׁתִּכָּנֵס לַטְּרַקְלִין.

כב. הוּא הָיָה אוֹמֵר: יָפָה שָׁעָה אַחַת בִּתְשׁוּבָה וּמַעֲשִׂים טוֹבִים בָּעוֹלָם הַזֶּה מִכָּל חַיֵּי הָעוֹלָם הַבָּא, וְיָפָה שָׁעָה אַחַת שֶׁל קוֹרַת רוּחַ בָּעוֹלָם הַבָּא מִכָּל חַיֵּי הָעוֹלָם הַזֶּה.

4:11　Rabbi Yonatan said: All who fulfill the Torah in poverty will in the end fulfill it in wealth, and all who neglect the Torah in wealth will in the end neglect it in poverty. [p. 144]

4:12　Rabbi Meir said: Do less business and busy yourself with Torah. And be humble before every person. Neglect Torah, and many causes for neglect will confront you. Toil in the Torah, and a great reward will be given you.

4:13　Rabbi Eliezer ben Ya'akov said: If you do one mitzvah, you acquire for yourself one advocate, and if you commit one sin, you acquire for yourself one prosecutor. Repentance and good deeds are as a shield against calamity. [p. 140]

4:14　Rabbi Yohanan HaSandlar said: Every assembly which is for the sake of Heaven will in the end be preserved; and those not for the sake of Heaven will not in the end be preserved. [p. 172]

4:15　Rabbi Elazar ben Shammua said: Let the honor of your student be as dear to you as your own; let the honor of your colleague be as your reverence for your teacher; and let your reverence for your teacher be as your reverence for Heaven. [p. 90]

4:16　Rabbi Yehudah said: Take care in talmud, for unintentional error in talmud is as serious as intentional sin. [p. 35]

4:17　Rabbi Shimon said: There are three crowns: the crown of Torah, the crown of priesthood, and the crown of royalty; but the crown of a good name is above them all. [p. 76]

4:18　Rabbi Nehorai said: Emigrate to a place of Torah, and don't say that it will come to you; for your fellow students will establish it as your possession. And "do not rely on your own understanding" (PROV 3:5). [p. 148]

4:19　Rabbi Yannai said: Beyond our grasp are the well-being of the wicked and the sufferings of the righteous.

4:20　Rabbi Matia ben Harash said: Be the first to greet all every person; and be a tail to lions, not a head to jackals. [p. 174]

4:21　Rabbi Ya'akov said: This world is like an anteroom before the world to come. Prepare yourself in the anteroom so that you may enter the banquet hall.

4:22　He used to say: Better is one hour of repentance and good deeds in this life than all the life of the world to come. And better is one hour of blissful spirit in the world to come than all the life of this world.

אבות: פרק ד, ה

כג. רַבִּי שִׁמְעוֹן בֶּן אֶלְעָזָר אוֹמֵר: אַל תְּרַצֶּה אֶת חֲבֵרְךָ בְּשַׁעַת כַּעֲסוֹ, וְאַל תְּנַחֲמֵהוּ בְּשָׁעָה שֶׁמֵּתוֹ מֻטָּל לְפָנָיו, וְאַל תִּשְׁאַל לוֹ בְּשַׁעַת נִדְרוֹ, וְאַל תִּשְׁתַּדֵּל לִרְאוֹתוֹ בְּשַׁעַת קַלְקָלָתוֹ.

כד. שְׁמוּאֵל הַקָּטָן אוֹמֵר: בִּנְפֹל אוֹיִבְךָ אַל־תִּשְׂמָח, וּבִכָּשְׁלוֹ אַל־יָגֵל לִבֶּךָ: "פֶּן־יִרְאֶה יְיָ וְרַע בְּעֵינָיו, וְהֵשִׁיב מֵעָלָיו אַפּוֹ."

כה. אֱלִישָׁע בֶּן אֲבוּיָ אוֹמֵר: הַלּוֹמֵד יֶלֶד לְמָה הוּא דוֹמֶה? לִדְיוֹ כְתוּבָה עַל נְיָר חָדָשׁ, וְהַלּוֹמֵד זָקֵן לְמָה הוּא דוֹמֶה? לִדְיוֹ כְתוּבָה עַל נְיָר מָחוּק.

כו. רַבִּי יוֹסֵי בַּר יְהוּדָה אִישׁ כְּפַר הַבַּבְלִי אוֹמֵר: הַלּוֹמֵד מִן הַקְּטַנִּים לְמָה הוּא דוֹמֶה? לְאוֹכֵל עֲנָבִים קֵהוֹת, וְשׁוֹתֶה יַיִן מִגִּתּוֹ, וְהַלּוֹמֵד מִן הַזְּקֵנִים לְמָה הוּא דוֹמֶה? לְאוֹכֵל עֲנָבִים בְּשׁוּלוֹת, וְשׁוֹתֶה יַיִן יָשָׁן.

כז. רַבִּי מֵאִיר אוֹמֵר: אַל תִּסְתַּכֵּל בַּקַּנְקַן אֶלָּא בְּמַה שֶּׁיֵּשׁ בּוֹ, יֵשׁ קַנְקַן חָדָשׁ מָלֵא יָשָׁן, וְיָשָׁן שֶׁאֲפִלּוּ חָדָשׁ אֵין בּוֹ.

כח. רַבִּי אֶלְעָזָר הַקַּפָּר אוֹמֵר: הַקִּנְאָה, וְהַתַּאֲוָה, וְהַכָּבוֹד, מוֹצִיאִין אֶת הָאָדָם מִן הָעוֹלָם.

כט. הוּא הָיָה אוֹמֵר: הַיְּלוֹדִים לָמוּת, וְהַמֵּתִים לִחְיוֹת, וְהַחַיִּים לִדּוֹן. לֵידַע וּלְהוֹדִיעַ וּלְהִוָּדַע, שֶׁהוּא אֵל, הוּא הַיּוֹצֵר, הוּא הַבּוֹרֵא, הוּא הַמֵּבִין, הוּא הַדַּיָּן, הוּא הָעֵד, הוּא בַּעַל דִּין, הוּא עָתִיד לָדוּן. בָּרוּךְ הוּא, שֶׁאֵין לְפָנָיו לֹא עַוְלָה, וְלֹא שִׁכְחָה, וְלֹא מַשּׂוֹא פָנִים, וְלֹא מִקַּח שֹׁחַד, וְדַע שֶׁהַכֹּל לְפִי הַחֶשְׁבּוֹן, וְאַל יַבְטִיחֲךָ יִצְרְךָ שֶׁהַשְּׁאוֹל בֵּית מָנוֹס לָךְ, שֶׁעַל כָּרְחֲךָ אַתָּה נוֹצָר, וְעַל כָּרְחֲךָ אַתָּה נוֹלָד, וְעַל כָּרְחֲךָ אַתָּה חַי, וְעַל כָּרְחֲךָ אַתָּה מֵת, וְעַל כָּרְחֲךָ אַתָּה עָתִיד לִתֵּן דִּין וְחֶשְׁבּוֹן לִפְנֵי מֶלֶךְ מַלְכֵי הַמְּלָכִים הַקָּדוֹשׁ בָּרוּךְ הוּא.

א. בַּעֲשָׂרָה מַאֲמָרוֹת נִבְרָא הָעוֹלָם, וּמַה תַּלְמוּד לוֹמַר? וַהֲלֹא בְּמַאֲמָר אֶחָד יָכוֹל לְהִבָּרְאוֹת? אֶלָּא לְהִפָּרַע מִן הָרְשָׁעִים, שֶׁמְּאַבְּדִין אֶת הָעוֹלָם שֶׁנִּבְרָא בַּעֲשָׂרָה מַאֲמָרוֹת, וְלִתֵּן שָׂכָר טוֹב לַצַּדִּיקִים, שֶׁמְּקַיְּמִין אֶת הָעוֹלָם שֶׁנִּבְרָא בַּעֲשָׂרָה מַאֲמָרוֹת.

ב. עֲשָׂרָה דוֹרוֹת מֵאָדָם וְעַד נֹחַ, לְהוֹדִיעַ כַּמָּה אֶרֶךְ אַפַּיִם לְפָנָיו, שֶׁכָּל הַדּוֹרוֹת הָיוּ מַכְעִיסִין וּבָאִין, עַד שֶׁהֵבִיא עֲלֵיהֶם אֶת מֵי הַמַּבּוּל.

ג. עֲשָׂרָה דוֹרוֹת מִנֹּחַ וְעַד אַבְרָהָם, לְהוֹדִיעַ כַּמָּה אֶרֶךְ אַפַּיִם לְפָנָיו, שֶׁכָּל הַדּוֹרוֹת הָיוּ מַכְעִיסִין וּבָאִין, עַד שֶׁבָּא אַבְרָהָם אָבִינוּ וְקִבֵּל שְׂכַר כֻּלָּם.

4:23 Rabbi Shimon ben Elazar said: Do not placate your friend in the hour of his anger, and do not console him in the hour when his dead lies before him, and do not question him in the hour of his vow, and do not try to see him in his hour of disgrace.

4:24 Shmuel HaKatan said: "If your enemy falls do not exult; If he trips, do not rejoice, lest the Lord see it and be displeased, and avert His wrath from him" (PROV 24:17–18). [p. 119]

4:25 Elisha ben Avuya said: Learning as a child, what is it like? Like ink written on new paper. Learning as an old person, what is it like? Like ink written on erased paper.

4:26 Rabbi Yose bar Yehudah of Kfar Bavli said: Learning from the young, what is it like? Like eating unripe grapes and drinking wine from the vat. Learning from the old, what is it like? Like eating ripe grapes and drinking aged wine.

4:27 Rabbi Meir said: Do not look at the bottle, but at what is in it. There are new bottles filled with aged wine, and old bottles that don't even have new wine.

4:28 Rabbi Elazar HaKappar said: Envy, lust, and ambition drive a person from the world. [p. 116]

4:29 He used to say: Those who are born, die; those who are dead, live again; and those who live again are judged. So know, make known, and have knowledge that He is God, He is maker, He is creator, He is knower, He is judge, He is witness, He is plaintiff, and He will in future make judgment. Blessed be He, in whose court there is no wrongdoing, no forgetting, no favoritism, no bribe-taking—for all is His. And know that all depends on the accounting. And do not heed your evil inclination promising you that sheol will be a place of refuge for you. For not by your choice were you created, do you live, will you die, and will you be called to account before the Supreme King of kings, the Holy One, blessed be He.

5:1 By ten utterances was the world created. What does this teach; for could not it have been created by one utterance? —The punishment of the wicked who destroy the world that was created by ten utterances, and the good reward of the righteous who sustain the world that was created by ten utterances.*

5:2 Ten were the generations from Adam to Noah, to make known how great His patience—for all these were provoking Him until He brought upon them the waters of the flood.*

5:3 Ten were the generations from Noah to Abraham, to make known how great His patience—for all these were provoking Him until Abraham our father received a reward for all of them.*

ד. עֲשָׂרָה נִסְיוֹנוֹת נִתְנַסָּה אַבְרָהָם אָבִינוּ, וְעָמַד בְּכֻלָּם, לְהוֹדִיעַ כַּמָּה חִבָּתוֹ שֶׁל אַבְרָהָם אָבִינוּ.

ה. עֲשָׂרָה נִסִּים נַעֲשׂוּ לַאֲבוֹתֵינוּ בְּמִצְרַיִם, וַעֲשָׂרָה עַל הַיָּם.

ו. עֶשֶׂר מַכּוֹת הֵבִיא הַקָּדוֹשׁ בָּרוּךְ הוּא עַל הַמִּצְרִיִּים בְּמִצְרַיִם, וְעֶשֶׂר עַל הַיָּם.

ז. עֲשָׂרָה נִסְיוֹנוֹת נִסּוּ אֲבוֹתֵינוּ אֶת הַקָּדוֹשׁ בָּרוּךְ הוּא בַּמִּדְבָּר, שֶׁנֶּאֱמַר "וַיְנַסּוּ אֹתִי זֶה עֶשֶׂר פְּעָמִים וְלֹא שָׁמְעוּ בְּקוֹלִי."

ח. עֲשָׂרָה נִסִּים נַעֲשׂוּ לַאֲבוֹתֵינוּ בְּבֵית הַמִּקְדָּשׁ, לֹא הִפִּילָה אִשָּׁה מֵרֵיחַ בְּשַׂר הַקֹּדֶשׁ, וְלֹא הִסְרִיחַ בְּשַׂר הַקֹּדֶשׁ מֵעוֹלָם, וְלֹא נִרְאָה זְבוּב בְּבֵית הַמִּטְבָּחַיִם, וְלֹא אֵרַע קֶרִי לְכֹהֵן גָּדוֹל בְּיוֹם הַכִּפּוּרִים, וְלֹא כִבּוּ הַגְּשָׁמִים אֵשׁ שֶׁל עֲצֵי הַמַּעֲרָכָה, וְלֹא נִצְּחָה הָרוּחַ אֶת עַמּוּד הֶעָשָׁן, וְלֹא נִמְצָא פְסוּל בָּעוֹמֶר וּבִשְׁתֵּי הַלֶּחֶם וּבְלֶחֶם הַפָּנִים, עוֹמְדִים צְפוּפִים וּמִשְׁתַּחֲוִים רְוָחִים, וְלֹא הִזִּיק נָחָשׁ וְעַקְרָב בִּירוּשָׁלַיִם מֵעוֹלָם, וְלֹא אָמַר אָדָם לַחֲבֵרוֹ צַר לִי הַמָּקוֹם שֶׁאָלִין בִּירוּשָׁלָיִם.

ט. עֲשָׂרָה דְבָרִים נִבְרְאוּ בְּעֶרֶב שַׁבָּת בֵּין הַשְּׁמָשׁוֹת, וְאֵלוּ הֵן, פִּי הָאָרֶץ, פִּי הַבְּאֵר, פִּי הָאָתוֹן, הַקֶּשֶׁת, וְהַמָּן, וְהַמַּטֶּה, וְהַשָּׁמִיר, הַכְּתָב, וְהַמִּכְתָּב, וְהַלֻּחוֹת, וְיֵשׁ אוֹמְרִים אַף הַמַּזִּיקִין וּקְבוּרָתוֹ שֶׁל מֹשֶׁה וְאֵילוֹ שֶׁל אַבְרָהָם אָבִינוּ, וְיֵשׁ אוֹמְרִים אַף צְבָת בִּצְבָת עֲשׂוּיָה.

י. שִׁבְעָה דְבָרִים בְּגוֹלֵם וְשִׁבְעָה בְּחָכָם, חָכָם אֵינוֹ מְדַבֵּר לִפְנֵי מִי שֶׁגָּדוֹל מִמֶּנּוּ בְּחָכְמָה וּבְמִנְיָן, וְאֵינוֹ נִכְנָס לְתוֹךְ דִּבְרֵי חֲבֵרוֹ, וְאֵינוֹ נִבְהָל לְהָשִׁיב, שׁוֹאֵל כָּעִנְיָן, וּמֵשִׁיב כַּהֲלָכָה, וְאוֹמֵר עַל רִאשׁוֹן רִאשׁוֹן וְעַל אַחֲרוֹן אַחֲרוֹן, וְעַל מַה שֶּׁלֹּא שָׁמַע, אוֹמֵר לֹא שָׁמַעְתִּי, וּמוֹדֶה עַל הָאֱמֶת. וְחִלּוּפֵיהֶן בְּגוֹלֵם.

יא. שִׁבְעָה מִינֵי פוּרְעָנִיּוֹת בָּאִים לָעוֹלָם עַל שִׁבְעָה גּוּפֵי עֲבֵרָה. מִקְצָתָן מְעַשְּׂרִין וּמִקְצָתָן אֵינָן מְעַשְּׂרִין, רָעָב שֶׁל בַּצּוֹרֶת בָּא, מִקְצָתָן רְעֵבִים וּמִקְצָתָן שְׂבֵעִים. גָּמְרוּ שֶׁלֹּא לְעַשֵּׂר, רָעָב שֶׁל מְהוּמָה וְשֶׁל בַּצּוֹרֶת בָּא, וְשֶׁלֹּא לִטּוֹל אֶת הַחַלָּה, רָעָב שֶׁל כְּלָיָה בָּא. דֶּבֶר בָּא לָעוֹלָם–עַל מִיתוֹת הָאֲמוּרוֹת בַּתּוֹרָה שֶׁלֹּא נִמְסְרוּ לְבֵית דִּין, וְעַל פֵּרוֹת שְׁבִיעִית. חֶרֶב בָּאָה לָעוֹלָם–עַל עִנּוּי הַדִּין, וְעַל עִוּוּת הַדִּין, וְעַל הַמּוֹרִים בַּתּוֹרָה שֶׁלֹּא כַהֲלָכָה. חַיָּה רָעָה בָּאָה לָעוֹלָם, עַל שְׁבוּעַת שָׁוְא וְעַל חִלּוּל הַשֵּׁם. גָּלוּת בָּאָה לָעוֹלָם–עַל עֲבוֹדַת

5:4 Ten trials tested Abraham our father, and he stood up to them all—so as to make known the love of Abraham our father.*

5:5 Ten miracles were wrought for our ancestors in Egypt and ten at the sea.*

5:6 Ten plagues the Holy One, blessed be He, brought upon the Egyptians in Egypt, and ten at the sea.*

5:7 With ten trials our ancestors tested the Holy One, blessed be He, in the wilderness. As it is said: "They have tested me these ten times, by not hearkening to my voice" (NUM 14:22).*

5:8 Ten miracles were wrought for our ancestors in the Temple. No woman ever miscarried from the scent of the holy flesh. Never did the holy flesh become putrid. Never was a fly seen in the slaughter house. Never did accidental impurity befall the high priest on Yom Kippur. Never did the rains extinguish the fire of the wood on the altar. No wind prevailed over the pillar of smoke. Never was unfitness found in the *omer*, or in the two loaves, or in the showbread. The worshipers stood packed, yet had space to prostrate themselves. No scorpion or snake ever caused harm in Jerusalem. Never did a man say to his fellow, "There is not enough place for me to lodge overnight in Jerusalem."*

5:9 Ten things were created on the eve of Shabbat at twilight: the mouth of the earth; the mouth of the well; the mouth of the donkey; the rainbow; the manna; the staff; the shamir; the script; the stylus; the tablets. And some say: evil spirits, too, and the grave of Moses, and the ram of Abraham our father. And some say: also tongs made with tongs.

5:10 Seven things mark the crude, and seven the wise. The wise do not speak before one who is greater in wisdom, nor interrupt the words of his colleague, nor rush to reply. Their questions are relevant, their answers to the point. They speak of first things first, and last things last. Of things they have not understood they say, "I do not understand," and they acknowledge the truth. The opposites mark the crude.

5:11 Seven kinds of calamity come into the world because of seven classes of sin: If some tithe and some do not, a famine comes from drought; some go hungry and some are full. If all do not tithe, a famine comes from riots and drought. If they also do not separate the ḥallah, an annihilating famine comes. Plagues come into the world because of capital crimes mentioned in the Torah that are not handed over to a court, and because of forbidden use of produce in a sabbatical year. The sword comes into the world because of delay of justice and perversion of justice, and because of teaching the Torah improperly. Wild beasts come upon the world because of false oaths and profanation of the Name. Exile comes to the world because of worship-

כּוֹכָבִים, וְעַל גִּלּוּי עֲרָיוֹת, וְעַל שְׁפִיכוּת דָּמִים, וְעַל שְׁמִטַּת הָאָרֶץ.

יב. בְּאַרְבָּעָה פְּרָקִים הַדֶּבֶר מִתְרַבֶּה, בָּרְבִיעִית, וּבַשְּׁבִיעִית, וּבְמוֹצָאֵי שְׁבִיעִית, וּבְמוֹצָאֵי הֶחָג שֶׁבְּכָל שָׁנָה וְשָׁנָה. בָּרְבִיעִית–מִפְּנֵי מַעְשַׂר עָנִי שֶׁבַּשְּׁלִישִׁית, בַּשְּׁבִיעִית–מִפְּנֵי מַעְשַׂר עָנִי שֶׁבַּשִּׁשִּׁית, בְּמוֹצָאֵי שְׁבִיעִית–מִפְּנֵי פֵּירוֹת שְׁבִיעִית, בְּמוֹצָאֵי הֶחָג שֶׁבְּכָל שָׁנָה וְשָׁנָה–מִפְּנֵי גֶּזֶל מַתְּנוֹת עֲנִיִּים:

יג. אַרְבַּע מִדּוֹת בָּאָדָם: הָאוֹמֵר שֶׁלִּי שֶׁלִּי וְשֶׁלְּךָ שֶׁלָּךְ–זוֹ מִדָּה בֵּינוֹנִית, וְיֵשׁ אוֹמְרִים זוֹ מִדַּת סְדוֹם. שֶׁלִּי שֶׁלָּךְ וְשֶׁלְּךָ שֶׁלִּי–עַם הָאָרֶץ, שֶׁלִּי שֶׁלָּךְ וְשֶׁלְּךָ שֶׁלָּךְ–חָסִיד, שֶׁלְּךָ שֶׁלִּי וְשֶׁלִּי שֶׁלִּי–רָשָׁע.

יד. אַרְבַּע מִדּוֹת בַּדֵּעוֹת, נוֹחַ לִכְעוֹס וְנוֹחַ לִרְצוֹת–יָצָא הֶפְסֵדוֹ בִּשְׂכָרוֹ, קָשֶׁה לִכְעוֹס וְקָשֶׁה לִרְצוֹת–יָצָא שְׂכָרוֹ בְּהֶפְסֵדוֹ, קָשֶׁה לִכְעוֹס וְנוֹחַ לִרְצוֹת–חָסִיד, נוֹחַ לִכְעוֹס וְקָשֶׁה לִרְצוֹת–רָשָׁע.

טו. אַרְבַּע מִדּוֹת בַּתַּלְמִידִים: מָהִיר לִשְׁמוֹעַ וּמָהִיר לְאַבֵּד–יָצָא שְׂכָרוֹ בְּהֶפְסֵדוֹ, קָשֶׁה לִשְׁמוֹעַ וְקָשֶׁה לְאַבֵּד–יָצָא הֶפְסֵדוֹ בִּשְׂכָרוֹ, מָהִיר לִשְׁמוֹעַ וְקָשֶׁה לְאַבֵּד–זֶה חֵלֶק טוֹב, קָשֶׁה לִשְׁמוֹעַ וּמָהִיר לְאַבֵּד–זֶה חֵלֶק רָע.

טז. אַרְבַּע מִדּוֹת בְּנוֹתְנֵי צְדָקָה, הָרוֹצֶה שֶׁיִּתֵּן וְלֹא יִתְּנוּ אֲחֵרִים–עֵינוֹ רָעָה בְּשֶׁל אֲחֵרִים, יִתְּנוּ אֲחֵרִים וְהוּא לֹא יִתֵּן–עֵינוֹ רָעָה בְּשֶׁלּוֹ, יִתֵּן וְיִתְּנוּ אֲחֵרִים–חָסִיד, לֹא יִתֵּן וְלֹא יִתְּנוּ אֲחֵרִים–רָשָׁע.

יז. אַרְבַּע מִדּוֹת בְּהוֹלְכֵי בֵּית הַמִּדְרָשׁ, הוֹלֵךְ וְאֵינוֹ עוֹשֶׂה–שְׂכַר הֲלִיכָה בְּיָדוֹ, עוֹשֶׂה וְאֵינוֹ הוֹלֵךְ–שְׂכַר מַעֲשֶׂה בְּיָדוֹ, הוֹלֵךְ וְעוֹשֶׂה–חָסִיד, לֹא הוֹלֵךְ וְלֹא עוֹשֶׂה–רָשָׁע.

יח. אַרְבַּע מִדּוֹת בְּיוֹשְׁבִים לִפְנֵי חֲכָמִים: סְפוֹג, וּמַשְׁפֵּךְ מְשַׁמֶּרֶת, וְנָפָה. סְפוֹג, שֶׁהוּא סוֹפֵג אֶת הַכֹּל; וּמַשְׁפֵּךְ, שֶׁמַּכְנִיס בְּזוֹ וּמוֹצִיא בְזוֹ; מְשַׁמֶּרֶת, שֶׁמּוֹצִיאָה אֶת הַיַּיִן וְקוֹלֶטֶת אֶת הַשְּׁמָרִים; וְנָפָה, שֶׁמּוֹצִיאָה אֶת הַקֶּמַח וְקוֹלֶטֶת אֶת הַסֹּלֶת.

יט. כָּל אַהֲבָה שֶׁהִיא תְּלוּיָה בְדָבָר, בָּטֵל דָּבָר בְּטֵלָה אַהֲבָה, וְשֶׁאֵינָה תְּלוּיָה בְדָבָר, אֵינָה בְּטֵלָה לְעוֹלָם. אֵיזוֹ הִיא אַהֲבָה שֶׁהִיא תְלוּיָה בְדָבָר? זוֹ אַהֲבַת אַמְנוֹן וְתָמָר, וְשֶׁאֵינָה תְּלוּיָה בְדָבָר? זוֹ אַהֲבַת דָּוִד וִיהוֹנָתָן.

ping the stars, forbidden sexual relations, the shedding of blood, and not leaving the earth fallow in the sabbatical year. [p. 150]

5:12 At four periods in the seven year cycle pestilence increases: in the fourth year, in the seventh year, at the conclusion of the seventh year, and every year at the conclusion of Sukkot. In the fourth year—for not giving the tithe for the poor in the third. In the seventh year—for not giving the tithe to the poor in the sixth year. At the conclusion of the seventh year—for violations regarding the produce of the seventh year. Every year at the conclusion of Sukkot—for stealing the harvest gifts for the poor.*

5:13 Four types of people. One who says: mine is mine and yours is yours— average (and some say—the character of Sodom); mine is yours and yours is mine—ignoramus; mine is yours, and yours is yours—saintly; yours is mine, and mine is mine—wicked.

5:14 Four types of temperament: Easy to anger, easy to appease—the loss is canceled by the gain. Hard to anger, hard to appease—the gain is canceled by the loss. Hard to anger, easy to appease—saintly. Easy to anger, hard to appease—wicked.

5:15 Four characters in students: Quick to understand and quick to forget—their gain is canceled by their loss. Slow to understand and slow to forget—their loss is canceled by their gain. Quick to understand and slow to forget—wise. Slow to understand and quick to forget—this is a misfortune.

5:16 Four types who give charity: One wants to give, but does not want others to give—an bad eye on others' possessions. One does not want to give, but wants others to give—an bad eye on his own possessions. One wants to give, and wants others to give—saintly. One does not want to give, and does not want others to give—wicked.

5:17 Four types who go to the house of study: Those who attend, but do not practice—they have the reward for attending. Those who practice, but do not attend—they have the reward for practice. Those who attend and practice— saintly. Those who neither attend nor practice—wicked.

5:18 Four types who sit before the wise: A sponge, a funnel, a strainer, and a sifter. The sponge soaks up everything. The funnel takes in at one end and lets out at the other. The strainer lets out the wine, and keeps the dregs. The sifter lets out the meal, and keeps the fine flour.

5:19 All love that is dependent on a particular thing, when the thing ceases, the love ceases. All love that isn't dependent on a particular thing, it will never cease. Which is a love dependent on a thing? The love of Amnon and Tamar. Which is a love not dependent on a thing? The love of David and Jonathan.

אָבוֹת: פֶּרֶק ה

כ. כָּל מַחֲלוֹקֶת שֶׁהִיא לְשֵׁם שָׁמַיִם סוֹפָהּ לְהִתְקַיֵּם, וְשֶׁאֵינָהּ לְשֵׁם שָׁמַיִם אֵין סוֹפָהּ לְהִתְקַיֵּם, אֵיזוֹ הִיא מַחֲלוֹקֶת שֶׁהִיא לְשֵׁם שָׁמַיִם? זוֹ מַחֲלוֹקֶת הִלֵּל וְשַׁמַּאי, וְשֶׁאֵינָהּ לְשֵׁם שָׁמַיִם? זוֹ מַחֲלוֹקֶת קֹרַח וְכָל עֲדָתוֹ.

כא. כָּל הַמְזַכֶּה אֶת הָרַבִּים, אֵין חֵטְא בָּא עַל יָדוֹ, וְכָל הַמַּחֲטִיא אֶת הָרַבִּים אֵין מַסְפִּיקִין בְּיָדוֹ לַעֲשׂוֹת תְּשׁוּבָה. מֹשֶׁה זָכָה וְזִכָּה אֶת הָרַבִּים, זְכוּת הָרַבִּים תָּלוּי בּוֹ, שֶׁנֶּאֱמַר: "צִדְקַת יְיָ עָשָׂה וּמִשְׁפָּטָיו עִם יִשְׂרָאֵל." יָרָבְעָם בֶּן נְבָט חָטָא וְהֶחֱטִיא אֶת הָרַבִּים חֵטְא הָרַבִּים תָּלוּי בּוֹ, שֶׁנֶּאֱמַר: "עַל חַטֹּאת יָרָבְעָם אֲשֶׁר חָטָא וַאֲשֶׁר הֶחֱטִיא אֶת יִשְׂרָאֵל."

כב. כָּל מִי שֶׁיֵּשׁ בּוֹ שְׁלֹשָׁה דְבָרִים הַלָּלוּ, הוּא מִתַּלְמִידָיו שֶׁל אַבְרָהָם אָבִינוּ, וּשְׁלֹשָׁה דְבָרִים אֲחֵרִים, הוּא מִתַּלְמִידָיו שֶׁל בִּלְעָם הָרָשָׁע: עַיִן טוֹבָה, וְרוּחַ נְמוּכָה, וְנֶפֶשׁ שְׁפָלָה—תַּלְמִידָיו שֶׁל אַבְרָהָם אָבִינוּ; עַיִן רָעָה, וְרוּחַ גְּבוֹהָה, וְנֶפֶשׁ רְחָבָה—תַּלְמִידָיו שֶׁל בִּלְעָם הָרָשָׁע, מַה בֵּין תַּלְמִידָיו שֶׁל אַבְרָהָם אָבִינוּ לְתַלְמִידָיו שֶׁל בִּלְעָם הָרָשָׁע? תַּלְמִידָיו שֶׁל אַבְרָהָם אָבִינוּ אוֹכְלִין בָּעוֹלָם הַזֶּה וְנוֹחֲלִין הָעוֹלָם הַבָּא, שֶׁנֶּאֱמַר: "לְהַנְחִיל אֹהֲבַי יֵשׁ וְאֹצְרֹתֵיהֶם אֲמַלֵּא," אֲבָל תַּלְמִידָיו שֶׁל בִּלְעָם הָרָשָׁע יוֹרְשִׁין גֵּיהִנָּם וְיוֹרְדִין לִבְאֵר שַׁחַת, שֶׁנֶּאֱמַר: "וְאַתָּה אֱלֹהִים תּוֹרִידֵם לִבְאֵר שַׁחַת אַנְשֵׁי דָמִים וּמִרְמָה לֹא יֶחֱצוּ יְמֵיהֶם וַאֲנִי אֶבְטַח בָּךְ."

כג. יְהוּדָה בֶן תֵּימָא אוֹמֵר: הֱוֵי עַז כַּנָּמֵר, וְקַל כַּנֶּשֶׁר, רָץ כַּצְּבִי, וְגִבּוֹר כָּאֲרִי לַעֲשׂוֹת רְצוֹן אָבִיךָ שֶׁבַּשָּׁמַיִם. הוּא הָיָה אוֹמֵר: עַז פָּנִים לְגֵיהִנָּם, וּבוֹשֶׁת פָּנִים לְגַן עֵדֶן. יְהִי רָצוֹן מִלְּפָנֶיךָ, יְיָ אֱלֹהֵינוּ וֵאלֹהֵי אֲבוֹתֵינוּ, שֶׁיִּבָּנֶה בֵּית הַמִּקְדָּשׁ בִּמְהֵרָה בְיָמֵינוּ, וְתֵן חֶלְקֵנוּ בְּתוֹרָתֶךָ.

כד. הוּא הָיָה אוֹמֵר: בֶּן חָמֵשׁ שָׁנִים לַמִּקְרָא, בֶּן עֶשֶׂר שָׁנִים לַמִּשְׁנָה, בֶּן שְׁלֹשׁ עֶשְׂרֵה לַמִּצְוֹת, בֶּן חֲמֵשׁ עֶשְׂרֵה לַגְּמָרָא, בֶּן שְׁמוֹנֶה עֶשְׂרֵה לַחוּפָּה, בֶּן עֶשְׂרִים לִרְדּוֹף, בֶּן שְׁלֹשִׁים לַכֹּחַ, בֶּן אַרְבָּעִים לַבִּינָה, בֶּן חֲמִשִּׁים לָעֵצָה, בֶּן שִׁשִּׁים לְזִקְנָה, בֶּן שִׁבְעִים לְשֵׂיבָה, בֶּן שְׁמוֹנִים לִגְבוּרָה, בֶּן תִּשְׁעִים לָשׁוּחַ, בֶּן מֵאָה כְּאִלּוּ מֵת וְעָבַר וּבָטֵל מִן הָעוֹלָם:

כה. בֶּן בַּג בַּג אוֹמֵר: הֲפֹךְ בָּהּ וַהֲפֹךְ בָּהּ דְּכֹלָּא בָהּ, וּבָהּ תֶּחֱזֵי וְסִיב וּבְלֵה בָהּ, וּמִנָּהּ לָא תָזוּעַ, שֶׁאֵין לְךָ מִדָּה טוֹבָה הֵימֶנָּה.

כו. בֶּן הֵא הֵא אוֹמֵר: לְפוּם צַעֲרָא אַגְרָא.

5:20 Any controversy for the sake of Heaven will in the end be preserved. And that not for the sake of Heaven will not in the end be preserved. Which is a controversy for the sake of Heaven? That of Hillel and Shammai. Which is a controversy not for the sake of Heaven? That of Koraḥ and all his band.

5:21 Those who lead multitudes to virtue, no sin will come through them. Those who lead multitudes to sin, they will never be able to do enough to make repentance. Moses was virtuous, and led many to virtue, and the virtue of many is ascribed to him. As it is said: "He did the righteousness of the Lord, and His judgments with Israel" (DEUT 33:21). Jeroboam, the son of Nevat, sinned and caused many to sin, and he was blamed for the sins of many. As it is said: "Upon the sins of Jeroboam that he committed, and that he caused Israel to commit" (1 KINGS 15:30).

5:22 All who possess these three things, praise as a disciple of our father Abraham. But if these three other things, they are disciples of the wicked Balaam. A good eye, a humble spirit, and a forbearing soul—a disciple of our father Abraham. A bad eye, a haughty spirit, and a greedy soul—a disciple of the wicked Balaam. What is the difference between the disciples of our father Abraham, and the disciples of the wicked Balaam? The disciples of our father Abraham enjoy this world and inherit the world to come. As it is said: "That I may cause those that love me to inherit substance, and that I may fill their treasuries" (PROV 8:21). The disciples of wicked Balaam inherit Gehinnom and descend to the deepest pit. As it is said: "For you, O God, will bring them down to the nethermost pit—those murderous, treacherous men; they will not live out half their days; but I will trust in you" (PS 55:24).

5:23 Yehudah ben Teima said: Be as bold as a leopard, as light as an eagle, as swift as a gazelle, and as brave as a lion to do the will of your Father in Heaven. He used to say: bold-faced to hell, shame-faced to heaven. May it be your will, O Lord our God and God of our ancestors, that your city will be rebuilt in our time, and give us a portion in your Torah. [p. 142]

5:24 He used to say: At age five, ready for Scripture; age ten, for Mishnah; age thirteen, for mitzvot; age fifteen, for Talmud; age eighteen, for marriage; age twenty, for career; age thirty, for might; age forty, for understanding; age fifty, for giving counsel; age sixty, for old age; age seventy, for white hair; age eighty, for valor; age ninety, for bent back; age one hundred, as if dead and already passed from the world.

5:25 Ben Bag Bag said: Turn it and turn it, for all is in it. Reflect on it, grow old and gray with it, and do not leave it, for you will have no better guide than it.

5:26 Ben Hei Hei said: As the travail, so the reward.

Kinyan Torah

THE FOLLOWING supplementary chapter to *Avot* is called *Kinyan Torah*, "The Acquisition of Torah," or the "Chapter of Rabbi Meir," after the first author quoted. It is found in traditional prayer books (*siddurim*) as the sixth chapter of the section entitled *Pirke Avot*. This additional chapter is not part of the tractate *Avot* in the Mishnah, and was likely put together hundreds of years after the original five chapters. It probably does contain some material from the time of the Mishnah. It was added to *Avot* in the prayer book to make "*Pirke Avot*," so that one chapter could be read on each of the six Sabbaths between Passover and Shavuot, as was the custom in ancient Babylonia. This remains the Sephardic custom, whereas the Ashkenazi custom is to read *Pirke Avot* throughout the summer months, until Yom Kippur.

Much of the material in this chapter, such as mishnah 5, either paraphrases passages in *Avot* or is in their spirit. As Rabbi Joseph Hertz noted, "And don't crave the table of princes, for your table is greater than their table," in 6:5 could be an allusion to 3:4, which says that when three gather for a meal and Torah is spoken of, holiness is present. If you speak of Torah at your table, and the prince does not, then your table is greater in that holiness is present. I would add that it's also greater because it's *your* table, for if you eat at the rich man's table you also—as the Stoics noted—have to accept the rich man's insults. Later in 6:5, "your crown is greater than their crown" may allude to the assertion in 4:17 that the crown of a good name is above the crown of royalty. The "greater" crown may also refer to the crown of Torah knowledge, which non-Jewish aristocrats won't have.

Some of the sayings in Chapter 6 are, however, a change in tone and emphasis from those in the Mishnah tractate *Avot*. Instead of hearing from men of the world engaged with building and sustaining a society and a culture, here we feel the confines of the schoolroom. Sometimes, the tone in this chapter is that of a lecturing schoolmaster: all who study will be exalted above everything in the world, those who don't study will be rebuked (6:1, 6:2).

In place of the fresh and incisive directives of the first five chapters, the sixth chapter provides a list of 48 virtues (6:6). The list is derived from *Avot*, and is an intriguing compilation. However, it also adds a note of unworldliness and of asceticism that goes against the grain of *Avot* and the Sages. In *Avot* 2:13, Yoḥanan ben Zakkai tells his students to go out into the world and see what is the good path that a person should stick to. Rabban Shimon ben Gamliel says in 1:17 that "the main thing is not the learning, but the doing." And Rabban Gamliel, son of Rabbi Yehudah haNasi says (2:2) that Torah study without work in the world is futile, and leads to sin. In Chapter 6, by contrast, we are told to minimize our involvement with anything outside of study. We are to minimize involvement with the world, as well as with business, sleep, pleasure and laughter. This foreshadows the medieval attitude of withdrawal from the world, rather than the Sages' commitment to courageous engagement with the world.

Even more extreme is 6:4, in which we are told that to live the life of Torah is to eat a morsel of bread, sleep on the ground, live a life of hardship, and toil in Torah. As others have noted in recent times, this mishnah is one of the most extreme expressions of asceticism that appears in the literature of Classical Judaism, and is discordantly out of tune with the mainstream views of the Sages, including those in *Avot*. The prooftext here is also particularly inappropriate, as "You will be happy and it will be well with you" in Psalm 128 describes the result of manual labor, and not of Torah study.

The Sages do advocate moderation, but within a balanced view of life, in which love and pleasure, friendship and joy, labor and the sacred rest of the Sabbath all have a part. This saying, 6:4, is probably a *baraita*, a saying from the time of the Mishnah that was excluded by Yehudah haNasi from the Mishnah—and in this case it would have been with good reason.

Kinyan Torah, Chapter 6 of *Pirke Avot*, contains much that is beautiful, but it does not approach the brilliance and grandeur of the original five chapters of *Avot*.

פרק ו

שָׁנוּ חֲכָמִים בִּלְשׁוֹן הַמִּשְׁנָה, בָּרוּךְ שֶׁבָּחַר בָּהֶם וּבְמִשְׁנָתָם.

א. רַבִּי מֵאִיר אוֹמֵר: כָּל הָעוֹסֵק בַּתּוֹרָה לִשְׁמָהּ, זוֹכֶה לִדְבָרִים הַרְבֵּה. וְלֹא עוֹד, אֶלָּא שֶׁכָּל הָעוֹלָם כֻּלּוֹ כְּדַאי הוּא לוֹ–נִקְרָא רֵעַ אָהוּב, אוֹהֵב אֶת הַמָּקוֹם, אוֹהֵב אֶת הַבְּרִיּוֹת, מְשַׂמֵּחַ אֶת הַמָּקוֹם, מְשַׂמֵּחַ אֶת הַבְּרִיּוֹת, וּמַלְבַּשְׁתּוֹ עֲנָוָה וְיִרְאָה, וּמַכְשַׁרְתּוֹ לִהְיוֹת צַדִּיק חָסִיד יָשָׁר וְנֶאֱמָן, וּמְרַחַקְתּוֹ מִן הַחֵטְא, וּמְקָרַבְתּוֹ לִידֵי זְכוּת, וְנֶהֱנִין מִמֶּנּוּ עֵצָה וְתוּשִׁיָּה בִּינָה וּגְבוּרָה. שֶׁנֶּאֱמַר: "לִי עֵצָה וְתוּשִׁיָּה אֲנִי בִינָה לִי גְבוּרָה." וְנוֹתֶנֶת לוֹ מַלְכוּת וּמֶמְשָׁלָה וְחִקּוּר דִּין, וּמְגַלִּין לוֹ רָזֵי תוֹרָה, וְנַעֲשֶׂה כְּמַעְיָן הַמִּתְגַּבֵּר, וּכְנָהָר שֶׁאֵינוֹ פוֹסֵק. וְהֹוֶה צָנוּעַ וְאֶרֶךְ רוּחַ, וּמוֹחֵל עַל עֶלְבּוֹנוֹ. וּמְגַדַּלְתּוֹ וּמְרוֹמַמְתּוֹ עַל כָּל הַמַּעֲשִׂים.

ב. אָמַר רַבִּי יְהוֹשֻׁעַ בֶּן לֵוִי: בְּכָל יוֹם וָיוֹם בַּת קוֹל יוֹצֵאת מֵהַר חוֹרֵב וּמַכְרֶזֶת וְאוֹמֶרֶת: אוֹי לָהֶם לַבְּרִיּוֹת מֵעֶלְבּוֹנָהּ שֶׁל תּוֹרָה! שֶׁכָּל מִי שֶׁאֵינוֹ עוֹסֵק בַּתּוֹרָה נִקְרָא נָזוּף, שֶׁנֶּאֱמַר: "נֶזֶם זָהָב בְּאַף חֲזִיר אִשָּׁה יָפָה וְסָרַת טָעַם." וְאוֹמֵר: "וְהַלֻּחֹת מַעֲשֵׂה אֱלֹהִים הֵמָּה וְהַמִּכְתָּב מִכְתַּב אֱלֹהִים הוּא חָרוּת עַל הַלֻּחֹת." אַל תִּקְרָא חָרוּת אֶלָּא חֵרוּת, שֶׁאֵין לְךָ בֶן חוֹרִין אֶלָּא מִי שֶׁעוֹסֵק בְּתַלְמוּד תּוֹרָה. וְכָל מִי שֶׁעוֹסֵק בְּתַלְמוּד תּוֹרָה הֲרֵי זֶה מִתְעַלֶּה, שֶׁנֶּאֱמַר: "וּמִמַּתָּנָה נַחֲלִיאֵל וּמִנַּחֲלִיאֵל בָּמוֹת."

ג. הַלּוֹמֵד מֵחֲבֵרוֹ פֶּרֶק אֶחָד, אוֹ הֲלָכָה אַחַת, אוֹ פָּסוּק אֶחָד, אוֹ דִבּוּר אֶחָד, אוֹ אֲפִילוּ אוֹת אַחַת, צָרִיךְ לִנְהָג בּוֹ כָּבוֹד, שֶׁכֵּן מָצִינוּ בְּדָוִד מֶלֶךְ יִשְׂרָאֵל, שֶׁלֹּא לָמַד מֵאֲחִיתֹפֶל אֶלָּא שְׁנֵי דְבָרִים בִּלְבָד, קְרָאוֹ רַבּוֹ אַלּוּפוֹ וּמְיֻדָּעוֹ. שֶׁנֶּאֱמַר: "וְאַתָּה אֱנוֹשׁ כְּעֶרְכִּי אַלּוּפִי וּמְיֻדָּעִי." וַהֲלֹא דְבָרִים קַל וָחֹמֶר: וּמַה דָּוִד מֶלֶךְ יִשְׂרָאֵל שֶׁלֹּא לָמַד מֵאֲחִיתֹפֶל אֶלָּא שְׁנֵי דְבָרִים בִּלְבָד, קְרָאוֹ רַבּוֹ אַלּוּפוֹ וּמְיֻדָּעוֹ, הַלּוֹמֵד מֵחֲבֵרוֹ פֶּרֶק אֶחָד אוֹ הֲלָכָה אַחַת אוֹ פָּסוּק אֶחָד אוֹ דִבּוּר אֶחָד אוֹ אֲפִילוּ אוֹת אַחַת עַל אַחַת כַּמָּה וְכַמָּה שֶׁצָּרִיךְ לִנְהָג בּוֹ כָּבוֹד. וְאֵין כָּבוֹד אֶלָּא תוֹרָה, שֶׁנֶּאֱמַר: "כָּבוֹד חֲכָמִים יִנְחָלוּ וּתְמִימִים יִנְחֲלוּ טוֹב." וְאֵין טוֹב אֶלָּא תוֹרָה, שֶׁנֶּאֱמַר: "כִּי לֶקַח טוֹב נָתַתִּי לָכֶם תּוֹרָתִי אַל תַּעֲזֹבוּ."

Sages taught thus in the language of the Mishnah; blessed be the One who chose them and their mishnah.

6:1 Rabbi Meir said: Everyone who occupies himself with Torah for its own sake merits many things; not only that, but he makes the entire world worthwhile. He is called beloved friend, a lover of God, a lover of humanity, one who gladdens God, and gladdens humanity. His Torah study clothes him in humility and reverence, and leads him to be righteous, pious, upright, and faithful. It distances him from sin, and draws him near goodness. From him come the benefits of counsel and resourcefulness, of understanding and courage. As it is said: "Mine are counsel and resourcefulness, I am understanding, courage is mine" (PROV 8:14). It gives him sovereignty and dominion and discerning judgment. It reveals to him secrets of Torah. He becomes an ever flowing fountain, a stream that never runs dry. He becomes modest, patient, and forgiving of affronts. It magnifies and exalts him over all creation.

6:2 Rabbi Yehoshua ben Levi said: Every day, a voice from heaven issues forth from Mount Horev, with a proclamation saying, "Woe to them, to the people who insult the Torah." And those who don't occupy themselves with Torah are called "rebuked." As it is said: "Like a gold ring in the snout of a pig is a beautiful woman bereft of sense" (PROV 11:22). And it is said: "The tablets were God's work, and the writing was God's writing, incised upon the tablets" (EX 32:16). Read not ḥarut, "incised," but ḥerut, "freedom," for no one is free except those who are occupied in the study of Torah. And all who occupy themselves in the study of Torah shall indeed be exalted. As it is said: "From Mattanah [gift] to Naḥaliel [heritage of God], and from Naḥaliel to Bamoth [heights]" (NUM 21:19).

6:3 One who learns from his companion one chapter, or one halakhah, or one verse, or one saying, or even one letter, must treat him with honor. For thus we find with David, King of Israel, who learned but two things from Aḥitophel, and called him his master, his guide, his close friend. As it is said: "But it is you, my equal, my guide, my close friend" (PS 55:14). Isn't this an inference from minor to major [kal va'homer]? If David, King of Israel learned but two things from Aḥitophel and called him his master, his guide, his close friend, how much more so must one who learns from his companion one chapter, or one halakhah, or one verse, or one saying, or even one letter, treat his companion with honor! And there is no honor but through Torah. As it is written: "The wise shall inherit honor" (PROV 3:35), and "the wholehearted shall obtain good" (PROV 28:11). And there is no good but through Torah. As it is written: "For I have given you a good doctrine, do not forsake my Torah" (PROV 4:2).

ד. כַּךְ הִיא דַּרְכָּהּ שֶׁל תּוֹרָה: פַּת בַּמֶּלַח תֹּאכַל, וּמַיִם בַּמְּשׂוּרָה תִּשְׁתֶּה, וְעַל הָאָרֶץ תִּישָׁן, וְחַיֵּי צַעַר תִּחְיֶה, וּבַתּוֹרָה אַתָּה עָמֵל. אִם אַתָּה עֹשֶׂה כֵן אַשְׁרֶיךָ וְטוֹב לָךְ–אַשְׁרֶיךָ בָּעוֹלָם הַזֶּה, וְטוֹב לָךְ לָעוֹלָם הַבָּא:

ה. אַל תְּבַקֵּשׁ גְּדֻלָּה לְעַצְמְךָ, וְאַל תַּחְמֹד כָּבוֹד, יוֹתֵר מִלִּמּוּדְךָ עֲשֵׂה, וְאַל תִּתְאַוֶּה לְשֻׁלְחָנָם שֶׁל שָׂרִים, שֶׁשֻּׁלְחָנְךָ גָּדוֹל מִשֻּׁלְחָנָם, וְכִתְרְךָ גָּדוֹל מִכִּתְרָם, וְנֶאֱמָן הוּא בַּעַל מְלַאכְתְּךָ שֶׁיְּשַׁלֶּם לְךָ שְׂכַר פְּעֻלָּתֶךָ.

ו. גְּדוֹלָה תּוֹרָה יוֹתֵר מִן הַכְּהֻנָּה וּמִן הַמַּלְכוּת, שֶׁהַמַּלְכוּת נִקְנֵית בִּשְׁלֹשִׁים מַעֲלוֹת, וְהַכְּהֻנָּה בְּעֶשְׂרִים וְאַרְבַּע, וְהַתּוֹרָה נִקְנֵית בְּאַרְבָּעִים וּשְׁמוֹנָה דְבָרִים. וְאֵלּוּ הֵן: בְּתַלְמוּד, בִּשְׁמִיעַת הָאֹזֶן, בַּעֲרִיכַת שְׂפָתַיִם, בְּבִינַת הַלֵּב, בְּאֵימָה, בְּיִרְאָה, בַּעֲנָוָה, בְּשִׂמְחָה, בְּטָהֳרָה, בְּשִׁמּוּשׁ חֲכָמִים, בְּדִבּוּק חֲבֵרִים, בְּפִלְפּוּל הַתַּלְמִידִים, בְּיִשּׁוּב, בְּמִקְרָא, בְּמִשְׁנָה, בְּמִעוּט סְחוֹרָה, בְּמִעוּט דֶּרֶךְ אֶרֶץ, בְּמִעוּט תַּעֲנוּג, בְּמִעוּט שֵׁנָה, בְּמִעוּט שִׂיחָה, בְּמִעוּט שְׂחוֹק, בְּאֶרֶךְ אַפַּיִם, בְּלֵב טוֹב, בֶּאֱמוּנַת חֲכָמִים, בְּקַבָּלַת הַיִּסּוּרִין, הַמַּכִּיר אֶת מְקוֹמוֹ, וְהַשָּׂמֵחַ בְּחֶלְקוֹ, וְהָעוֹשֶׂה סְיָג לִדְבָרָיו, וְאֵינוֹ מַחֲזִיק טוֹבָה לְעַצְמוֹ, אָהוּב, אוֹהֵב אֶת הַמָּקוֹם, אוֹהֵב אֶת הַבְּרִיּוֹת, אוֹהֵב אֶת הַצְּדָקוֹת, אוֹהֵב אֶת הַמֵּישָׁרִים, אוֹהֵב אֶת הַתּוֹכָחוֹת, וּמִתְרַחֵק מִן הַכָּבוֹד, וְלֹא מֵגִיס לִבּוֹ בְּתַלְמוּדוֹ, וְאֵינוֹ שָׂמֵחַ בְּהוֹרָאָה, נוֹשֵׂא בְעֹל עִם חֲבֵרוֹ, וּמַכְרִיעוֹ לְכַף זְכוּת, וּמַעֲמִידוֹ עַל הָאֱמֶת, וּמַעֲמִידוֹ עַל הַשָּׁלוֹם, וּמִתְיַשֵּׁב לִבּוֹ בְּתַלְמוּדוֹ, שׁוֹאֵל וּמֵשִׁיב שׁוֹמֵעַ וּמוֹסִיף, הַלּוֹמֵד עַל מְנָת לְלַמֵּד וְהַלּוֹמֵד עַל מְנָת לַעֲשׂוֹת, הַמַּחְכִּים אֶת רַבּוֹ, וְהַמְכַוֵּן אֶת שְׁמוּעָתוֹ, וְהָאוֹמֵר דָּבָר בְּשֵׁם אוֹמְרוֹ. הָא לָמַדְתָּ כָּל הָאוֹמֵר דָּבָר בְּשֵׁם אוֹמְרוֹ מֵבִיא גְאֻלָּה לָעוֹלָם, שֶׁנֶּאֱמַר: "וַתֹּאמֶר אֶסְתֵּר לַמֶּלֶךְ בְּשֵׁם מָרְדְּכָי."

ז. גְּדוֹלָה תּוֹרָה שֶׁהִיא נוֹתֶנֶת חַיִּים לְעֹשֶׂיהָ בָּעוֹלָם הַזֶּה וּבָעוֹלָם הַבָּא, שֶׁנֶּאֱמַר: "כִּי חַיִּים הֵם לְמֹצְאֵיהֶם וּלְכָל בְּשָׂרוֹ מַרְפֵּא;" וְאוֹמֵר: "רִפְאוּת תְּהִי לְשָׁרֶּךָ וְשִׁקּוּי לְעַצְמוֹתֶיךָ." וְאוֹמֵר: "עֵץ חַיִּים הִיא לַמַּחֲזִיקִים בָּהּ וְתֹמְכֶיהָ מְאֻשָּׁר." וְאוֹמֵר: "כִּי לִוְיַת חֵן הֵם לְרֹאשֶׁךָ וַעֲנָקִים לְגַרְגְּרֹתֶיךָ;" וְאוֹמֵר: "תִּתֵּן לְרֹאשְׁךָ לִוְיַת חֵן עֲטֶרֶת תִּפְאֶרֶת תְּמַגְּנֶךָּ." וְאוֹמֵר: "כִּי בִי יִרְבּוּ יָמֶיךָ וְיוֹסִיפוּ לְךָ שְׁנוֹת חַיִּים;" וְאוֹמֵר: "אֹרֶךְ יָמִים בִּימִינָהּ בִּשְׂמֹאולָהּ עֹשֶׁר וְכָבוֹד;" וְאוֹמֵר: "כִּי אֹרֶךְ יָמִים וּשְׁנוֹת חַיִּים וְשָׁלוֹם יוֹסִיפוּ לָךְ."

6:4 Thus is the way of Torah: Eat a morsel of bread with salt, drink water by the measure, and sleep upon the ground. Live a life of hardship, and toil in the Torah. If you do thus, "Happy shall you be and it shall be well with you" (PS 128:2). "Happy shall you be"—in this world. "And it shall be well with you"—in the world to come.

6:5 Do not seek greatness for yourself, and don't covet honor; let your deeds exceed your learning. And don't crave the table of princes, for your table is greater than their table, and your crown is greater than their crown. And your employer can be relied upon to pay you the reward for your labors.

6:6 Torah is greater than priesthood and kingship, for kingship is acquired through thirty achievements, and priesthood through twenty-four, but the Torah is acquired through forty-eight things. These are: by study, by attentive listening, by well-ordered speech, by an understanding heart, by awe, by reverence, by humility, by joy, by purity, by attending upon the sages, by attachment to friends, by critical discussion with students, by diligence, by Scripture, by Mishnah, by limiting business affairs, by limiting worldly engagement, by limiting pleasure, by limiting sleep, by limiting conversation, by limiting laughter, by patience, by a good heart, by trust in the Sages, by accepting afflictions, by recognizing one's place, by rejoicing in one's lot, by making a fence for one's words, by not claiming credit for one's self, being beloved, loving God, loving humanity, loving righteousness, loving integrity, loving rebukes, and shrinking from honors, not being brash with one's learning, not rejoicing in giving directives, helping with the burden of a colleague, judging him in a favorable light, guiding him to truth, guiding him to peace, being diligent in study, asking and answering, listening and expanding upon, learning in order to teach, learning in order to do, increasing the wisdom of one's teacher, being precise concerning one's received traditions, and reporting a saying in the name of the one who said it. For thus you have learned: whoever reports a saying in the name of the one who said it brings deliverance to the world. As it is said: "And Esther reported it to the King in the name of Mordecai" (ES 2:22).

6:7 Great is the Torah, for it gives life to those who practice it, both in this world and in the world to come. As it is said: "They are life to him who finds them, healing for his whole body" (PROV 4:22). And it says: "It will be a cure for your body, a tonic for your bones" (PROV 3:8). And it says: "It is a tree of life to all who grasp it, and whoever holds onto it is happy" (PROV 3:18). And it says: "For they are a graceful wreath upon your head, a necklace about your throat" (PROV 1:9). And it says: "For through me your days will increase, and years be added to your life" (PROV 10:11). And it says: "In her right hand is length of days, in her left, riches and honor" (PROV 3:16). And it says: "For they will bestow on you length of days, years of life and well-being" (PROV 3:2).

ח. רַבִּי שִׁמְעוֹן בֶּן יְהוּדָה מִשּׁוּם רַבִּי שִׁמְעוֹן בֶּן יוֹחַאי אוֹמֵר: הַנּוֹי, וְהַכֹּחַ, וְהָעֹשֶׁר, וְהַכָּבוֹד, וְהַחָכְמָה, וְהַזִּקְנָה, וְהַשֵּׂיבָה, וְהַבָּנִים–נָאֶה לַצַּדִּיקִים וְנָאֶה לָעוֹלָם. שֶׁנֶּאֱמַר: "עֲטֶרֶת תִּפְאֶרֶת שֵׂיבָה בְּדֶרֶךְ צְדָקָה תִּמָּצֵא;" וְאוֹמֵר: עֲטֶרֶת זְקֵנִים בְּנֵי בָנִים וְתִפְאֶרֶת בָּנִים אֲבוֹתָם. וְאוֹמֵר: "תִּפְאֶרֶת בַּחוּרִים כֹּחָם וַהֲדַר זְקֵנִים שֵׂיבָה;" וְאוֹמֵר: "וְחָפְרָה הַלְּבָנָה וּבוֹשָׁה הַחַמָּה, כִּי מָלַךְ יְיָ צְבָאוֹת בְּהַר צִיּוֹן וּבִירוּשָׁלַיִם וְנֶגֶד זְקֵנָיו כָּבוֹד." רַבִּי שִׁמְעוֹן בֶּן מְנַסְיָא אוֹמֵר: אֵלּוּ שֶׁבַע מִדּוֹת שֶׁמָּנוּ חֲכָמִים לַצַּדִּיקִים, כֻּלָּם נִתְקַיְּמוּ בְּרַבִּי וּבְבָנָיו.

ט. אָמַר רַבִּי יוֹסֵי בֶּן קִסְמָא: פַּעַם אַחַת הָיִיתִי מְהַלֵּךְ בַּדֶּרֶךְ וּפָגַע בִּי אָדָם אֶחָד, וְנָתַן לִי שָׁלוֹם, וְהֶחֱזַרְתִּי לוֹ שָׁלוֹם. אָמַר לִי: רַבִּי מֵאֵיזֶה מָקוֹם אָתָּה. אָמַרְתִּי לוֹ: מֵעִיר גְּדוֹלָה שֶׁל חֲכָמִים וְשֶׁל סוֹפְרִים אָנִי. אָמַר לִי: רַבִּי רְצוֹנְךָ שֶׁתָּדוּר עִמָּנוּ בִּמְקוֹמֵנוּ וַאֲנִי אֶתֵּן לְךָ אֶלֶף אֲלָפִים דִּנְרֵי זָהָב וַאֲבָנִים טוֹבוֹת וּמַרְגָּלִיּוֹת. אָמַרְתִּי לוֹ: אִם אַתָּה נוֹתֵן לִי כָּל כֶּסֶף וְזָהָב וַאֲבָנִים טוֹבוֹת וּמַרְגָּלִיּוֹת שֶׁבָּעוֹלָם, אֵינִי דָר אֶלָּא בִּמְקוֹם תּוֹרָה. וְכֵן כָּתוּב בְּסֵפֶר תְּהִלִּים עַל יְדֵי דָוִד מֶלֶךְ יִשְׂרָאֵל: "טוֹב לִי תוֹרַת פִּיךָ מֵאַלְפֵי זָהָב וָכָסֶף." וְלֹא עוֹד, אֶלָּא שֶׁבִּשְׁעַת פְּטִירָתוֹ שֶׁל אָדָם אֵין מְלַוִּין לוֹ לְאָדָם לֹא כֶסֶף, וְלֹא זָהָב, וְלֹא אֲבָנִים טוֹבוֹת וּמַרְגָּלִיּוֹת, אֶלָּא תוֹרָה וּמַעֲשִׂים טוֹבִים בִּלְבַד, שֶׁנֶּאֱמַר: "בְּהִתְהַלֶּכְךָ תַּנְחֶה אוֹתָךְ, בְּשָׁכְבְּךָ תִּשְׁמוֹר עָלֶיךָ וַהֲקִיצוֹתָ הִיא תְשִׂיחֶךָ." בְּהִתְהַלֶּכְךָ תַּנְחֶה אוֹתָךְ–בָּעוֹלָם הַזֶּה, בְּשָׁכְבְּךָ תִּשְׁמוֹר עָלֶיךָ–בַּקֶּבֶר, וַהֲקִיצוֹתָ הִיא תְשִׂיחֶךָ–לָעוֹלָם הַבָּא. וְאוֹמֵר: "לִי הַכֶּסֶף וְלִי הַזָּהָב נְאֻם יְיָ צְבָאוֹת."

י. חֲמִשָּׁה קִנְיָנִים קָנָה לוֹ הַקָּדוֹשׁ בָּרוּךְ הוּא בְּעוֹלָמוֹ. וְאֵלּוּ הֵן: תּוֹרָה קִנְיָן אֶחָד, שָׁמַיִם וָאָרֶץ קִנְיָן אֶחָד, אַבְרָהָם קִנְיָן אֶחָד, יִשְׂרָאֵל קִנְיָן אֶחָד, בֵּית הַמִּקְדָּשׁ קִנְיָן אֶחָד. תּוֹרָה מִנַּיִן? דִּכְתִיב: "יְיָ קָנָנִי רֵאשִׁית דַּרְכּוֹ קֶדֶם מִפְעָלָיו מֵאָז." שָׁמַיִם וָאָרֶץ מִנַּיִן? דִּכְתִיב: "כֹּה אָמַר יְיָ הַשָּׁמַיִם כִּסְאִי וְהָאָרֶץ הֲדֹם רַגְלַי אֵי זֶה בַיִת אֲשֶׁר תִּבְנוּ לִי וְאֵי זֶה מָקוֹם מְנוּחָתִי," וְאוֹמֵר: "מָה רַבּוּ מַעֲשֶׂיךָ יְיָ כֻּלָּם בְּחָכְמָה עָשִׂיתָ מָלְאָה הָאָרֶץ קִנְיָנֶךָ." אַבְרָהָם מִנַּיִן? דִּכְתִיב: "וַיְבָרְכֵהוּ וַיֹּאמַר בָּרוּךְ אַבְרָם לְאֵל עֶלְיוֹן קוֹנֵה שָׁמַיִם וָאָרֶץ." יִשְׂרָאֵל מִנַּיִן? דִּכְתִיב:

6:8   Shimon ben Yehudah, in the name of Rabbi Shimon bar Yohai said: Beauty, strength, wealth, honor, wisdom, age, gray hair, and children are becoming to the righteous and becoming to the world. As it is said: "Gray hair is a crown of glory; if it is obtained by the way of righteousness" (PROV 16:31). And it says: "The glory of youths is their strength; the majesty of old men is their gray hair" (PROV 21:29). And it says: "The ornament of the wise is their wealth" (PROV 14:24). And it says: "Grandchildren are the crown of their elders, and the glory of children is their parents" (PROV 17:6). And it says: "Then the moon shall be ashamed, and the sun shall be abashed. For the Lord of Hosts will reign on Mount Zion and in Jerusalem, and the Presence will be revealed to His elders" (IS 24:23). Rabbi Shimon ben Menasia said: These are seven qualities that the sages attributed to the righteous; all were realized in Rabbi [Yehudah haNasi] and his sons.

6:9   Rabbi Yose ben Kisma said: Once I was walking along the way and a man encountered me and said, "Shalom," and I answered, "Shalom." He said to me, "Rabbi, what place do you come from?" I said, "From a great city of sages and scribes." He said to me, "Rabbi if you are willing to live with us in our place, I will give you a million gold dinars and precious stones and pearls." I said to him, "Even if you give me all the money and gold and precious stones and pearls that are in the world, I can only live in a place of Torah." For thus it is written in the Book of Psalms by the hand of David, King of Israel: "I prefer the Torah you proclaimed to thousands of gold and silver pieces" (PS 119:72). Not only that, but in the hour of departure from this world, a person is not accompanied by silver and gold, nor precious stones and pearls, but only by Torah and good deeds. As it is written: "When you walk, it will lead you, when you lie down it will watch over you, and when you awake it will talk with you" (PROV 6:22). "When you walk it will lead you"—in this world, "when you lie down it will watch over you"—in the grave, "when you wake it will talk with you"—in the world to come. And it is said: "Silver is Mine, gold is Mine, declared the Lord of Hosts" (HAG 2:8).

6:10   Five possessions the Holy One, Blessed be He, made His own in this world. Torah is one possession, heaven and earth is one possession, Abraham is one possession, Israel is one possession, the Temple is one possession. How do we know this of Torah? Because it is written: "The Lord created me at the beginning of His course as the first of His works of old" (PROV 8:22). How do we know this of heaven and earth? Because it is written: "Thus said the Lord: the heaven is My throne and the earth is My footstool: where could you build a house for Me, what place could serve as My abode?" (IS 66:1) And it says: "How manifold are Your works, O Lord, in wisdom You made them all; the earth is full of Your possessions" (PS 104:24). How do we know this of Abraham? Because it is written: "And he blessed him, saying blessed be Abram of God Most High, owner of heaven and earth" (GEN 14:19). How do we know this of Israel? Because it is written: "Till your people pass over,

"עַד יַעֲבֹר עַמְּךָ יְיָ עַד יַעֲבֹר עַם זוּ קָנִיתָ." וְאוֹמֵר: "לִקְדוֹשִׁים אֲשֶׁר בָּאָרֶץ הֵמָּה וְאַדִּירֵי כָּל חֶפְצִי בָם." בֵּית הַמִּקְדָּשׁ מִנַּיִן? דִּכְתִיב: "מָכוֹן לְשִׁבְתְּךָ פָּעַלְתָּ יְיָ מִקְדָּשׁ אֲדֹנָי כּוֹנְנוּ יָדֶיךָ." וְאוֹמֵר: "וַיְבִיאֵם אֶל גְּבוּל קָדְשׁוֹ הַר זֶה קָנְתָה יְמִינוֹ."

יא. כָּל מַה שֶּׁבָּרָא הַקָּדוֹשׁ בָּרוּךְ הוּא בָּעוֹלָמוֹ, לֹא בְרָאוֹ אֶלָּא לִכְבוֹדוֹ, שֶׁנֶּאֱמַר: "כֹּל הַנִּקְרָא בִשְׁמִי וְלִכְבוֹדִי בְּרָאתִיו יְצַרְתִּיו אַף עֲשִׂיתִיו," וְאוֹמֵר: "יְיָ יִמְלֹךְ לְעֹלָם וָעֶד."

O Lord, till the people pass over, whom you have acquired" (EX 15:16). And it says: "For the holy ones that are on the earth, they are the excellent, in whom all is my delight" (PS 16:3). How do we know this of the Temple? Because it is written: "The place You made Your abode, O Lord, the sanctuary, O Lord, which Your hands established" (EX 15:17). And it says: "He brought them to His holy realm, the mountain, His right hand had acquired" (PS 78:54).

6:11 All that the Holy One, Blessed be He, created in His world, he created only for His glory. As it is said: "All that is called by my name, for my glory I have created, formed, and made it" (IS 43:7). And it says: "The Lord will reign for ever and ever" (EX 15:18).

Commentary Topics

CHAPTER ONE

Chapter Five

Subject Index